Companies and Markets

IMI *information service*
Sandyford, Dublin 1ᶜ
Telephone 2078513 Faᵛ

Companies and Markets

Understanding Business Strategy
and the Market Environment

*Bryan Lowes, Christopher Pass and
Stuart Sanderson*

Copyright © Bryan Lowes, Christopher Pass and Stuart Sanderson, 1994

First published 1994

Blackwell Publishers
108 Cowley Road
Oxford   OX4 1JF
UK

238 Main Street
Cambridge, Massachusetts 02142
USA

British Library Cataloguing in Publication Data
A CIP catalogue record for this book is available from the British Library.

Library of Congress Cataloging-in-Publication Data
Lowes, Bryan.
    Companies and markets : understanding business strategy and the market environment / Bryan Lowes, Christopher Pass and Stuart Sanderson.
        p.   cm.
    Includes index.
    ISBN 0–631–19098–8. — ISBN 0–631–19099–6 (pbk.)
    1. Corporate planning.   2. Marketing—Management.   3. Strategic planning.   I. Pass, C. L.   II. Sanderson, Stuart.   III. Title.
    HD30.28.L68   1994
    658.4'012—dc20   94–1735
                                                                    CIP

Typeset in 11 on 13 pt Plantin
by Graphicraft Typesetters Ltd., Hong Kong
Printed and bound in Great Britain by
Hartnolls Limited, Bodmin, Cornwall

This book is printed on acid-free paper

Contents

Figures

Tables

Boxes

Preface

Business strategy is concerned with the formulation of long-term plans by a firm to achieve its business objectives. These plans have economic, organizational, marketing and financial dimensions so that business strategy is inevitably holistic in approach seeking to integrate functional activities in order to develop appropriate policies for dealing with the firm's changing environment. One of the more important facets of this environment is the economic climate facing firms, in particular changes in market demand, technology and costs, and market competition.

The purpose of this book is to provide students and practitioners of business policy with an in-depth understanding of the various *economic* factors which impinge upon strategic decision-making, particularly in the two key areas of the choice of the firm's *strategic direction* and the formulation of its *competitive strategies*. The book is designed for students on MBA and DMS courses, as well as intermediate and final year undergraduate students of business studies, who may have been introduced to some basic microeconomics prior to studying business policy but who now require a more detailed, industrial economics-orientated presentation of material dealing with issues such as vertical integration, conglomerate expansion and the 'forces driving competition' in markets. Thus, the intent is to harness concepts and ideas from industrial economics with a view to providing the strategist with a richer analytical framework on which to formulate appropriate strategies for the achievement of corporate success.

Bryan Lowes, Christopher Pass, Stuart Sanderson

Introduction

This book is concerned with two key areas of corporate decision-making, the *strategic direction* of the company and the formulation of *competitive strategy*. The 'strategic' company in essence consists of a bundle of 'internalized' resources under the direction of top management which can, at its discretion, be deployed between a number of product and geographic markets and, over time, be expanded and repositioned in accordance with actual and perceived opportunities for profit gain. One key strategic decision for a company is thus to decide on which business activities and markets to operate in. Another key issue is the formulation of competitive strategy, since no matter how few or many markets the company chooses to be in its corporate prosperity will depend fundamentally on how well it succeeds in the individual product markets making up its business. The decisions a company makes in respect of strategic direction and competitive strategy will be influenced by various other 'internal' and 'external' factors: the company's 'mission' (corporate objectives), the resources available to it and its competencies, and its competitive advantages over rival suppliers.

Markets provide the 'backdrop' to a company's activities as it strives for competitive success. A market (defined as consisting of a group of product offerings which buyers view as substitutes) is characterized by a number of interrelated elements, in particular: *structure* (the degree of seller and buyer concentration, the condition of entry and exit etc.), *conduct* (the nature and intensity of competition in the areas of price, promotion, new products etc.) and *performance* (including market supply costs, price and profit levels etc.). Together these factors will have an important influence on the 'attractiveness' of the markets in which the company currently operates (or proposes to enter or leave).

The book is organized as follows. Chapter 1 introduces the concept of 'strategic direction' and the contextual framework in which it is applied. Chapters 2–5 then examine the 'generic' expansion routes available to a company: horizontal growth (chapter 2), vertical growth (chapter 3), conglomerate growth (chapter 4) and internationalization (chapter 5). The second main section of the book deals with competitive strategy. Chapter 6 introduces the market structure–conduct–performance schema which can be used by decision-makers to identify the 'attractiveness' of a market. Chapter 7 looks at how firms respond to the relative attractiveness of markets by entering or leaving a market. Chapter 8 explores key facets of competitive strategy formulation. Chapters 9 and 10 are concerned more specifically with how companies can create and sustain competitive advantages over rival suppliers. Chapter 11 provides a summary of the book's main issues. Finally, there is a Technical Appendix.

Acknowledgements

We would like to thank Chris Barkby for her patience and efficiency in typing the manuscript, and Tim Goodfellow of Blackwell Publishers for his enthusiastic support of the work.

Bryan Lowes, Christopher Pass, Stuart Sanderson

1

Strategic Direction: Background

Business strategy is concerned with decisions and actions taken by a firm in order to achieve its objectives and purposes. Thus, strategy is concerned with fundamental questions affecting firms such as: What do we want to be? What are we presently? How do we get to where we want to be? The answers to these questions are bound up in products, processes, technologies, skills and values. Strategy is also concerned with performance in terms of how well a company is performing, how well others are performing and what can be done to improve the company's performance. Specifically, three key areas can be identified which together interlock all aspects of a firm's activities:

1 *Objective-setting*: determining the general long- and short-term goals of the firm (e.g. increasing the rate of return on capital employed, or increasing earnings per share). In order to achieve these objectives the firm has to ensure an efficient and coordinated effort from the various operational divisions of the firm: marketing, production etc. through appropriate management and organization structures and management control and reward systems.
2 *Strategic direction*: deciding what business activities the firm should operate in, and where; e.g. continue its existing activities, divest some of them and/or diversify into new product markets; remain a national supplier or globalize its operations. As part of the process of determining the firm's strategic direction it must choose its growth mode: deciding for each particular area of activity the most appropriate means of expanding its business interests; for example, internal/ organic growth or external growth via mergers, take-overs and strategic alliances such as joint ventures.
3 *Competitive strategy*: deciding, on the basis of an evaluation of the firm's own competitive strengths and weaknesses *vis-à-vis* those of

its rivals and what customers require, the best means of establishing a position of competitive advantage over rival suppliers (through lower prices, innovative products etc.).

Thus, strategy is concerned with goal-directed behaviour and accordingly the process begins with the development of purpose or mission within which companies will set performance targets.

Business Objectives

Business objectives are the goals which a firm sets for itself in respect of profit returns, sales and asset growth etc. which in turn determine the strategic and operational policies it adopts. Many companies seek to operationalize their long-term aims and objectives in the form of an explicit written document – a Mission Statement. Mission statements are designed to give substance to the perceived purposes of the company and provide all employees with an indication of what they are attempting to achieve through their collective endeavours.

The firm may pursue a single objective or multiple objectives; objectives may be operationalized in 'maximization' or 'satisfactory' target level terms; the time frame in which objectives are pursued may be short term or long term. Thus, it can be seen that objective-setting can be a complex matter. Critical factors affecting the setting of objectives include who controls decision-making in the firm and the various constraints – institutional, financial and environmental etc. – impinging upon this process.

Economic theories of the firm emphasize that firms which are owner-controlled will tend to pursue single- or multi-period profit maximization; likewise, theories of finance suggest that the operational goal of the firm will be to maximize the value of the firm (shareholders' wealth) over the long term. Firms which are management-controlled will tend to pursue objectives such as multi-period sales revenue maximization and asset growth maximization. In this latter case, although shareholders are the owners of the firm, there is a *de facto* 'divorce of ownership from control' enabling the appointed representatives of the shareholders, namely members of the Board of Directors, to make the key decisions affecting the firm's business. In general, shareholdings are too fragmented and shareholders, as 'outsiders', too remote from the 'seat of power' as to be able to exercise control over the business, thus leaving the incumbent managers relatively free to run the company as they see fit. Obviously shareholders' interests cannot be ignored since directors can be removed at the Annual General Meeting (AGM) if the firm is badly managed and dividends are not paid. However, within this constraint, managers will be able to set objectives which enhance their own interests – sales revenue maximization and asset growth maximization objectives, since these goals result in 'bigger' firms and big firms generally pay higher salaries to managers and accord them more power and status.

An alternative framework to the largely normative maximization view of objective-setting is provided by the 'organizational' or 'behavioural' school which argues that the decision-making process at work in most firms tends to produce objectives which are couched in 'satisfactory' terms. Objectives tend to reflect organizational bargaining between the various divisions of the firm – marketing, production, finance etc., which results in the specification of objectives which are generally 'acceptable' (i.e. satisfactory) to all participants, rather than optimal for one group alone.

In addition to the various internal interest groups within the organization described above, certain (generally external) stakeholder groups such as customers and the broader community have an interest in the firm's operations. For example, customers require safe, efficient and inexpensive products while the community would expect the firm to minimize pollution associated with its production and distribution tasks. Their views and concerns may need to be embodied in the firm's objectives.

In practice, examination of directors' statements at AGMs reveals a strong concern in most companies with increasing earnings per share as a measure of corporate 'success'. This is, of course, a profit-related yardstick but one which nonetheless requires the firm to increase its sales and asset base over time in order to provide a sustainable platform for profit growth.

Company Management and Organization

In order to set and achieve the firm's objectives the firm's senior managers will need to develop patterns of interaction between employees, that is, the firm will need to establish an appropriate organizational structure. This organizational structure then provides a framework for the management processes of organizing and directing the human and physical resources of the firm as a means of implementing strategic decisions.

Management

Four key management roles can be identified:

1   *Planning* how to carry out the various activities which are required to achieve the firm's objectives. This involves establishing an action programme and an appropriate organizational structure within which

tasks can be subdivided (e.g. into production, personnel, marketing and finance); delegating responsibility for the tasks; and instituting pay and reward systems. The organizational structure which the firm adopts will inevitably follow from its strategy and plans.

2 *Coordination* of the tasks being undertaken, which involves synchronizing and balancing work loads and ensuring effective collaboration between the various departments and groups within the organization.

3 *Control*, by comparing current performance with that planned in order to monitor progress of the work. Such comparisons reveal where additional resources may be needed to achieve desired performance or when plans may need to be modified in the light of experience. Such control requires clear lines of authority and responsibility within the organization so that senior managers can identify who within the organization is responsible for particular tasks and who needs to be held accountable for their achievement.

4 *Motivation* of the members of the organization, encouraging them to work effectively in performing their assigned tasks. Here again clear lines of authority and responsibility are important if appropriate financial rewards and promotions are to be awarded for successful achievement and appropriate leadership styles adopted which enthuse and galvanize workers. Whilst these roles are important they are often difficult to discern from the study of individual managers. Managers tend to be action orientated rather than the reflective thinkers which strategy formulation would suggest. There is considerable evidence that companies have deliberate strategies and also have emergent strategies as they respond to environmental change. Thus the strategic decision-making appears to be incremental within a broad framework or mission of purpose.

The success of a firm in achieving superior performance and creating and sustaining competitive advantage depends upon how well the firm undertakes the above management roles and the effectiveness of the organization in facilitating these management tasks. The firm's organizational structure, in particular, must not only ensure an efficient use of the firm's existing resources but must also be sufficiently adaptable to anticipate and respond to changing market conditions.

Company organization

Companies can be organized in a number of different ways in seeking to pursue their profit and growth objectives, in particular management activities may be grouped by function, by product group, by geographical area or by holding company arrangements.

1 *Functional structures* group activities into departments by management functions (production, marketing etc.) with formal coordination of these activities at the apex of the pyramid-shaped organization.
Such structures provide a generally effective means of coordination
both within departments and across the organization as a whole,
when there is a single product or service. However, functional structures become less appropriate when an organization diversifies – it
can be difficult to adapt functions to possibly varying product or
service requirements since the centralization of authority in this model
tends to encourage uniformity.

2 *Multi-divisional structures* have separate groups or divisions of the
firm each responsible for a group of similar products or serving a
separate market. Each group or division will have its own management team and its own separate production, marketing etc. functions, coordinated by the chief executive of the group or division.

  Although this structure duplicates management functions, potentially losing some economies of scale, it enables their activities to
be tailored to the requirement of a particular product and its market.
It is, therefore, said to be an appropriate structure for a diversified
organization. The locus of authority and coordination occurs at a
relatively decentralized level (compared with functional structures),
thereby facilitating swift adjustment to changing market conditions.

  Return on capital may be a particularly useful objective for
companies organized along such divisional lines, with autonomous
divisions based on products or geographic areas and a head office
at the top where senior managers coordinate and appraise the goals
and policies of divisions and allocate resources to the self-contained
divisions. With a central objective of return on capital it is possible
to establish fairly clear-cut unequivocal targets for different divisions
couched in terms of return on capital expected, making due allowance
for different growth rates in different markets and the different degrees
of risk involved. Senior managers at head office can then reward
divisional managers and allocate capital resources to competing
divisions on the basis of their performance measured in terms of
return on capital.

3 *Holding company structures* are highly devolved multi-divisional structures in which constituent companies operate as independent companies. The constituent companies are completely or partially owned
by a holding company. Little direct control is exercised by the holding
company other than receipt of profits and the holding company confines itself to acquisitions and divestment. Holding companies often
arise out of merger or acquisition activity and the product range,
production facilities and management structures of the constituent
companies are often left largely unchanged by the holding company.

Strategic Analysis

In seeking ways to achieve its objectives a firm needs a framework for identifying its internal *strengths* and *weaknesses* and the external *opportunities* open to it and the *threats* it faces, which can be used by corporate planners in formulating the firm's overall business strategy, (a SWOT analysis).

Internal appraisal

The internal appraisal of a firm's strengths and weaknesses involves looking at the firm's current resources: the amount and quality of these resources, how well they are being managed in terms of achieving operating economies and developing core skills, and how the firm's resources match up to the requirements of the market-place, as identified by the external appraisal of threats and opportunities. This kind of audit typically reveals a 'checklist' of strengths and weaknesses of the firm as seen by its incumbent management (but their perception could be endorsed or changed by employing the services of an 'outside' team of management consultants). For example, the analysis may reveal that the firm is especially strong in production but that the firm's products have failed to sell well because of poor marketing. This can then be remedied by upgrading the marketing function with a more careful focus on understanding customer needs. It is increasingly important for companies to be aware of their capabilities. The essence of strategy is matching capability to the environment. These capabilities have their origin in intellectual property and are often difficult to recognize and develop.

External appraisal

The appraisal of the firm's external environment involves looking at the immediate *threats* and *opportunities* encountered in the firm's present markets, but also at the long-term strategic possibilities open to the firm for developing its business interests in other directions. A typical threat facing a firm in its existing market is loss of business to competitors and new entrants (due possibly, as in the example above, to the firm's poor marketing), but for firms possessing competitive advantage (lower costs, superior products) over rivals, opportunities abound, particularly in expanding markets. The ultimate threat facing firms in an existing market is, of course, the danger of market obsolescence, i.e. the market itself goes into decline as new substitute products emerge. In consequence, careful attention needs to be paid to the identification of opportunities for successful diversification, where, for example, the firm's core internal skills can be 'carried over' and transferred to new markets.

Having drawn up a 'checklist' of possible key strategic factors, caution needs to be exercised in interpreting them. For example, many feature-film-makers in the 1950s who made movie films for screening through cinemas (often their own vertical chains), initially saw the advent of television as a 'threat' to their traditional business and refused TV companies permission to screen their films. The reality was and still is, of course, that television is simply another form of viewing, representing an 'opportunity' for market development and concentric diversification, i.e. the basic materials and skills involved in film-making (actors, film crews etc.) are the same irrespective of whether a film is being produced for the cinema or television; the key thing, strategically, is the perception of the true dimensions of the market which is being supplied. (See chapter 2.)

Strategic Direction

The product–market matrix provides a framework for highlighting and analysing the various growth opportunities open to the firm which can be used by senior managers in formulating a firm's business strategy.

The broad options

Figure 1.1 shows the matrix which depicts products on one axis and markets on the other. By way of example let us consider a firm specializing in the production of rayon, a man-made fibre, in the UK, which is currently sold to UK textile fabricators to be made up into clothing. The matrix indicates four main ways that the firm can develop its business:

1 *Market penetration:* It can seek to achieve a greater penetration of its existing market, increasing its share of the textile fabrication market by various competitive means – low costs and prices, product differentiation.
2 *Market development:* The firm can aim to develop new markets for its existing products, capitalizing on the firm's production expertise. In the example above, the firm could adapt rayon for use as a packaging material for products such as crisps and cigarettes, or the firm could globalize its operations selling rayon into international markets.
3 *Product development:* The firm can seek to develop new products for its existing markets, exploiting the firm's marketing strengths. The rayon firm mentioned above could, for example, add other synthetic fibres to its product range, or blend together rayon with natural wool to create 'hybrid' fabrics of various strengths and dexterity for use by clothiers.

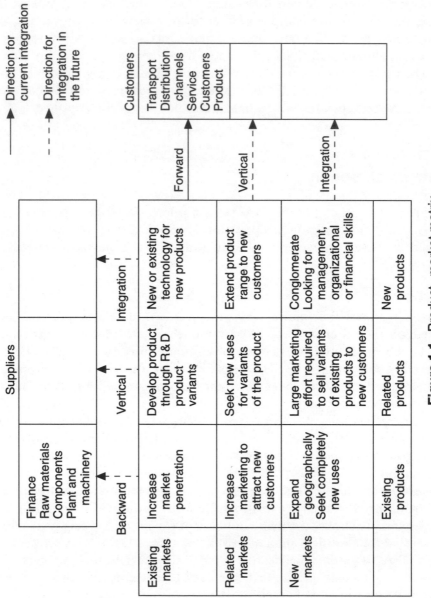

Figure 1.1 Product–market matrix
Source: Ansoff (1968)

4 *Diversification:* The firm could aim to diversify away from its existing activity by developing new products for new markets. The rayon firm might decide that the clothing industry overall had too little long-term growth potential, or that it had become too competitive to make decent profit returns. In this case, divestment of its original business interests or a gradual move away from rayon production into, say, the electronics industry may be considered.

Generic growth strategies

Consideration of the product and market opportunities delineated in the product–market matrix would lead a firm to consider four generic growth strategies:

1 *Horizontal growth:* Horizontal growth involves increasing sales by producing and/or distributing more of the firm's existing products. Expansion through horizontal growth may be advantageous because it enables the firm to reduce its production and distribution costs by securing economies of scale and because it removes or reduces competitive pressures and increases the firm's control over the market. However, if the firm already has a large share of its existing market and the market itself is slow growing, static or declining, the opportunities for further growth are limited. (See chapter 2.)

2 *Vertical growth:* Vertical growth involves the firm undertaking a number of successive stages in the supply of a product. Backward integration occurs when a firm begins producing raw materials which were previously supplied to it by other firms (e.g. a camera producer making glass lenses); forward integration occurs when a firm undertakes further finishing of a product, final assembly or distribution (e.g. an oil company which sells petrol through its own petrol stations).

From the firm's point of view, vertical integration may be advantageous because it enables the firm to reduce its production and distribution costs by linking together successive activities, or because it is vital for it to secure reliable supplies of inputs or distribution outlets in order to remain competitive.

Like horizontal expansion, however, vertical integration offers only limited growth potential for the firm since firms are ultimately locked into the fortunes of the end-markets they serve. (See chapter 3.) If these markets are static or declining, firms must seek new growth opportunities through diversification.

3 *Diversification:* Diversification or conglomerate growth involves the firm expanding into a range of different product areas which leads to it operating in a number of markets rather than a single market. Diversification may be 'concentric' or 'pure', the former involving

some carry over of production or marketing functions (e.g. two firms which utilize a common technological base – razor blades and garden spades both produced from stainless steel and sold through the same outlets – supermarkets), whilst in the latter case the products are entirely unrelated (e.g. cars and cement). The main attraction of diversification as a growth strategy is the ability to spread risks and broaden the firm's profit-earning potential. Specifically, a one-market firm is vulnerable not only to erratic, cyclical profit returns resulting from the business cycle, but worse still, its very survival may be threatened by a declining customer base as the firm's product moves into the final stages of the product life cycle. Diversification is thus the main way the firm can reduce its exposure to business risk and fluctuating profitability, whilst reorientating its activities away from mature and declining markets into new areas offering sustained growth and profit opportunities.

On the other hand, diversification into too many disparate areas can lead to loss of 'focus' and control problems as the firm moves further away from its established expertise in production and marketing. (See chapter 4.)

4   *Internationalization:* Internationalization involves the firm expanding into overseas markets. This could take the form of horizontal international expansion, offering the firm's existing products in overseas markets; vertical international expansion, developing overseas supply sources for inputs or overseas outlets for its products; and conglomerate international expansion. International expansion can take a number of forms: exporting, strategic alliances with foreign partners (licensing, joint ventures etc.) and wholly owned direct investment in manufacturing plants, sales subsidiaries etc. International growth provides additional sales opportunities for firms constrained by the small size of their national markets and serves to reduce their dependency on a single national market to generate profits. (See chapter 5.)

Internal and External Growth

As well as deciding the directions in which to grow (horizontal, vertical, conglomerate or international), a firm must also determine the extent to which it expands by means of internal/organic growth and/or external growth.

Internal growth

Internal growth may be based upon expanding the firm's *existing* production and distribution facilities or could involve the establishment of new, 'greenfield' plants and distribution networks.

The advantages of organic growth include the ability to capitalize on the firm's existing core skills and knowledge, use up spare production capacity and more closely match available resources to the firm's expansion rate over time. Internal growth may be the only alternative in cases where no suitable acquisition exists or where the product is in the early phase of the product life cycle. The disadvantages of organic growth are that in relying too extensively on internally generated resources, the firm may fail to develop acceptable products to sustain its position in existing markets, whilst existing skills and know-how may be too limited to support a broader based expansion programme.

External growth

The main forms of external growth are (1) merger and take-over, and (2) various forms of strategic alliance, e.g. joint ventures, licensing and franchising.

Mergers and take-overs   Merger, or amalgamation, involves the combining together of two or more firms into a single business on a basis that is mutually agreed by the firms' managements and approved by their shareholders.

Take-over, or acquisition, involves the acquisition by one firm of some other firm. For companies listed on the stock market this involves the acquiring firm either buying in the open market, or bidding for the voting shares in the target firm. Unlike a merger which is usually arranged by mutual agreement between the two firms' managements, a take-over is often resisted by the target firm's management so that the bidder must convince shareholders that selling out to the acquirer, or taking shares in it in the case of a share exchange, is of benefit to them. Although a 51 per cent stake in the target company would be sufficient to allow the acquiring company to exercise effective control, generally it would wish to take full control so as to be free from the 'interference' of minority interests.

In general terms, mergers and take-overs allow a firm to expand more rapidly and in a more cost-effective way than internal expansion, whilst augmenting and widening the firm's resource base. Additionally, they have some more specific attractions. For example, in the case of horizontal growth, a merger with, or take-over of, a competitor can enable a firm to exploit economies of scale through rationalization of the two firms' operations and to increase its market share. The alternative of attempting to improve market share through price and product differentiation competition may be prohibitively expensive by comparison. Likewise, in the case of conglomerate expansion, the firm may simply not have the expertise to develop products in non-related areas, whereas external growth allows a firm to move into new activities by acquiring a customized operation and related resource capabilities.

Mergers and take-overs, however, are not without their complications. For example, the merged or acquired firms may have to be integrated into the one controlling organization which may require a major streamlining of operations and the creation of new management structures. If this is not done effectively, efficiency may be impaired and financial resources strained.

Strategic alliances   Strategic alliances, broadly defined, are cooperative arrangements between businesses (each of which continues to retain its own individual identity) which enables them to obtain access to technologies, know-how, capital and markets to augment their own resources and capabilities whilst allowing each partner to focus and concentrate its efforts on its core business strengths.

One such strategic alliance is the *joint venture*, which involves the creation of a business owned jointly by two (or more, in some cases) independent firms who continue to function separately in all other respects but pool their resources in a particular line of activity. Firms set up equity-based joint ventures for a variety of reasons. The combining together of the resources of the two firms may facilitate the establishment of a larger scale operation giving the joint venture access to economies of scale and increasing its penetration of the market. A joint venture is often a particularly effective way of exploiting complementary resources and skills, with one firm, for example, contributing new technology and products and the other marketing expertise and distribution channels. In the international context, joint ventures with local partners are often used by multinational companies as a means of entering unfamiliar foreign markets.

Joint ventures are usually a less expensive way of expanding a firm's business interests than full mergers and take-overs, whilst also allowing firms to withdraw from a particular activity more easily. On the other hand, they involve partners in a deeper commitment to the business than can be allowed for within the confines of a contractual arrangement. The main problem with joint ventures centres on the need to secure agreement between the two partners (especially if it is a 50–50 arrangement) as to how the business should be managed and developed.

Another strategic alliance, *licensing*, involves the assignment by one firm to another firm or number of firms of the right to use its technology or distribution network or to produce its product. Licences are contractual arrangements which are entered into usually for a specified period of time, with the licensee paying a lump sum payment and/or a royalty or fee for the rights assigned. For an innovating firm with limited financial resources of its own, licensing offers a means of obtaining extensive national and international sales potential and a quick return on its risk capital. The danger is that the firm, by providing actual and potential (long-run) competitors with its know-how etc., will lose control of core technology and products to rival producers. To safeguard this and also to provide greater technological collaboration between firms working both in complementary and diverse areas, a 'cross-licensing' arrangement may be established involving the reciprocal licensing of each other's products or technology. More pro-activity cross-licensing agreements may be used to enhance the effectiveness of production and marketing alliances.

Franchising involves the granting by one firm to another firm or number of firms of the right/s to supply its products. A franchise is a contractual arrangement which is entered into for a specified period of time, with the franchisee paying a royalty to the franchisor for the rights assigned.

Franchises are a form of co-partnership, offering mutual benefits. They allow the franchisor to expand sales rapidly and widely, sometimes on a global basis, without having to raise large amounts of capital, by building on the efforts of a highly motivated team of entrepreneurs. Individual franchisees are usually required to contribute the bulk of the investment in physical assets and hence have a personal interest in the success of the venture. On the franchisee's side, he/she obtains access to an innovative product or novel selling method with the franchisor providing back-up technical assistance, specialized equipment and advertising and promotion.

Finally, *functional alliances* provide opportunities for firms to collaborate in specific functional areas such as production, marketing and R & D:

1 *Joint production agreements* enable partners to optimize the use of their own resources, to share complementary resources and to take advantage of economies of scale by, for example, each agreeing to specialize in the production of particular components or finished products.
2 *Co-marketing or co-promotion agreements* enable partners to maximize their marketing efforts by obtaining wider sales coverage and the benefit of partners' local marketing expertise.
3 *Joint R & D agreements* facilitate the input of different mixes of technical expertise and know-how in solving problems and in progressing projects, allowing partners to reduce the expense and risks involved in R & D work.

Choosing a Strategy

The foregoing represents a series of choices which firms have when determining strategic direction. Of interest is the way in which firms choose particular strategies. The act of choosing is bounded by company perceptions of risk, corporate culture, financial and other objectives, the range of available alternatives and the company's view of its own strengths and weaknesses. Although the process is essentially one of matching corporate capability to environmental opportunities, it is often hard to discern. This is because rarely are strategic decisions taken once. The process tends to be an iterative one with companies 'testing out' ideas to see what fits. Furthermore strategic decisions may not be located in one place but may be an aggregate of a series of decisions taken at different times and in different places. The process can appear to be muddled, but it must be remembered that strategic decision-making, like politics, is often the art of the possible as senior managers and departments have to be persuaded.

Constraints on Growth

The text above under the heading 'Strategic Direction' drew attention to various potential *external* growth constraints, in particular the growth rates of the firm's existing markets. However, it was noted that the firm is not necessarily limited to particular markets, industries or countries and may pursue growth by expanding existing product lines and by innovation, product development and diversification, or may seek external growth through mergers or acquisitions. Consequently, demand conditions need not set an upper limit on the growth rate of the firm.

Even where firms have an established position in rapidly growing markets they may still be unable to fulfil their growth potential because of *internal* financial and managerial constraints. In order to expand productive capacity firms require finance, and this finance may be raised either internally or externally. Internal financing can be hindered by too rapid a growth rate which depresses profitability. Furthermore, if too much of the firm's profits are retained to finance expansion and insufficient paid out in dividends this can have the effect of depressing the share price and leaving the firm vulnerable to a take-over bid. External capital sources may also pose a constraint because of imperfections in the capital market. The faster the firm attempts to expand the more it will be driven to accept high-risk investments and the more it may have to rely on fixed interest debt, and capital markets may demand a high-risk premium in providing capital. These pressures may force the firm to limit its rate of expansion to that which available finance allows.

Even when a company has plenty of customers and finance, its rate of growth may be constrained by managerial capacity. If managers of a firm are completely absorbed in day-to-day problems of marketing and production then they will not have time to plan for future developments and seek out new market opportunities, nor will they have the time to manage additional new product or market innovations. Rapid expansion can only be managed where managerial resources can be released from other uses as experience is gained in existing activities and previously complex work becomes routine. This poses internal managerial limits to growth. It is possible to expand management capacity by hiring additional managers but a firm's management is a team with experience of working together, and it takes time for newly recruited managers to be trained and gain enough experience to become effective team members. Consequently there is a limit to how many new managers can be absorbed into the management team over a short period of time, to facilitate growth.

Having said this, the firm may be able to access various co-partnership arrangements such as joint ventures, licensing and franchising which ease these constraints.

Rationalization and Retrenchment

Whilst a firm may seek to expand its business in one or more of the various ways discussed above, it may also choose to rationalize or re-structure other parts of its business as and when required. Where the firm's aim is to improve operating efficiency or to reduce overcapacity then it may close high-cost plants and concentrate production in larger, more modern plants; or it may involve the streamlining of a firm's organizational structure and reducing overhead costs. Insofar as redundancies associated with rationalization may have traumatic effects on the morale of remaining workers and also involve the firm in considerable expenditure on redundancy payments, it may prefer to sell surplus plants or businesses as going concerns to others. Furthermore, firms may choose to divest operating units or whole business divisions as part of a strategic re-thinking of its business/product portfolio. Divestment in this case may reflect a number of considerations, including a desire to pull out of an unprofitable, loss-making activity deemed to be incapable of turnround, the wish to shed peripheral businesses in order to release cash and managerial resources which could be more effectively redeployed in the firm's other activities; or a major re-think of a firm's strategic position involving a retrenchment back to 'core' businesses.

In some cases the firm can divest itself of a surplus business by selling that business to a former competitor or another firm seeking to enter the market. Alternatively, the firm may sell the business to its existing management team (a so-called 'management buy-out') or demerge the business by forming a separate new company (giving the firm's existing shareholders shares in the new company).

References

Ansoff, H. I., 1968. *Corporate Strategy*, Penguin.

Further Reading

Grant, R. M., *Contemporary Strategy Analysis*, Blackwell, 1991.
Jauch, L. R. and Glueck, W. F., *Business Policy and Strategic Management*, 5th edn, McGraw-Hill, 1988.
Porter, M. E., *Competitive Strategy*, Free Press, 1980.
Porter, M. E., *Competitive Advantage*, Free Press, 1985.
Luffman, G., Sanderson, S., Lea, E. and Kenny, B., *Business Policy*, Blackwell, 2nd edn, 1991.
Thompson, J. L., *Strategic Management*, Chapman and Hall, 1990.

2
Horizontal Expansion

Firms seeking to grow can choose one of four broad growth directions: horizontal expansion, vertical expansion, conglomerate growth and internationalization. These four growth modes are explored in the present and three subsequent chapters.

Horizontal expansion takes place when a company expands sales of its existing products in its existing market. This can be achieved through organic growth with the company securing sales either because the market itself is growing, or because the company is able to win customers away from competitors thus increasing its market share. Alternatively, the company can achieve horizontal growth through mergers and take-overs, merging with and taking over competitors as a means of achieving sales growth and an increase in its market share. In this chapter the advantages and disadvantages of horizontal growth for the firm are discussed, and the implications of market concentration for industry cost and price levels are identified. First, however, it is important for the firm to identify in strategic terms precisely what constitutes a 'market' or 'industry'.

Delineating the Market

Crudely speaking, an 'industry' may be defined as a group of related goods or services. For example, the 'beer/brewing industry' might be defined as consisting of bitter and mild ales, lagers, stouts and ciders. However, 'beer' might be seen also as constituting part of a wider – bigger – industry, the 'alcoholic beverages industry' which includes spirits and wines as well as beer. Thus, there are specification problems with respect to how widely or narrowly a particular industry is defined.

Industrial classifications

In order to codify and measure economic activity at various levels of aggregation and disaggregation governments use a 'standard industrial classification' (SIC). In the UK, the SIC comprises ten major Divisions (agriculture, metal goods/engineering etc.), sixty Classes (metal manufacture, man-made fibres etc.), 222 Groups (iron and steel, non-ferrous metals etc.) and 334 Activities (aluminium, adhesives etc.). Individual plants or establishments are assigned to divisions, classes etc. on the basis of four main criteria: (1) nature of the process; (2) principal raw material; (3) intended use of goods; and (4) type of service.

In practice, the first two criteria tend to predominate so that activities, or their equivalent 'industries', are derived on the basis of their *supply* characteristics, in particular the use of common raw materials and processes of manufacture. Such a classification provides a useful source of information on industry structure and statistical details of employment, output and investment by the industrial sector. However, from the firm's point of view, SIC data usually needs to be reinterpreted in order to provide more meaningful specifications of 'markets', defined in terms of groups of products which are regarded by *buyers* as close substitute products. To illustrate, glass jars and metal cans are assigned to different industries by the SIC (Division 2, Activity 'glass containers', Division 3, 'packaging products of metal', respectively), but might be regarded by a user of packaging materials such as a coffee manufacturer as substitute products.

Product substitutability

It is appropriate to think of a market as consisting of a group of products which are substitutable to a greater or lesser degree; one market is then distinguished from another market by a 'gap' in the chain of substitutes. There are difficulties, however, in determining the relationship between products. Products may be closely related in the sense that they are regarded as substitutes by consumers, or they may be close in that the factors of production used in each are similar – i.e. there is substitutability on the supply side of the market. If products are substitutable for both consumers and producers we have no trouble in deciding that they belong in the same market. It is more often the case, however, that the degree of closeness on the two sides is different; for example, men's shoes are poor substitutes for women's shoes from the standpoint of consumers. Yet the shoes are produced in much the same way, utilizing similar materials, machinery etc. and (often) produced by the same firms.

Market definition thus raises the important question as to how narrow or wide the scope of the market should be. One method of identifying discrete markets, suggested by economic theory, is the 'cross-elasticity of demand' test:

$$\text{cross-elasticity of demand} = \frac{\text{percentage change in quantity of X demanded}}{\text{percentage change in the price of Y}}$$

If a fall (rise) in the price of Y causes a fall (rise) in the demand for product X, then buyers regard X and Y as close substitutes and they may be regarded as falling within a single market.

There are practical difficulties, however, in evoking the cross-elasticity of demand test; e.g. price-demand data is often unavailable or insufficiently precise to derive meaningful calculations. Thus companies and public policy agencies are forced to employ more empirically orientated concepts such as 'reasonable interchangeability' and 'customary use', which emphasize factors other than price (product quality attributes, type of end-use etc.), to define market limits. Because of their subjectivity, relying extensively on trade and consumer opinion, such 'tests' tend to define markets narrowly and may ignore important dynamic influences. Theodore Levitt (1960) coined the term 'marketing myopia' to describe situations where firms define their markets in excessively narrow terms and so fail to perceive market opportunities presented by demographic or technological changes.

Geographic scope provides a further dimension to the analysis of markets. Spatially, a market may be local, regional, national or international in scope, depending on such considerations as transport costs, product characteristics and the homogeneity of buyer tastes. For example, because of a high ratio of transport costs to value added, cement and plasterboard markets tend to be localized. Likewise, Bavarian beer caters for a specialized regional taste, whilst Coca Cola, by contrast, is sold worldwide as a global brand.

The strategic market

By putting together the product and geographic elements of a market it is possible for a company to identify its 'strategic market', defined by Kay (1990) as 'the smallest area within which it is possible to be a viable competitor'. Figure 2.1 summarizes the essence of Kay's proposition. The demand and supply characteristics have to be seen in relation to the potential economies of scale and scope available to firms in any market sector. For example, in some market sectors such as motor-car assembly, production technology may allow unit costs to fall significantly as production volumes expand, whereas in other market sectors economies of scale are exhausted at relatively low levels of output. In addition, firms may secure economies of scope by sharing common inputs or

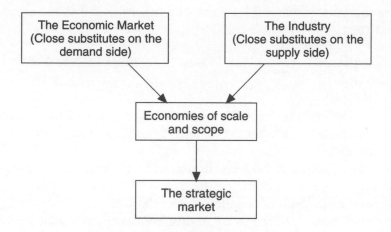

Figure 2.1   Markets and industries
Source: Kay (1990)
By Permission of Oxford University Press

jointly promoting or distributing products. The availability of economies of scale and scope determine the firm's capacity for exploiting demand and supply characteristics and the size and breadth of its strategic market.

The strategic market has both a product and a geographic dimension. The strategic product market is the minimum feasible product range which may be offered in a given geographic market. (See box 2.1.)

Box 2.1   The strategic market for motor cars

In serving the national and continental European car markets, companies such as Rover and Peugeot market a wide selection of cars ranging from small saloons like the Mini Metro and Peugeot 205, light saloons such as the Rover 1.4 and Peugeot 309, medium saloons such as the Montego and Peugeot 405 and large saloons such as the Rover 800 and Peugeot 605. By contrast, luxury car manufacturers such as Mercedes and Jaguar offer a much narrower product range. The strategic market area is the minimum market territory which may be feasibly served with a given product range. For example, volume car manufacturers like Rover and Peugeot can survive by serving primarily their national and European markets. By contrast, luxury car manufacturers such as Mercedes and Jaguar need to sell globally in order to be economically viable. Breadth in one dimension may offset narrowness in another. Thus, the motor car industry can be sub-divided into a number of 'strategic groups' of firms, with each group operating in a different sector of the market. (See chapter 8, text under the heading 'Structure Within Industries'.)

Over time the dimensions of the strategic market may change. For example, rising consumer incomes and changing tastes may create a demand for product diversity, lessening the opportunities for offering standardized products. Similarly, changes in manufacturing technology, in particular the development of flexible manufacturing processes, have reduced the significance of economies of scale and have enabled smaller scale firms to compete with low-cost volume manufacturers. Likewise, product innovation has also served to re-define existing markets and create new markets.

Market Concentration

Once market boundaries have been specified it is then possible to determine the extent to which the production of a particular good or service is controlled by the leading suppliers (seller concentration) and the extent to which the purchase of a product is controlled by the leading buyers (buyer concentration).

The significance of market concentration for companies lies in its effect on the nature and intensity of competition. Structurally, as the level of seller concentration in a market progressively increases 'competition between the many' becomes 'competition between the few' until at the extreme, the market is totally monopolized by a single supplier. In terms of market conduct, as supply becomes concentrated in fewer and fewer hands, suppliers may seek to avoid mutually ruinous price competition and channel their main marketing efforts into sales promotion and product innovation, activities which offer a more profitable and effective way of establishing competitive advantage over rivals.

Buyer concentration can also affect the competitive situation. In many markets (particularly end-consumer markets), buyers are too small to influence supply conditions, but in others (particularly in intermediary goods markets and in retailing), buying power is concentrated and purchasers are able to obtain bulk-buying discounts, extended credit or other concessions from suppliers.

Measuring concentration

Market size and concentration can be measured in a number of ways. Generally, the size of the market and of the firms serving a market will be measured in terms of sales revenue. However, other size measures may be adopted, in particular physical output (barrels per day etc.), value added, numbers employed and capital employed. Each of these size measures is likely to give slightly different results in measuring both the size of the market and the relative importance of firms serving that

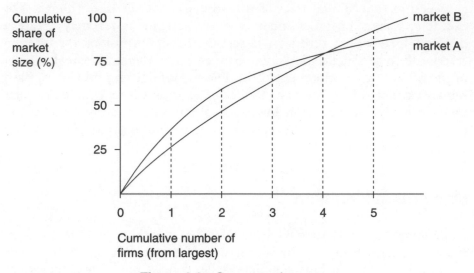

Figure 2.2   Concentration curve

market. Selection of an appropriate size variable is important in measuring market concentration. For example, industries such as grocery retailing tend to measure size in terms of sales turnover, since this is the primary measure of success in that industry. Some industries such as oil refining, where the final products bear a heavy tax burden and are produced through long vertically integrated production chains, may find sales turnover less relevant than value added. Other industries such as steel which are highly capital-intensive may tend to measure the relative size of firms in terms of capital employed.

Concentration measures are concerned with measuring the size distribution of firms in a market. Several measures of market concentration seek to measure seller or buyer concentration. The most common of these measures is the concentration ratio, which records the percentage of a market's sales (or assets or numbers employed) accounted for by a given number of the largest firms in that market. In the UK it has been usual to estimate the concentration ratio for the three or (more recently) five largest firms; whereas in the US the four-firm concentration ratio tends to be employed.

However, the concentration ratio only records seller concentration at one point along the cumulative concentration curve, as figure 2.2 indicates. This makes it difficult to compare concentration curves for two different markets, like A and B in the figure, where their concentration curves intersect. For example, using a three-firm concentration ratio, market A is more concentrated, whilst using a five-firm ratio, market B is shown to be more concentrated.

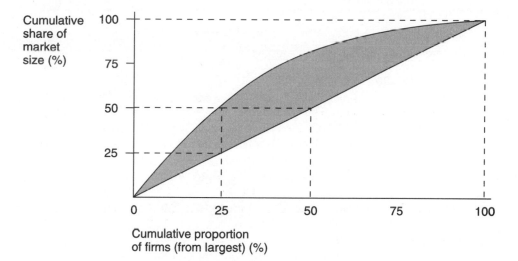

Figure 2.3   Relative concentration (Lorenz) curve

Concentration measures like the concentration ratio are known as absolute concentration measures since they are concerned with the market shares of a given (absolute) number of firms. By contrast, relative concentration measures are concerned with inequalities in the share of the total number of firms producing for the market. Such irregularities can be recorded in the form of a relative concentration (Lorenz) curve as in figure 2.3. The diagonal straight line shows what a distribution of complete equality in firm shares would look like, so the extent to which the Lorenz curve deviates from this line gives an indication of relative seller concentration. For example, the diagonal line shows how one might expect 50 per cent of market sales to be accounted for by 50 per cent of the total firms, whilst in fact 50 per cent of market sales are accounted for by the largest 25 per cent of total firms, as the Lorenz curve indicates.

Box 2.2 shows the market shares of the leading suppliers of a number of products in the UK.

Limitations of concentration measures

The above measures offer some indication of the size distribution of sellers in a market and therefore of the degree of monopoly or oligopoly market structure. However, these measures on their own do not offer a complete picture of market power. For example, they do not measure the market dominance of vertically integrated or conglomerate firms whose potential for price-squeezing competitors (see chapter 3) or cross-subsidizing a subsidiary can (see chapter 4) enhance the subsidiary's market power, despite its modest market share. Nor do the measures

Box 2.2   Market concentration: some UK examples

Market	Leading suppliers
Household gas	British Gas 100%
Sugar	British Sugar 52%, Tate and Lyle 40%, Imports 8%
Frozen food products	Birds Eye (Unilever) 22%, Ross Young 20%, Findus 5%, Other branded and 'Own label' 53%
Coffee	Nestlé 47%, General Foods 18%, Brooke Bond (Allied Lyons) 6%, 'Own label' 24%, Other brands 5%
Mains cables	DCC 24%, BICC 21%, Pirelli 14%, Sterling 14%, GEC 10%, Others 18%
Cakes	RHM 23%, Allied Lyons 11%, Memory Lane 3%, McVities 3%, Other branded 24%, 'Own label' 34%
Amplifiers	Pioneer 8%, Rotel 7%, Arcam 6%, Akai 6%, Sony 6%, Technics 6%, Other branded 61%
Shampoos	Proctor and Gamble 28%, Elida Gibbs 15%, Smith Kline Beecham 10%, Alberto Culver 5%, Other branded and 'Own label' 42%
Portable radios	Sony 32%, Morphy Richards 13%, Philips/Pye 11%, Roberts Radio 7%, Panasonic 6%, Grunding 5%, Other branded 26%
Household detergents	Proctor and Gamble 45%, Unilever 44%, Other branded and 'Own label' 11%

Source: *Retail Business*

give any direct indication of the height of entry barriers protecting existing firms from potential competitors since they merely measure the size distribution of existing sellers.

In addition, the measures are generally based upon shares of the national market for a product, not allowing for imports, thus they can be misleading where markets for products are international in scope, with strong international competition. The definition of the market employed can also have a significant effect upon the concentration measures. By taking a narrow definition of a market, e.g. men's high-quality woollen suit material, only a few suppliers would be relevant, with high market shares. By contrast taking a broader market definition, e.g. clothing, many more suppliers would be embraced and market shares lower. Finally, most concentration measures are based on production census data where industries are often arbitrarily defined in terms of their use of common raw materials or technical processes which, as noted earlier, do not fully reflect cross-elasticities of demand and product substitutability in the eyes of consumers.

Advantages of Horizontal Expansion

Horizontal expansion may be advantageous to firms if it permits them
to lower unit costs by exploiting economies of scale, and to increase
their market share, enabling them to exercise greater control over market
conditions. There are, however, limits to horizontal expansion as a growth
strategy for the firm. Overall market demand may be static or declining,
necessitating firms to seek new growth opportunities through diversification (see chapter 4). In addition, firms' ability to increase market share
by merger and take-over may be restricted by competition policy. In the
UK, for example, mergers and take-overs which take a firm's market
share of a product above 25 per cent may be challenged by the Office
of Fair Trading if there are grounds for believing that competitive processes and market efficiency may be adversely affected. (See chapter 7.)

In this section two aspects of horizontal expansion are discussed: costs
and profitability. These are of particular concern to the firm. Other
horizontally related aspects of firm efficiency such as advertising expenditures, innovation and 'organizational slack' are discussed in later
chapters.

Horizontal expansion and firm's costs

Economies of scale   Economies of scale refer to the reduction in the
unit costs of the firm (in production, marketing, finance, R & D etc.) as
its scale of operations is increased. Economies of scale are an important
means of establishing cost advantages over rival suppliers and potential
entrants to the market. Lower costs not only enable firms to survive
price wars but help boost profitability in more stable trading conditions.

There are available in most industries economies of scale so that
producing a greater quantity of output reduces average or unit costs.
Figure 2.4 depicts a typical long-run average cost curve for a firm. OX
is the scale of output at which average cost is minimized and economies
of scale are exhausted. Thereafter, diseconomies of scale may set in
giving the cost curve a U-shaped configuration (shown by the dotted U
line), although empirical studies indicate that in many industries long-
run firm cost curves tend to be L-shaped (as shown by the dashed L
line). In such cases there is a critical level of output at which costs are
minimized (the 'minimum efficient scale') with constant returns at output levels greater than this.

Economies of scale may operate both at the level of the individual
plant and at the level of the firm (operating a number of plants).
Economies of scale fall into five major groups:

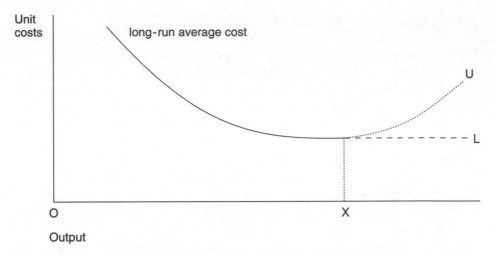

Figure 2.4 Unit costs and economies of scale

1 *Production economies:* These arise from operating larger plants where
sufficient workers are employed to allow operatives to specialize in
particular parts of the total job, so increasing their proficiency and
reducing training time. Economies can also arise from the use of
larger and technically more efficient specialist plant, e.g. in oil refining and motor-car assembly. Large-scale production also makes it
easier to balance production lines so as to minimize surplus capacity
when linking together production processes embodying indivisible
machinery and equipment with different capacities. Additionally, large
manufacturers may benefit from economies of increased dimensions
– for certain items of capital equipment such as boilers and storage
tanks. Furthermore, as scale of production is increased, superior
techniques of production may be utilized, employing automatic
machinery rather than manually operated machines. Large factories
can utilize specialist materials-handling equipment such as conveyor
belts to link production processes, and avoid costly manhandling.
Large producers are able to spread the cost of custom-built tools
over a larger output, so ensuring smaller tooling costs per unit, e.g.
body-component moulds and dies in the motor car industry.
Companies handling large orders will experience less lost production
time whilst machines are adjusted and set up for the order; indeed,
where volumes are large enough to justify a special mass-production
line, set-up time may become negligible. Finally, on the buying side
larger companies benefit from the skills of specialized buying staff
and can often obtain better discounts by buying their raw materials
and services in bulk.

2 *Marketing and distribution economies:* Large single- or multi-plant
   companies can afford to employ trained specialist sales staff, and are
   able to deploy them so as to use their sales forces to the full; e.g. by
   arranging sales territories which minimize unproductive travelling
   time between customer calls. Economies may also be achieved in
   product promotion, e.g. in printing sales leaflets, and in using mass-
   advertising media such as television which are generally suitable only
   for large promotions, but which reduce the cost per person reached.
   In distributing products the large company can maintain a national
   distribution network, possibly with regional depots, and thus organize deliveries to customers more efficiently. It can also effect economies in materials-handling by using fork-lift trucks, and so on, and
   can utilize larger transport units such as oil tankers and lorries.
3 *R & D economies:* Large companies can afford to spend considerable
   amounts of money on R & D and such large-scale R & D tends to
   lower the cost of developing new products and production processes.
4 *Financial economies:* Since they offer greater security, large companies
   generally find it easier to obtain further funds from share issues or
   from loans, and can obtain funds on more advantageous terms. Small
   firms are at a particular disadvantage in raising capital, especially
   when they have only a brief trading history.
5 *Managerial economies:* Division of labour can also be beneficial in
   improving management efficiency by allowing managers to specialize
   in the various functional areas of production, finance, and so on.
   In addition, large companies can afford to employ full-time staff
   specialists in such areas as computer programming, market research,
   and forecasting.

These internal economies of scale may be augmented by the existence
of various external economies of scale which are outside the immediate
influence of any individual firm, but which can lead to decreasing long-
run costs for all firms in the industry. For example, if a college concentrated on training large numbers of, say, computer programmers to serve
the needs of local computer businesses, then the individual employer
would have a supply of trained programmers available with a resulting
reduction in the firm's own (internal) training costs.

Diseconomies of scale   Economies of scale like those above lead one
to expect that unit costs will generally fall as a company increases the scale
of its output. However, at very high output levels a company may begin
to encounter diseconomies of scale, which cause its unit costs to rise.
These diseconomies, it is argued, arise from the problems of coordination
which result when a company grows to be very large and complex. A
company can become more difficult to manage as it grows and as communication channels between senior managers and their subordinates

lengthen. This may result in confusion and misunderstandings, leading to a loss of efficiency. Also labour relations may become strained as managers become increasingly remote from the workers they manage.

These problems are not insurmountable, however, and by breaking down the company into smaller semi-autonomous departments or divisions and improving communications channels, it is possible to avoid the worst problems of size.

The potential to realize economies of scale can be limited for a variety of reasons. In some industries the nature of the product and the processes of manufacture, or technology, may be such that diseconomies of scale are encountered at modest output levels. On the demand side, total market demand may be insufficient to permit firms to attain minimum efficient scale, or firms' individual market shares may be too small. Where consumers demand a wide variety of products this mitigates against standardization and long production runs.

Minimum efficient scale (MES) is the level of output at which economies of scale are exhausted and constant returns to scale are encountered. In industries where the MES is large relative to the total size of the market, one would expect to find high degrees of seller concentration, for the market may only support a few firms of MES size. In terms of figure 2.4 (see above), size OX is the minimum optimal size of firm. Two important questions immediately come to mind. First, how large is OX in relation to the size of the market? If it is half of the market size, the market can support only two firms of optimal size; if it is one-fiftieth of market size, the market is large enough to support fifty firms of optimal size, and so on. Second, how steep is the cost curve to the left of OX? The answer to this question tells one what cost disadvantage is suffered by firms of sub-optimal size – or in other words, how important quantitatively are the economies of scale. Box 2.3 presents data on the MES in a number of UK industries.

The size of the market is an important factor in setting limits to the scale of operations. Where economies of scale are important, the domestic market may be too small to support even one plant of optimal size. Here, however, allowance must be made for exports. Small countries can overcome the disadvantage of a small domestic market and succeed in concentrating a high proportion of activity in plants of optimal size because of success in export markets. On the other hand, as noted above, where consumers demand product variety such that many small segmented markets for a product exist, scale economies are unachievable. In some situations economies of scale are so significant that costs are only minimized when the entire output of an industry is supplied by a single producer. Such situations are termed natural monopolies.

The firm's definition of its 'strategic market' will be conditioned by these factors of market size and scope and the potential for realizing economies of scale.

Box 2.3 Minimum efficient scale (MES) in selected UK industries: the Pratten study

Pratten's study (1971) of economies of scale in manufacturing industry was one of the most comprehensive undertaken for the UK, and covered 30 product groups. Some of his results are shown here. There are considerable variations across the industries as to the importance of the relationship between economies of scale and concentration; e.g. the UK aircraft industry could never approach optimum size producing for the relatively small UK market alone because it would need to have more than a 100 per cent market share of its UK market to fully exploit scale economies. Conversely, a bread-maker would need only a 1 per cent share of the UK market. However, overall, twenty-one of the thirty cases considered would need to have at least a 20 per cent share of the UK market to operate at MES.

Industry and plant/product	MES	
	in absolute terms	as % of UK output
Aircraft (a type of aircraft)	over 50	over 100%
Steel (plant making range of rolled products)	4 million tons per year	80%
Motor cars (firm making range of models)	1 million cars per year	50%
Sulphuric acid (plant)	1 million tons per year	30%
Detergent (plant)	70,000 tons per year	20%
Beer (brewery)	1 million barrels per year	3%
Bread (bakery)	30 sacks per hour	1%
Bricks (plant)	25 million bricks per year	0.5%

Source: Pratten (1971)

The potential cost disadvantage to firms seeking to enter a market on a small scale, *vis-à-vis* large established firms, can also serve as a barrier to entry in certain industries. If the MES of production and distribution is large in relation to total market size then firms face the choice of either (1) meeting the high initial capital requirements to attain an economic production/sales volume and so substantially increasing total market supply, thereby driving down market price after entry; or (2) entering the market on a smaller, sub-optimal scale and bearing substantial cost disadvantages. (See chapter 6.)

The importance of economies of scale *per se* as a determinant of market structure and cost efficiencies needs to be qualified in the light of recent developments in process technology. In many industries the introduction of flexible manufacturing systems has enabled relatively small firms to achieve many of the productivity and cost savings associated with large-scale operations. For example, the introduction of 'mini' steel mills in the 1970s not only allowed smaller steel-makers to match the supply costs of their larger competitors, but also allowed them to accommodate changes in demand for individual steel products more rapidly without loss of efficiency.

Economies of scope   Economies of scope can reduce the average costs of firms by increasing the number and variety of goods and service produced and sold. A building society can sell insurance, pensions and other financial services as well as mortgages. Such economies can arise because the firm employs specialist factors of production which are capable of widening the variety of their outputs. For example, specialist marketing personnel can market more than one variety of product thus spreading their costs across more products and lowering the average cost of the marketing operation. The same argument would apply to plant and equipment capable of producing a variety of products or brands. For example, a manufacturer of baked beans could utilize its plant to produce not only beans sold under the manufacturer's brand name but also beans sold as 'own labels' by food retailers, the extra throughput obtained serving to reduce average production costs.

For larger firms which are big enough to employ specialist plant, equipment and personnel, the combining of economies of scale and economies of scope may enable the firm to significantly lower its average total costs. The combined effects of scale and scope which can result in lower costs and thus prices has been shown to be a key factor in the success of companies in brewing, pharmaceuticals and petrol as well as many public utilities such as gas and water.

Economies of scope are relevant to the strategic notion of 'sweating the assets' to achieve cost reductions and enhanced profitability. To take the building society example above, by cross-selling a range of financial services utilizing existing branch networks and staff, the business is in a better position to optimize returns from its current asset base. Similarly, oil companies such as Esso and Shell have sought to increase the income from their prime urban petrol station sites by not only selling a wide range of motoring accessories but also establishing 'mini shops' selling sweets, tobacco, magazines, barbeques etc. Strategically, the concept of economies of scope is also linked to the growth of the firm through concentric diversification (see chapter 4).

Experience curve effects   A further compelling reason for increasing market share and thus output is the effect of cumulative increases in output on costs which goes beyond that of 'conventional' economies of scale. If costs per unit decline with cumulative output growth then the company with the largest market share has the potential to be the highest profit earner through having the lowest unit costs. In the late 1960s the Boston Consultancy Group showed that costs could fall by as much as 30 per cent if output doubled. This so-called 'experience curve' effect is brought about by companies learning to do things more efficiently and improvements in the use of technology, serving to reinforce underlying economies of scale (see chapter 9). Hence, there would appear to be an advantage in having strategies which are aimed at increasing market share.

Experience effects probably work best in capital-intensive mass-production industries which tend to have steeply sloped cost curves. Service industries or fragmented goods industries are probably less amenable to experience effects. What it is probably true to say is that in the appropriate industry it pays a company to build market share rapidly when the curve is at its steepest at the growth stage of the product life cycle. However, relentless pursuit of cost economies can have negative strategic effects; e.g. over-concentration on process technology to the neglect of consumer needs may result in consumer rejection of the product despite its low price.

Competitive implications of cost advantages   Where a firm is able to secure cost advantages through economies of scale, economies of scope and experience curve effects then it has the choice of whether to exploit its unit cost advantages by charging a lower price than rivals and gaining market share at their expense or to charge prices which match rivals' prices and secure high price–cost margins and profits.

For example, in figure 2.5 firm A operates with substantial profit margins at current industry prices, firm B is also profitable but firm C is making losses. A could drive C out of business by dropping prices. If, however, A wants high margins C could stay in business. The danger for A is that firm B might wish to increase its market share at the expense of A. If C cannot increase its share then it will have to find some other strategy such as differentiation to stay in the market (see chapter 10).

Horizontal expansion, profitability and cash flow

Profitability   Horizontal expansion by firms can have an important impact on profits whether done organically or by take-over or merger. There is empirical evidence from the Profit Impact of Market Strategies

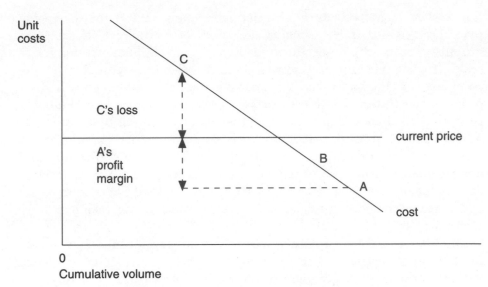

Figure 2.5 Costs and strategic options

(PIMS) project that this is indeed so. However, the PIMS data indicates that various other factors impact on profitability. The PIMS database was established in 1975 and has been expanded over the years to include, currently, some 3,000 business units in North America and Europe. The database includes firms with quite different profit profiles. PIMS seeks to identify the reasons for differences in corporate performance between firms. According to PIMS data the variability in a businesses profitability is accounted for by three main factors which explain around 75 per cent of the variability. These are shown in figure 2.6.

The data show that businesses with high profitability had:

− high relative market share in each segment served;
− high product quality;
− high capacity utilization;
− high productivity;
− relatively low direct costs;
− low investment intensity (investment to turnover ratio).

The results are not without controversy as other researchers have found low-market-share companies with high profitability. There is, of course, the proposition that quality will be important in any event and will eventually, if relatively high, drive up market share. It must be remembered, however, that for the practising manager a number of the variables in figure 2.6 are not under his/her control such as market growth, concentration and customer power. Thus, the art is to assemble

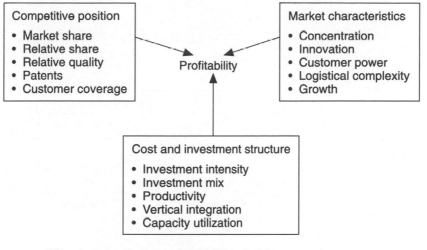

Figure 2.6   Factors determining business performance
Source: PIMS (1992)

those strategic variables which are to some degree under control into the most potentially effective strategy.

Cash flow

Whilst the earlier discussion has been concerned with profits or profitability, for many firms cash flow is of prime importance. In the short run firms can survive loss of profits as long as they are liquid, i.e. they have enough cash to pay their debts. The relationship between cash flow, market share and market growth can be seen in the Boston Consulting Group product portfolio matrix. Figure 2.7 shows the matrix which depicts market growth rate on one axis and the product's relative market share on the other; the matrix indicates that the higher the market's growth rate, the greater will be the capital investment required and hence cash used, whilst the greater the product's market share, the greater will be the profit earned and hence cash generated. The four market growth/share segments relate to four product types:

1 *Cash cow.* A product (which is usually in the mature phase of the product life cycle) which has a low growth rate so that it requires little new investment to support it and has a high market share yielding a high profit return.
2 *Star.* A product which has a high growth rate and needs a considerable amount of new investment to keep up with market demand, and has a high market share, often yielding sufficient cash to make

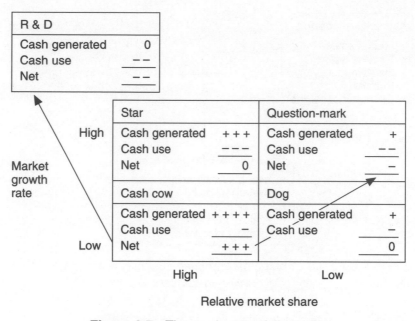

Figure 2.7 The product portfolio matrix
Source: Adapted from Henderson (1973)

its operations self-financing. Star products are usually relatively new products in the growth phase of the product life cycle and, with proper handling, hopefully will become the firm's cash cows of the future.

3 *Question-mark.* A product which has a high growth rate and so requires heavy cash injections to support it, and a low market share providing only a modest profit return, if at all. Such products are a cash drain but they have 'star' potential if their market shares can be improved.

4 *Dog.* A product which has both a low growth rate and a low market share and which lacks potential for future development. Such products are prime candidates for withdrawal from the market or divestment if a suitable buyer can be found.

Cash cows are the firm's primary source of internal funds for investing in R & D and the financing of new products to replenish the firm's portfolio of (question-mark) products as older products decline and unsuccessful ones are withdrawn. Thus, it is important for the firm to have a 'balanced' portfolio of products some of which are cash generators and others which are cash users if it is to survive and thrive over the longer term.

Horizontal Expansion and Market Power

Market dominance is a situation where a firm possesses a high market share, both in absolute terms and relative to the market shares of its competitors. A high market share is an important means of increasing profits both by underpinning a firm's ability to take full advantage of the cost reductions available from exploiting economies of scale, but also because of the potential it offers to exercise some degree of 'control' over the market. Firms which are monopolists or which have a high market share giving them a degree of monopoly or 'market power' are effectively 'price-makers'. The dominance of their product brands and consumer loyalty to those brands and the absence of powerful competition allows them considerable discretion over the prices they charge for their products. This enables them to generate high price–cost margins and a large return on their capital employed. By contrast in more atomistic markets with a significant number of smaller suppliers, none of which has a high market share, the firms will effectively be 'price-takers'. Prices in such markets will be determined by the broad interaction of market demand and supply conditions and individual suppliers are forced to accept the market price as a datum which limits their price–cost margins and return on capital employed to levels comparable with those of their competitors.

Market dominance and profitability

Traditional market theory views market dominance with scepticism. Specifically, in the extreme cases of complete monopoly versus perfect atomistic competition, market theory demonstrates that monopoly tends to lead to higher prices and lower output levels than atomistic competition. The brief analysis which follows provides an overview of the competition versus monopoly issue. A more detailed exposition is contained in the Technical Appendix at the back of this book. Figure 2.8 shows the conventional contrast between price and output levels in monopoly and atomistic markets. As the sole industry supplier the monopolist faces a downward sloping market demand curve (DD) and the sale of additional units of his product forces down the price at which all units can be sold. This gives the monopolist an incentive to restrict output in order to keep prices high. If the objective of the monopolist is profit maximization he will aim to expand his sales and output up to the point where the last unit produced and sold adds as much to revenues as to costs, i.e. he will produce at that price–output combination which equates marginal revenue (MR) and marginal cost (MC). Consequently the monopolist would supply quantity 0Qm and charge a price 0Pm. At this price the monopolist's average costs (AC), which includes

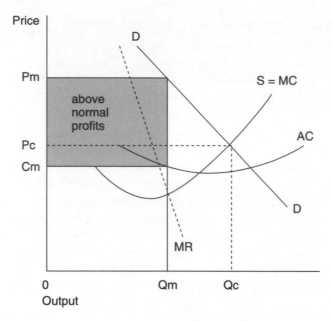

Figure 2.8   Monopoly and atomistic markets compared

a 'normal' profit return, are 0Cm; giving a high price–cost margin per unit sold of PmCm and large above-normal profits as indicated by the shaded area. The monopolist's ability to maintain high prices and secure high profits over the longer term is dependent upon not only the lack of immediate competition but also, critically, the inability of new competitors to break into the market and compete away these profits because of barriers to entry (see chapter 6). By contrast, atomistic markets are characterized by a large number of small suppliers each offering an identical product and easy entry conditions. In such markets prices are determined by the interaction of market demand (DD) and the collective outputs of the many small firms supplying the market (S). Since no one firm is large enough to influence this price they must all accept the 'ruling' market price (0Pc) and at this price a total quantity 0Qc would be supplied. Thus, conventional market theory predicts that monopoly leads to a higher price and a lower output than does atomistic competition.

However, the conclusion that atomistic markets yield superior results is crucially dependent on the assumption that cost structures are identical for small competitive firms and large monopolistic firms. But as the previous section on economies of scale made clear, this is not usually the case. Where industries are characterized by significant economies of scale large firms are able to produce at lower costs than smaller firms. The economies of scale factor thus opens up the possibility that a concentrated market may be technically more efficient than an atomistic market, producing a greater total output at a lower price.

Furthermore, large-scale monopolistic firms often have a greater incentive to invest and develop new production processes, since they are better able to finance research into new technology and are better able to fully exploit it. This means that any relative cost advantages accruing to monopolistic firms through economies of scale may be reinforced by absolute cost advantages deriving from process innovation.

In practice, most markets lie between these two extremes. In some (monopolistically competitive) markets there are a large number of small firms, but since they do not offer identical products each firm has a limited amount of pricing discretion over its differentiated brand of the product. In other (oligopolistic) markets a small number of large firms supply the majority of the market and thus may be able collectively to raise prices to monopoly levels through formal collusion and price leadership (see the Technical Appendix).

Judging the 'reasonableness' of profit rates

Support for the contention that firms in markets with high levels of seller concentration and high entry barriers are able to achieve above-normal profits can be found in various empirical studies of the relationship of profit rates to concentration levels, including those of Bain, Mann, and Collins and Preston for the US and Cowling and Waterson, Geroski, and Hitiris for the UK. (For a review of these and other studies see Hay and Morris (1991) and George, Joll and Lynk (1992).)

However, there are problems in interpreting profit/concentration data. Assuming that there is a positive correlation between concentration and profitability can this be attributed to monopolistic exploitation as conventional theory maintains, or does it reflect superior efficiency on the part of the dominant firm or firms? Demsetz (1973), for example, argues that firms with superior efficiency will have both high market shares and high profitability. This highlights the need to take a dynamic view of market processes. To quote Demsetz, 'if rivals seek better ways to satisfy buyers or to produce a product, and if one or a few succeed in such endeavours then the reward for their entrepreneurial efforts is likely to be some (short term) monopoly power, and this may be associated with increased industry concentration'. These sentiments reflect the earlier views of the Austrian economists, most notably Schumpeter (1965), who argue that all competition involves a process of 'creative destruction' and that where dominant firms arise from innovative performance which destroys their rivals' market positions then the resulting monopolies are not necessarily harmful. This is to be contrasted with a situation in

---

Box 2.4 Profitability and market concentration: some examples

Monopolies and Mergers Commission

- *BPB (plasterboard report, 1990)* – market share 76 per cent, rate of return on capital employed 37 per cent (1985–9).

MMC comment: BPB's high level of profitability was due in part to 'improved efficiency, coupled with high and rapidly expanding demand', but was also due in part to the fact that BPB 'was able to charge its customers prices higher than would have been the case in conditions of more normal competition, and this, we find, was a step taken by BPB to exploit the monopoly situation'. (paragraph 9.105).

- *Intermed (artificial lower limbs report, 1989)* – market share 70 per cent, rate of return on capital employed 53 per cent (1985–7).

MMC comment: 'We have considered whether these returns were higher than would normally be expected in a low risk business of this nature, conducted as it is with completely creditworthy customers' (mainly the National Health Service). The MMC concluded that 'the prices obtained are higher than would have been achieved in the absence of the monopoly situation' (paragraph 8.12).

- *Nestlé (soluble coffee report, 1991)* – market share 47 per cent, rate of return on capital employed 42 per cent (1985–9).

MMC comment: 'It may be regretted that no other firm has to date proved as effective a competitor as Nestlé, but this is no reason to conclude that Nestlé's performance is against the public interest . . . its high profitability need not lead us to penalise that success in a market characterised by a wide degree of choice. Its high profitability should indeed be seen as an incentive for other firms to compete in this lucrative market.' (paragraph 7.79).

---

which a high rate of return is obtained through monopolistic pricing. (See box 2.4.)

It is, of course, possible that society will remain worse off under concentrated markets, even if monopolists achieve scale economies and innovate; the benefits of large-scale production and innovation may not outweigh the costs of monopolistic exploitation, monopolistic firms not sharing efficiency gains with consumers but appropriating these gains for themselves in the form of above-normal profits or dissipating them in the form of organizational slack/X-inefficiency (see chapter 9). Where a firm increases its market share through internal, organic growth meeting and beating competition, rather than by means of merger with, and take-over of, rivals which eliminates competition, the overall result is likely to be more favourable to the public interest since the former route forces firms to share their efficiency gains with consumers in order to gain market share.

Summary

Firms can seek to capitalize on their existing production and marketing know-how by expanding sales of their existing products in their present markets. Where present markets are fast growing this can offer the firm a profitable expansion path; however, where the firm's existing markets are small, slow growing or declining, horizontal expansion may offer only limited opportunities for further expansion although it may be possible for firms to sustain growth by internationalizing their operations (see chapter 5). Horizontal growth often enables the firm to increase its profitability by taking advantage of the lower unit costs associated with large-scale production and distribution. Horizontal growth which results in a firm achieving a high market share may give the firm better control of its market and reduces competitive encroachment upon its profits. Through these means the firm can develop a competitive advantage over rivals and the detailed manner it which in can do so is discussed further in chapters 8, 9 and 10.

Questions

1   Indicate some of the problems encountered in defining the boundaries of a particular product market.
2   (a) How might 'market concentration' be measured? (b) What are the possible advantages and disadvantages of the measures identified in part (a)?
3   Examine the nature and significance of economies of scale.
4   Discuss the main reasons why firms seek to expand horizontally.
5   Why might the monopolization of a market lead to adverse consequences for resource allocation efficiency?
6   Examine the possible associations between a firm's market share and its profitability/cash flow.

References

Demsetz, H., 1973. 'Industry Structure, Market Rivalry and Public Policy', *Journal of Law and Economics*, vol. 16.

Henderson, B. D., 1973. 'The Experience Curve Reviewed: The Growth Share Matrix of the Product Portfolio', Boston Consulting Group.

George, K. D., Joll, C. and Lynk, E. L., 1992. Chapters 5, 6 and 11, *Industrial Organization*, Routledge, 4th edn.

Hay, D. A. and Morris, D. J., 1991. Chapters 2, 8 and 15, *Industrial Economics and Organization*, 2nd edn, Oxford University Press.

Kay, J., 1990. 'Identifying the Strategic Market', *Business Strategy Review*, vol. 1, no. 1.

Levitt, T., 1960. 'Marketing Myopia', *Harvard Business Review*, July–August.

Pratten, C. F., 1971. *Economies of Scale in Manufacturing Industry*, Cambridge University Press.

Profit Impact of Market Strategies (PIMS), 1992. Database established 1975.

Retail Business (various issues), Economist Intelligence Unit.

Schumpeter, J., 1965. *Capitalism, Socialism and Democracy*, George Allen and Unwin.

Further Reading

Grant, R. M., chapters 2 and 3, *Contemporary Strategy Analysis*, Blackwell, 1991.

Luffman, G., Sanderson, S., Lea, E. and Kenny, B., chapters 6 and 9, *Business Policy*, Blackwell, 2nd edn, 1991.

3

Vertical Expansion

Vertical expansion involves a firm undertaking a number of successive stages in the supply of a product, as opposed to operating at only one stage. Backward ('upstream') integration occurs when a firm begins producing materials which were previously supplied to it by other firms (e.g. a camera producer making glass lenses). Forward ('downstream') integration occurs when a firm undertakes further finishing of a product, final assembly or distribution (e.g. an oil company which sells petrol through its own petrol stations). The firm may integrate vertically through organic growth by establishing new supply sources or outlets, or it may choose to expand vertically by merger with, or take-over of, established suppliers or distributors. In the case of complete vertical integration the firm actually *owns* earlier or later stage activities. On the other hand, quasi-integration may be achieved through contractual arrangements such as exclusive dealing and franchises. In this chapter the advantages and disadvantages for the firm of vertical integration are discussed, and some of the public policy issues raised by vertical relationships are addressed. First the nature of vertical integration and the concept of the 'value chain' will be discussed.

Vertical Firms and Markets

The extent to which a particular firm is vertically integrated need not coincide with the extent to which a series of vertically linked markets are integrated. From the firm's perspective the degree of vertical integration relates essentially to the number of production and distribution stages or vertically linked markets the firm operates in. Thus, the more stages the firm is involved in the more vertically integrated the firm is said to be. However, a series of vertically linked markets may be populated by a

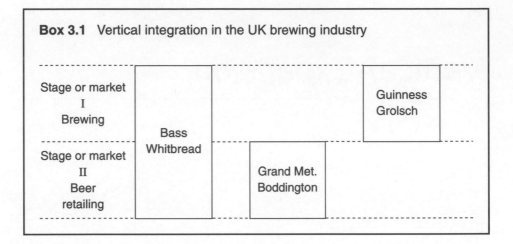

Box 3.1   Vertical integration in the UK brewing industry

mixture of fully vertically integrated firms, partially integrated firms which operate in a more limited number of the vertically linked markets, and single-stage firms (see box 3.1), buying their inputs from and selling their outputs to, other firms.

In the last analysis, where *all* firms operate across two or more vertically linked stages then these stages may cease to be viewed as 'separate' markets but rather as a single integrated market or industry embracing all stages. The distinction between the two situations described above can have important implications for competitive relationships. Where some firms in the chain of activities are dependent on other firms as sources of inputs or outlets for their products then a completely integrated firm may be able to exercise market power over non-integrated competitors by virtue of its dominance of a particular stage (see below). By contrast, when all firms are fully vertically integrated then no one firm can act to deprive its competitors of either raw materials or outlets since each firm has its own, although, of course, any one firm may exercise market power by holding a large share of the single integrated market.

Conceptual Frameworks for Analysing Vertical Markets

Markets and hierarchies

Many industries involve two or more successively linked vertical operations with firms operating at different stages in the chain of activities, firms at earlier stages selling to firms at later stages. However, with vertical integration by firms successive stages of production and distribution are brought under a single managerial supervision and markets are bypassed. As Coase (1937) notes, if there were no economies of integration there would be no need for firms, since factors of production would always be completely coordinated and organized by the market alone. However, the firm can sometimes coordinate resources more efficiently than the market and achieve economies of integration such as reducing stockholding by coordinating throughput volume at different stages to minimize interstage stocks. Coase argues that identification of a 'stage' of a vertical productive process is a matter of finding where these economies of integration finally disappear and at which point a market relationship with the next 'stage' can intervene.

Coase's idea that transactions can be effected through markets or embodied within the firm, was developed further by Williamson (1971) who explored when an internal organization or hierarchy is likely to displace the market in terms of two concepts: (1) 'transaction costs' and (2) the extent of uncertainty about cost and demand conditions. Transaction costs are those costs which are associated with buying and selling in a market and include the costs of finding satisfactory input suppliers and distributors for products, and the costs of negotiating, concluding and monitoring contracts with other firms. Williamson argues that internal organizations will tend to displace the market where these transaction costs are high and where there is considerable uncertainty about, for example, the reliability of input supplies. Under these circumstances firms may choose to integrate vertically in order to minimize transaction costs and reduce uncertainty.

The value chain

Strategically, it is useful to view successively linked vertical activities as constituting a 'value-added' chain. Figure 3.1 illustrates the value-added chain for a range of petrochemical products, focusing on the particular example of a plastic bread bin. The chain begins with the extraction of crude oil from land- and sea-based oil wells; crude oil is then transported by pipeline or shipped to an oil refinery which is located either close to the oil wells or in some major industrial centre. At the refinery crude oil is 'cracked', i.e. broken down into various 'primary' base materials such as ethylene, butadiene and propylene. These primary derivatives are then processed and combined with chemicals and other materials to form 'secondary' materials such as polythene and phenol. These materials in turn are processed further, combined with other materials and subjected to various treatments and assembly operations before finally emerging as finished products, such as plastic bread bins, pharmaceuticals, tyres etc.

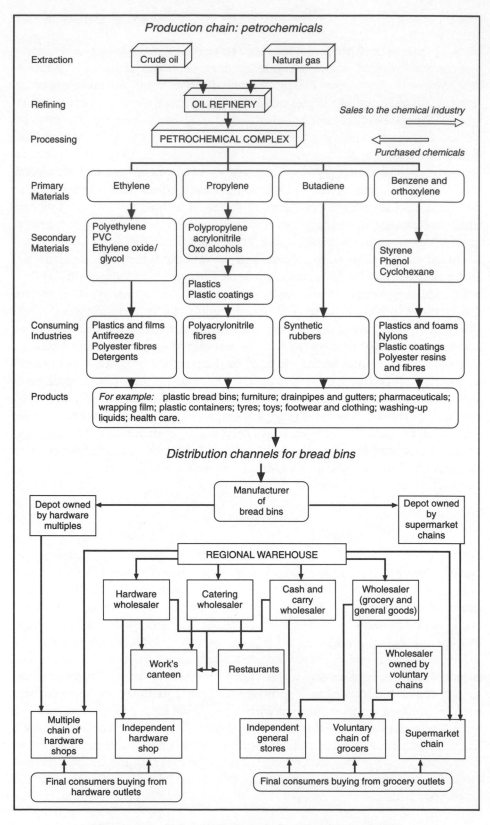

Figure 3.1 Value-added chain for plastic bread bins

Distribution channels provide the pathways to markets. They incorporate a sequence of value-adding activities which assist the passage of goods to the final consumer. A fundamental problem exists because manufacturers typically produce large quantities of a limited variety of goods, while customers normally desire a limited quantity of a broad range of goods. Consequently, a number of distribution tasks must be undertaken to ensure that goods of appropriate quality and form are provided to customers in the right quantities at the right time and at convenient locations. Market information must be gathered, storage must be provided for inventories, large quantities (e.g. pallets) must be broken down into smaller lots (e.g. individual packs), outlets need to be operated close to consumers and credit and service facilities have to be established. The main activities of wholesaling and retailing plastic bread bins are illustrated in figure 3.1.

As the figure illustrates, there are a number of possible distribution channel structures for moving bread bins to the final consumer. The pathways employed reflect the relative costs and marketing effectiveness of the various systems and also depend upon 'tradition' in the trade and the characteristics of the markets being served.

A firm can operate at any one stage or across a number of stages of the value-added chain above. However, industry-wide value-added chains are often too broad in identifying important sources of competitive advantage for firms. Thus, as Porter (1980) argues, the value chain of the particular firm should be the appropriate unit of analysis for the firm. Value is the amount buyers are willing to pay for what a firm provides them, and is measured by total revenue obtained. A firm's profitability depends upon the extent to which the value it commands exceeds the costs involved in creating the product. The value chain consists of 'value activities' (the physically and technologically distinct activities performed by the firm) used to create a product which buyers are prepared to purchase at the prices on offer, and 'margin' which is the difference between total revenue and the collective cost of performing the value activities.

Primary and support activities

Value activities can be divided into two broad types, 'primary activities' and 'support activities' as indicated in figure 3.2. Primary activities are those activities which involve the production of a good or service and its sale and movement to the buyer as well as after-sales facilities, whilst support activities provide purchased inputs, technology, human resources and various firm-wide information functions which support the primary activities.

In the Porter schema there are five broad categories of primary activities:

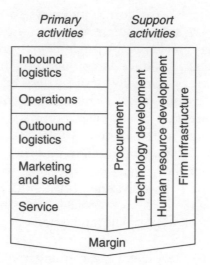

Figure 3.2 The Porter value chain
Source: Porter (1980)

1 *Inbound logistics activities* which involve receiving, storing and disseminating inputs to the product manufacturing process (e.g. materials handling, warehousing, stock control etc.).
2 *Operations activities* involving the transformation of inputs into products (e.g. machining, assembly, packaging etc.).
3 *Outbound logistics* activities associated with storing and distributing the product (e.g. finished goods warehousing, order processing, delivery etc.).
4 *Marketing and sales* activities associated with generating customer demand for the firm's products such as advertising and sales promotion etc.
5 *Service activities* such as installation, repairs and parts supply etc. which help maintain the value of the product.

Due attention to primary activities is important in the context of establishing and maintaining competitive advantages (lower costs, superior products etc.) over rival suppliers. Differences in the value chains of major competitors reflect the emphasis each firm places upon particular activities as its major competitive strength, so that, for example, one firm in a market may rely primarily upon the efficiency of its production operations, whilst another may emphasize marketing expertise. Importantly, the scope of an individual firm's value chain has to be considered in the context of the industry value-added chain in which the firm operates. Some firm's value chains may encompass only one stage of the industry (e.g. in terms of figure 3.1 an oil exploration firm or hardware store), whilst other firm's value chains may embrace several industry stages (e.g. in terms of figure 3.1 a petrochemical firm). The emphasis of a firm's primary activities will be influenced by the 'length' of its value chain (i.e. the number of industry stages embraced) and upon whether the activities are undertaken near the beginning of the industry value-added chain or towards the end. Thus, for example, an oil exploration firm would place particular emphasis upon its inbound logistics and operations whereas a hardware store would place particular stress upon marketing and sales, and service activities.

Contractual Forms of Vertical Coordination

The coordination of successively related production and distribution activities can be achieved, as noted above, through markets at the one extreme and by vertical integration within a firm at the other. In between these extremes other 'looser' possibilities exist. Several institutional arrangements may be employed, including long-term supply and distribution contracts, franchising and futures markets. These devices seek to reduce transaction costs or uncertainty and provide some of the advantages expected of vertical integration.

Long-term contracts

Long-term supply or distribution contracts provide a means for a firm to secure inputs and distribution outlets through legal contracts tying the firm to particular suppliers and distributors. Often a firm will use a single outside supplier for each particular material or component with the supplier operating a 'just-in-time' (JIT) system, delivering batches of materials or components just as they are needed for production or assembly operations. Such an arrangement serves to minimize the firm's stockholding of materials or components, with consequent cost savings. Similar arrangements with distributors serve to economize on finished product stocks by matching the production or assembly of products with deliveries to customers. Since long-term supply contracts often embody predefined quality standards for materials or components such contracts also serve to reduce the costs of goods-inward inspection. Moreover, there is an increasing tendency in some industries to involve suppliers in the firm's new product and process development efforts, consulting them at an early stage on the implications for material or component supply. Such long-term contractual arrangements have been widely employed amongst others by Japanese car manufacturers. However, JIT contracts leave a firm vulnerable to production losses occasioned by delivery hold-ups or component defects and for this reason some firms prefer dual sourcing of key inputs.

Sometimes long-term supply contracts can take the form of exclusive dealing arrangements whereby a firm agrees with a supplier or distributor that the latter will not supply to or distribute for any other firm over a specified time period. They are sometimes also known as Loyalty Agreements, Tying Agreements or Requirements Contracts and usually involve the user or distributor undertaking to obtain from the firm its total requirements of the product.

Franchises

Long-term contracts with distributors could involve the firm granting rights to supply its products through other firms by means of franchise arrangements. The franchisee pays a royalty to the franchisor for the rights to supply the franchisor's products. Examples of franchises include the McDonald Burger and Kentucky Fried Chicken diner chains, Tie Rack and Dyno-Rod.

Franchises are a form of co-partnership, offering mutual benefits. They allow the franchisor to expand sales rapidly and widely, sometimes on a global basis, without having to raise large amounts of capital, by building on the efforts of a motivated team of entrepreneurs. Individual franchisees are usually required to contribute the bulk of the investment in physical assets and hence have a personal interest in the success of the venture. On the franchisee's side, he/she obtains access to an innovative product or novel selling method, with the franchisor providing back-up, technical assistance, specialized equipment and advertising and promotion. In order to maximize distribution of the product a franchisor will generally enter into non-exclusive franchise arrangements with a number of firms. However, where the franchisor needs to retain a high degree of control over the distribution of its product it may enter into an exclusive franchising arrangement with just one distributor.

Futures contracts

Another means for the firm to reduce uncertainty about quantities, qualities and prices of raw materials is to enter into futures contracts. Futures markets enable buyers to negotiate forward delivery contracts on specified quantity, quality and price terms. However, organized futures markets generally only cover a limited range of commodity-type raw materials such as cotton, iron ore, tea etc.

Advantages of Vertical Integration

Firms undertake vertical integration because they are motivated either by considerations of efficiency in terms of the availability of technological joint economies and the ability to bypass imperfect markets, or the strategic need to ensure a reliable supply of factor inputs and market access.

Cost and profit considerations

There are certain costs involved in coordinating resources by means of market transactions which can be eliminated by integration.

Production costs   The cost advantages of integrating processes are most obvious in cases where technologically complementary production processes can be carried out in quick succession in a single plant. For example, the integration of making pig-iron, converting iron into steel, and shaping steel into semi-finished products – all in a single plant – permits considerable savings in the total fuel requirement for heating the iron and steel. If all functions are performed in a single plant, neither the pig-iron nor the steel ingots have to get cold and then be reheated before passing to the next production process. Equally in a vertically integrated organization it becomes possible to treat metals with finishes before they are exposed to oxygen corrosion. Again, the ability to turn pulp into newsprint without the need for the drying and reconstitution that would be involved if the pulp had to be delivered to a different organization between processes, represents a considerable cost-saving.

A second form of production savings arises from the easier consultation, planning and coordination of adjacent processes that is made possible in a vertically integrated organization. Forward scheduling is facilitated, the economies of longer production runs may be achieved and a steadier pattern of production activity and/or more intensive utilization of capacity and spreading of overheads may ensue. Inventory or stock levels may be kept at a lower level than would apply where unintegrated activities were carried on. Specifically, a firm may be able to practise JIT supply arrangements at each phase in the production process, minimizing the amount of buffer stock held between production processes to avoid production disruptions caused by materials shortages. Because of better coordination the buffer stocks held by a vertically integrated firm would generally be smaller than the stocks it would need to carry when supplied with materials or components by independent suppliers, even compared to firms relying on external JIT contracts.

Similar considerations apply to issues of component quality and reliability and the vertically integrated firm will often be in a better position to assure product quality by making its own components than by relying on external suppliers, even where it lays down rigorous quality standards for external suppliers. Intra-group trading should also allow costs of distribution to be lowered through easier storage and handling, and possibly more economical delivery arrangements. In some cases ownership of distribution outlets may be necessary if required standards of service for a complex product are to be provided.

Transaction costs   There are various 'transaction costs' involved with dealing at 'arm's length' with outside parties which may be eliminated or reduced through integration. Firms, for example, incur costs in finding satisfactory input suppliers and distributors for their products and in negotiating, concluding and monitoring contracts with other firms. These economies arise from overcoming the lack of information between unintegrated firms. If there is a high degree of interdependence among successive stages of production, coordinating responses to changes in market conditions may be difficult to secure if the separate stages are operated independently. The conditions for long-term contracts with suppliers are very difficult to negotiate in order to allow for uncertainties, whilst short-term contracts, relying exclusively on market (price) signals, tend to be costly in terms of negotiation time and involve further lags before the new arrangements can be brought into existence. Other information problems involve uncertainties about whether the other party can fulfil all the terms of contract, including meeting delivery dates, technical specifications and so forth. Integration can also be important in accommodating periodic design and/or volume changes in response to changing market circumstances and in long-run investment planning.

With long-term contracts there is the dilemma between, on the one hand, providing for sufficient flexibility in the terms of the contract to meet changed conditions, and on the other, avoiding contractual ambiguities which may, at a future time, involve further bargaining. Short-term contracts facilitate adaptive decision-making but deter suppliers from investing compared with long-term arrangements that permit the supplier to recoup his investment. With vertical integration, therefore, it is possible that the conflict between efficient investment and efficient decision-making may be avoided. Williamson (1971) suggests that with vertical integration adaptations to changing market conditions become an occasion for cooperative adjustment rather than opportunistic bargaining.

Internalization of control achieved by vertical integration has the further advantage of reducing bargaining costs and haggling over the exchange price for materials or components. Minor conflicts over differences of interpretation of supply terms between independent firms can often only be settled by means of haggling or litigation over the contract conditions. By contrast, within an integrated firm, disputes between divisions of the firm over the terms on which they supply one another can be more easily resolved by senior management arbitration.

However, although a firm may avoid some transaction costs by vertical integration this may not represent a 'pure' saving in such costs since they may be offset, wholly or in part, by the higher administrative and other costs involved in running a vertically integrated business.

Make or buy   In some cases internalizing input supply may be profitable if the unit cost of production to the firm is less than the external supply price. If the price of an input exceeds its costs of production, it may prove profitable for the firm to integrate backward and make the input itself. However, if there are economies of scale in the production of the input, integration and self-production is only profitable if the firm's typical requirement for the input is sufficiently large to realize these economies and produce for itself at a cost which is below the external supply price. If the firm's typical requirement for the input is too small to achieve scale economies, production for self-consumption only is uneconomical. However, even here the possibility exists that the firm could produce an efficient rate of output, consume some units itself, and sell the remainder to other buyers.

In some market situations buying-in costs may be inflated by the application of monopoly surcharges by powerful suppliers. In such circumstances firms have a stronger incentive to make their own materials and components.

The decision to 'make or buy' is not a mutually exclusive pair of alternatives and sometimes a firm can choose to both make and buy. For example, the large firm can sometimes realize savings by keeping an integrated division, supplying most of its normal requirements of some raw material or component, operating at or near the optimal level, whilst it displaces the burden of market fluctuations – the cost of idle capacity – onto independent suppliers. To realize such private economies, however, the buyer must be sure that he himself will not be caught in a squeeze when he attempts to expand his open market purchase in times of short supply.

Stage profitability   A firm may be able to enhance its profitability by downstream integration into higher value-added activities. For example, the French flat glass producer St Gobain has integrated forward into glass fabrication and distribution: profit margins from chopping up glass for doors and windows and delivering them to tight specifications and schedules are larger than from basic glass-making. Similarly, chemical companies such as Hoechst have found it profitable to move downstream into 'specialist' petrochemical product and paint applications.

The need to 'balance' inputs and outputs between stages   In some industrial situations, stage 'balancing' considerations might mitigate against vertical integration. In the case of many consumer goods, especially nondurables, there are considerable economies of scale to the distributor from handling a large number of lines, only a few of which will be supplied by any one manufacturer. Thus forward integration into retailing is unlikely under these circumstances. Similarly, backward integration may not be feasible or an economical use of resources in industries where technical progress in the supply industry is faster than a processor can keep up with, or where one process offers greater scale advantages than its related activity. This latter issue of balancing input–output relationships between stages is an important one. Tin can manufacturers, for example, have in general not found it economical to integrate backward to produce their own steel strip for tinplating largely because steel firms producing a variety of intermediary products can attain economies of scale in production which permit them to sell steel strip to the can-makers at a lower price than the can-maker's cost of producing steel would be.

Control of inputs and markets   The desire to achieve stability and reliability in the flow of some input is often cited as an important motive for vertical integration. Because of the existence of market imperfections the price mechanism may fail to function efficiently in coordinating supply and demand. By controlling the production of an input, a firm can channel this production to its own use, thereby ensuring continuity of supply. In general, a firm will attempt to exercise control over certain inputs that are crucial to its viability. For example, if there are no or few substitutes for the input, then a disruption in that input's supply could seriously curtail output. In a sense, the input is essential in the production of the firm's product; attempts to use substitute inputs would lead to sharply increased costs. The longer-term strategic requirement of maintaining essential supplies may override immediate cost factors. Similarly, suppliers may undertake forward integration into their market outlets in order to secure a more effective control over demand for their products. (See box 3.2.)

Firms may also seek to extend their control of inputs and markets for defensive reasons when they are confronted by powerful suppliers and buyers who can excessively limit their own market discretion. A firm may also find it convenient to have a bridgehead on the opposite side of the market as a check on costs, profit margins or market conditions. This need not be a substantial operation, but it can always be expanded upon if large independent suppliers or customers offer terms that are considered to be unreasonable, and the suppliers or customers will, of course, be aware of this.

A firm may undertake integration if it is threatened with foreclosure from the other side of the market. If one firm tries to increase its own market power by pre-empting sources of supply or markets, its rivals will

Box 3.2   Vertical integration in the UK housing finance market

The explosive growth in the UK housing market in the mid-1980s together with financial deregulation resulting from the Building Societies Act 1986 and the Financial Services Act 1986 encouraged a number of the major building societies to integrate backwards into the estate agency business. The table below shows the number of estate agency branches owned by selected building societies and banks in late 1990 as a result of acquiring established estate agencies and setting up new ones.

Institution	Branches
Halifax BS	640
Lloyds Bank (Black Horse)	500
Nationwide Anglia BS	430
Abbey National	420
Woolwich BS	120
Leeds BS	110

   This move by building societies and banks was partly to protect their mortgage business since estate agents are often the first point of contact for people entering the housing market and generally organize mortgages for customers. Thus, buying estate agents provided the building societies and banks with relatively secure distribution channels for mortgage business. In addition, these institutions were able to use their agency branches to sell other lucrative financial services such as life-assurance policies linked to mortgages. See also box 3.3, 'Vertical disintegration in the UK housing finance market'.

be certain to take vigorous counter-measures, perhaps by invading the opposite side to secure an integrated supply or market subsidiary.

   Even though it may face no direct threat of foreclosure, a large firm may integrate vertically in response to any circumstance which places it at a disadvantage in its cross-market relations. If oligopolistic suppliers, for instance, maintain strong collusive control over price, the large buyer will generally consider bypassing the dominant sellers and creating a satellite source of supply. Similarly, if some intermediary producers are themselves subjected to a 'price squeeze' by their suppliers they may undertake backward integration (see below).

   These and other strategic considerations may override cost factors. Thus, for example, a firm in a thin and unreliable resource market may make its own supplies even at a higher cost, the additional cost burden being in effect an insurance premium against production losses caused by shortages of materials. However, in time, greater experience may bring down the cost, and the integration may be a success even on the strictest financial reckoning.

The firm will probably use forward or backward integration, not as a short-run bargaining tactic, but as a response to permanently unfavourable terms of trade. Once undertaken, the commitment is not easily revoked. The feasibility of backward or forward integration in view of cost conditions, market accessibility and the like, will presumably be known to sellers and buyers, and they will adapt their policies in the long run to the threshold terms that will just fail to induce a firm on the other side of the market to move in on their own. It may be, of course, that the short-term threat of changing suppliers will be a more potent weapon in the hands of the large buyer than the long-term threat of backward integration, and that short-run bargaining tactics will dominate the sellers' behaviour also. But cross-market integration will remain as an ultimate check to joint profit maximization by firms on the other side.

Vertical integration can take the form of a merger between an existing buyer and an existing seller, or the buyer may set up an independent source of supply. The former is the more probable result when the motive for integration is the avoidance of foreclosure by rivals. When a firm wishes to bypass a collusive agreement on the opposite side of the market it is more likely to establish new capacity to replace a previously existing market relationship. In this case there is new entry and expansion of capacity in the industry across the market.

Some or all of the above factors may explain the level of firm integration at particular points in time. Vertical integration can also be viewed as a dynamic industry process with the degree of integration varying over the industry's 'life span'. In the early days of an industry there is often no specialist supply industry so that manufacturers must engage in some backward integration producing their own semi-finished goods or components. Equally a manufacturer of a sophisticated new product may integrate forwards to control the distribution of the product to ensure its resale under satisfactory conditions. In time, as a specialist supply industry develops, and independent distributors acquire expertise, manufacturers can, if they choose, run down their own vertical involvement. Examples of vertical disintegration of this sort through time can be found in food packaging with the growth of Metal Box, and in photographic goods where Kodak, in the 1930s, decided it was no longer necessary to own its own retail outlets as other retailers were now providing satisfactory distribution of its product.

At the other end of the life cycle for a product or industry, as the rate of expansion of the market decreases, there may be an increase in both horizontal and vertical integration. The vertical integration here may be a reflection of the particular horizontal competitive pressures for market shares which will often encourage attempts particularly to increase control over outlets. By contrast, Harrigan (1980) argues that vertical integration tends to reduce in the mature phase of the industry life cycle and to be lower towards the end of the cycle as declining profitability forces managers to concentrate on short-term profit targets and cut back new capital investment. At this time investment in reinforcing integrative relationships becomes difficult to justify and managers are forced to re-assess the extent to which the firm's vertically integrated assets are appropriate to the new market conditions. (See below under the heading 'Some Dangers of Vertical Integration for the Firm'.)

Transfer-pricing

Transfer prices are the internal prices at which factor inputs, components and products are transacted between the branches or subsidiaries of a vertically integrated firm. Vertically integrated firms often seek to retain a divisional structure of the firm, and make divisional managers responsible for their own profits. Each division is a profit centre in its own right, with efficient managers being rewarded in line with their divisional performance. However, divisional autonomy creates problems of transfer-pricing. What price should be charged by one division for the product it sells to another? Should the sister division be compelled to buy at the price asked? The pricing and purchasing policies adopted will affect divisional profitability and so management morale, and influence the long-run efficiency of the integrated firm.

Transfer-pricing policy often has as its prime objective the maximization of group profits. A second objective is to permit divisional managers to profit-maximize as autonomous units. The transfer price rules which senior group management lay down must be such that both of these objectives can be pursued simultaneously, otherwise sub-optimizing will occur, with divisional managers maximizing their unit performance at the expense of overall company profit. The transfer price charged may be set by reference to the prices ruling in outside markets for inputs and products (arm's-length pricing). Where a factor input, component or product being transferred has a competitive market such that the purchasing division could secure its supplies from a sister division or from an outside source, then the transfer price will generally be set at the open market price. The purchasing division can then choose to purchase some or all of its supplies from its sister division at the market price, and the producing division can supply all or part of the purchasing division's requirement as it chooses. Neither purchasing nor supply division is compelled by group management to purchase or supply internally. Such arm's-length pricing would serve to reflect the underlying market values of the factor inputs, components or products transferred.

However, many factor inputs, components or products have either an imperfect external market or no external market so that internal administered prices must be set. Here the transfer price may be set at a lower or higher level than the going market price according to some internal accounting convention (e.g. cost of production plus standard profit mark-up) and the desired 'profit split' between the firm's activities. Such administered transfer prices would generally be designed to achieve the firm's overall profit goals, but in transfer-pricing decisions there may often be an inherent conflict between the overall goals of the firm and the goals of its sub-units. For example, if one cost centre is allowed to transfer components at cost of production plus a specific mark-up, then it has little incentive to minimize its production costs. Again, where a profit centre does not have discretion over its buying or selling prices but must buy or sell some or all of its inputs or outputs to other sub-units at transfer prices established by headquarters, then the profit performance of the sub-unit will not depend solely upon the efforts of local managers, making it difficult to evaluate the performance of sub-group managers and motivate them to improve efficiency.

Transfer-pricing gives a firm added flexibility in pricing its products. It may deploy transfer-pricing to gain a competitive advantage over rival suppliers (to 'price-squeeze' a non-integrated rival – see below). In various other ways transfer prices may be set at artificial levels which reflect price discrimination strategies. An exporting company may charge a higher price for its product in one export market than it does in other countries where it faces stiffer competition, so recovering a disproportionate amount of its overheads from the market.

Multinational firms can use transfer prices to boost their after-tax profits, by transfer-pricing across national frontiers so that the greater part of the firm's profits are received in a low-taxation economy. By inflating the price it pays for components or services imported from overseas subsidiaries, the multinational can reduce its recorded profit in high-tax countries. Such inflated transfer prices also serve to remit surpluses back to the parent company from subsidiaries located in countries which limit the repatriation of profits through exchange controls.

Some Dangers of Vertical Integration for the Firm

Whilst vertical integration can produce certain benefits for a firm, it also involves certain drawbacks:

Loss of flexibility and cost-effectiveness

Vertical integration may reduce a firm's flexibility and blunt cost-effectiveness. The temptation to procure inputs exclusively from subsidiaries may lead the firm to ignore (or be unaware of) profitable external buying opportunities, or the availability of superior parts or components from outside suppliers. Similarly, ownership of *particular* types of distribution outlets (e.g. 'specialized' shops) may make a firm myopic to changes in distribution channels (e.g. a switch of primary demand away from 'specialist' outlets to purchases in supermarkets). Moreover, 'captive' buying and selling arrangements may breed complacency and lack of attention to cost control with the result that the firm's underlying cost structure suffers from 'X-inefficiency'. This may well be compounded by the use of inappropriate transfer-pricing procedures which mask cost-inefficiencies.

Further, the firm needs to consider its cost situation alongside the broader picture of its portfolio of brands and its position in the value chain in terms of profit generation. Examination of the 'make or buy' decision in this context may well suggest *vertical disintegration as market conditions change*. Thus, for example, the UK regional brewers Boddington and Greenalls have quit brewing to concentrate on their pub retailing operations in response to a number of factors:

- primary demand for their self-brewed products was insufficient to maintain brewery throughput at break-even levels;
- an increasing proportion (over a half) of their drinks sales were accounted for by bought-in lager brands ('Heineken' and 'Stella Artois' bought from Whitbread in the case of Boddingtons);
- there was greater scope for adding value and improving profitability through extending their retail pub chains, using their bargaining power to obtain bought-in brands at favourable price discounts and investing in amenities to build market share.

However, firms must be aware that they need an appropriate skill base to successfully realize added value in the assets they retain.

Exposure to cyclical demand fluctuations

Vertical integration often increases the exposure of the firm to *cyclical* demand tendencies, rippling back up the chain from fluctuations in final demand (box 3.3). A vertically integrated firm, having balanced its various production phases to a given capacity or throughput level, is then highly vulnerable to changes in demand levels. Decreases in demand are likely to leave it with excess production capacity at *all* production phases and can result in the build-up of excessive interprocess stocks. By contrast, increases in demand can leave the firm unable to respond since it lacks adequate capacity at *all* stages of production. This can be partly offset by using, in the case of inputs, outside suppliers as 'buffers' and, in the case of outputs, finding new distribution outlets or developing new downstream production applications.

Box 3.3 Vertical disintegration in the UK housing finance market

As presented in box 3.2, the boom in UK house sales from the mid-1980s onwards encouraged many building societies, banks and insurance groups to acquire estate agents. However, the slump in the housing market in the late 1980s and early 1990s (see table below) led to many of these groups making losses on their estate agency business. For example, in March 1993 the Abbey National disclosed that it had lost a total of £226 million on estate agency since it acquired its business in 1987 of which operating losses constituted £88 million and goodwill write-offs, £126 million. Such losses have caused some building societies and other financial institutions to sell off their estate agencies, generally at a significant discount off the original purchase price. In late 1990 Abbey National's Cornerstone chain totalled some 420 branches but this had been reduced to around 355 branches by 1993. In 1993, Abbey National announced the sale of the complete business. In 1992 Abbey gained around £500 million of business through the Cornerstone chain but found it was getting a similar flow of business through other agents that it did not own.

Loans for house purchase (building societies and banks)

	£ billion
1984	16.6
1985	18.9
1986	24.6
1987	25.0
1988	34.6
1989	31.2
1990	30.6
1991	25.4

Where firms operate with a high ratio of fixed to variable costs the 'make or buy' decision may be critical, especially in the context of cyclical downturns. Vertical disintegration may be necessary to convert a fixed cost into a variable cost and thus reduce the firm's exposure to declining volumes. For example, a holiday travel operator which owns its own fleet of aeroplanes could divest the fleet and use leasing arrangements to meet its transportation requirements.

Market obsolescence

Even this strategy, however, cannot insulate the firm from the 'ultimate threat', that of market obsolescence. A decline in primary demand resulting from a shift in the pattern of final demand or the introduction of new technologies and products leaves the firm 'locked into' a falling sales base. In order to avoid being locked in, the firm may actively cultivate progressive disintegration, shedding marginal upstream or downstream activities. Like horizontal expansion, vertical integration as a corporate strategy needs to be looked at alongside opportunities to diversify into *new* products and *new* markets.

Vertical Integration and Market Power

Public interest in vertical integration has centred on the possible effects of such integration as a source and carrier of market power.

Market 'distortions' and vertical integration

In general, entry into a vertically integrated industry is more difficult than would be entry into one of its component horizontal stages, at least by the amount of extra capital costs. Vertical integration converts what in its absence would be variable costs into fixed costs by substituting investment in fixed equipment for current outlays on purchases. Where the integration of existing firms is complete rather than partial, a potential entrant may have no opportunity to enter at one horizontal stage, because no supplying (or buying) market exists to serve him (or which he could serve). In some cases this must be accepted as a consequence of large efficient scale, just as large horizontal size must be accepted. In others, the integration may exist primarily because of its importance as an entry-limiting device. Firms possessing a significant degree of market power at one stage in a production chain can, by integrating backward or forward, spread that power to lower and higher stages and put competitors (particularly non-integrated rivals) at a disadvantage by, for example, applying a price squeeze or by a refusal to supply (see below under the heading 'Price-squeezing').

It is important to note, however, that vertical integration *alone* is insufficient to distort market processes and that it is the existence of *horizontal market power* and *entry barriers* at some stage of the integrated

Example

STAGE A	*Firm 1*	*Firm 2*	. . .	*Firm 100*
Market share	1%	1%		1%
STAGE B	*Firm 1*	*Firm 2*	. . .	*Firm 100*
Market share	1%	1%		1%
STAGE C	*Firm 1*	*Firm 2*	. . .	*Firm 100*
Market share	1%	1%		1%

enterprise which creates the potential for 'abuse'. Where *horizontal* dominance is absent, vertical integration cannot create market power, as the Example above demonstrates.

The production of a particular product comprises three processes, A, B and C: these initially constitute *separate* 'stages'. Stages A, B and C are atomistically organized with 100 small firms each contributing only 1 per cent to total output, and individual inputs and outputs between stages are balanced.

Assume now that each stage A firm merges with *one* stage B firm and *one* stage C firm. All that has happened is that *all* firms are now vertically integrated. The fundamental point is that the market is *still* atomistically organized; there are still 100 independent sources of supply, each contributing only 1 per cent of the output of the combined stages.

Foreclosure

Where one firm has market dominance of a particular stage and is protected by barriers to entry then it is in a position to adopt predatory tactics against non-integrated rivals. Assume that stage B in the Example above is monopolized by one firm which has taken over the other 99 stage B firms, giving it a market share in stage B of 100 per cent, while it continues to operate as a small player in stage A and stage C markets. It is now in a position to prevent the entry of new competitors, foreclosing access to the market. It can do so by depriving competitors of access to outlets, as in the example above where the monopoly firm at stage B can refuse to buy from any of the supplying firms at stage A. Alternatively, it can deprive competitors of access to inputs as in the example above where the monopoly firm at stage B can refuse to sell to any of the customer firms at stage C. The extent of foreclosure depends critically on the following:

1   An effective limitation on the establishment of *new* input sources and outlets, i.e. barriers to entry encountered *separately* at the input and outlet stages which prevent entry at that stage, and which operate *independently* of vertical integration, e.g. the exclusive ownership of scarce raw materials, patent protection on a key manufacturing process, government regulations (planning and licensing controls on the number and location of businesses) restricting the number of new sources of supply or points of sale.
2   In the case of existing suppliers, the degree of market dominance. Acquisition of the majority of input suppliers or outlets by a dominant firm may result in the foreclosure of competitors (provided, however, condition (1) above also applies). In the case of potential entrants, if *all* existing input suppliers and outlets are *collectively*

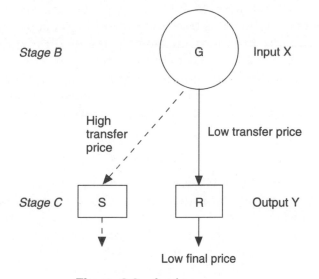

Figure 3.3 A price squeeze

controlled by existing suppliers (even though *individually* none of them is in a position of dominance), entrants are effectively denied market access (again, provided condition (1) above also applies).

Price-Squeezing

Where firms do not seek to foreclose markets to actual and potential competitors they may be in a position to circumscribe the power of competitors through predatory transfer-pricing aimed at price-squeezing their non-integrated competitors. Figure 3.3 illustrates how a price squeeze supposedly can be applied by a vertically integrated firm to injure non-integrated rivals.

Firm G is a monopoly supplier of input X at stage B, and is also engaged, along with other manufacturers, in the production of product Y at stage C. Firm G is shown as circle G and its stage C manufacturing operation as square R. The other manufacturers at stage C, who are dependent on firm G for their inputs, are shown by the square S.

A 'squeeze' is applied, it is alleged, if firm G charges competing firms at the second (manufacturing) level a *high transfer price* for input X, thereby raising their raw material cost base, and sells its finished product at the output level at a *low price* in hard competition with its non-integrated rivals. Thus, firm G in controlling both the input and output level prices has the power to determine for its competitors the profit spread between the stages, making it difficult for them to survive at the second, and for them the *only*, level of operation. However, firm G's ability to squeeze is due to the monopolization of the input stage, i.e. the lack of alternative sources of supply. Whilst it is true that integration enables an integrated firm to separate the market at the input stage, had the non-integrated manufacturers been able to draw on alternative sources of supply, the ability to discriminate would have been limited or even impossible. The real vice would appear to be the *monopoly* of the *input stage* and the *barriers to entry* operating to buttress that monopoly position.

Market dominance and the supply chain

The ability of firms to practise foreclosure and price-squeezing depends in essence upon the differential extent to which firms are vertically integrated and the extent to which firms at any one stage are dominant. In situations where there are mixes of market power different outcomes can arise. In the scenario developed from the Example above, two extreme situations were shown: the first was of a monopoly seller at stage B in the industry supplying many small buyers, and the second was of a monopsony buyer at stage B purchasing from many small suppliers.

The most extreme example of market power is one where a monopoly seller of materials or components confronts a monopsony buyer. In these situations of bilateral monopoly each firm exercises a degree of 'countervailing power' in curbing the market power of the other. The final terms and prices at which products are transacted between two bilateral monopolists depends upon their relative bargaining strength, although since they are mutually dependent upon one another they need to exercise some restraint in the interests of continued co-existence.

In practice, most vertical markets are characterized by a degree of concentration with small numbers of large oligopoly sellers and/or small numbers of large oligopsony buyers (bilateral oligopoly). The relative power of firms at each stage of the industry in relation to firms at other stages depends upon the extent to which they are able to collude in order to exercise a degree of collective monopoly power over a particular stage of the industry.

Alongside changes in ownership and control a firm may employ a range of other forms of vertical coordination such as long-term supply/distribution contracts to extend its influence over the market. For example, exclusive dealing contracts can be used to deprive rival suppliers of distribution outlets by committing those outlets exclusively to the one firm's products. Similarly, 'full-line forcing', where a supplier encourages distributors to stock not only his principal products but also other products from his range, can also serve to discourage distributors from stocking rival suppliers' products. Finally, 'aggregated rebates' may also be used to deprive rival suppliers of distribution outlets by offering distributors a discount on their *total* purchases from the supplier so as to encourage distributors to place all their regular orders with the one supplier. The ability to enforce these arrangements depends largely upon the effects of the supplier's threat to 'refuse to supply', which again depends upon the firm's market dominance of one market stage in the supply chain.

Summary

There are a number of reasons why firms integrate. First, companies may integrate for strategic reasons to secure sources of materials or market outlets in order to reduce uncertainty. Second, firms may integrate in order to secure efficiency gains which serve to lower production and distribution costs. Finally, firms may integrate for predatory reasons with a view to increasing their market power by foreclosing markets to present competitors and heightening entry barriers to potential competitors. However, firms must be mindful of the need to avoid being excessively tied to input sources and outlets and of its vulnerability to changes in demand. In particular, integration may leave the firm locked into the fortunes of a *specific* market and as such offers only limited opportunities for growth compared to diversification. The implications of vertical integration for competition, resource allocation and final product price will depend upon which of these motives predominate and how firms behave once they have integrated, which in turn will be influenced by the countervailing power of the firms' customers and suppliers.

Questions

1 Define and discuss the concept of the 'value chain'.
2 In what ways can vertical integration enable a firm to reduce its supply costs?
3 Discuss the main reasons why firms seek to expand vertically.
4 What are the possible disadvantages of vertical integration for a firm?
5 Why might vertical integration in a market lead to adverse consequences for resource allocation efficiency?
6 What is transfer-pricing? What considerations might a firm take into account when deciding upon a particular transfer-pricing system?

References

Coase, R. H., 1937. 'The Nature of the Firm', *Economica*, vol. 14.
Harrigan, K. R., 1980. *Strategies for Declining Industries*, D.C. Heath & Co.
Porter, M. E., 1980. *Competitive Strategy*, Free Press.
Williamson, O. E., 1971 'Vertical Integration of Production: Market Failure Considerations', *American Economic Review*, Paper and Proceedings, May.

Further Reading

George, K. D., Joll, C. and Lynk, E. L., chapter 3, *Industrial Organization*, Routledge, 4th edn, 1992.

Grant, R. M., chapters 6 and 7 ('Value Chain Sections'), *Contemporary Strategy Analysis*, Blackwell, 1991.

Harrigan, K. R., *Strategies for Vertical Integration*, Lexington Books, 1983.

Hay, D. A. and Morris, D. J., chapters 6 and 10, *Industrial Economics and Organization*, Oxford University Press, 2nd edn, 1991.

Luffman, G., Sanderson, S., Lea, E. and Kenny, B., chapter 9, *Business Policy*, Blackwell, 2nd edn, 1991.

Thompson, J. L., chapters 11 and 17, *Strategic Management*, Chapman and Hall, 1990.

4

Conglomerate Expansion

Conglomerate expansion or diversification is the expansion of a firm into a range of different product areas which involves it operating in a number of markets rather than a single market. Diversification may be 'concentric', based upon some carry over of production and marketing functions, by adding a new business which utilizes the firm's existing technological or marketing expertise. For example, a producer of stainless steel garden implements may add cutlery or razor blades to its product range. Alternatively, diversification may be 'pure', involving the firm expanding into unrelated product areas, e.g. a car producer expanding into the cement business.

Diversification may take the form of organic (internal) growth, or firms may choose to expand by external growth, merging with or taking over established firms. 'Concentric' diversification via internal growth often arises as a result of new discoveries and applications made by the firm's R & D activities as an extension of its existing technological expertise. For example, many producers of basic chemicals such as ICI have extended their businesses into areas of chemical derivatives, such as paint and pharmaceuticals. In the case of 'pure' diversification, mergers and take-overs often offer the better prospects of a successful entry into a new area. The distinction between concentric and pure diversification is, of course, somewhat arbitrary since most firms seek to justify their diversification programmes as offering some related concentric benefits on the production, marketing and financial fronts.

In this chapter the nature of conglomerate firms – and the motives for diversification – are examined and the public policy implications of diversification are discussed. In addition, attention is focused on the management of conglomerates and issues relating to the restructuring of the firm involving both expansion and divestment.

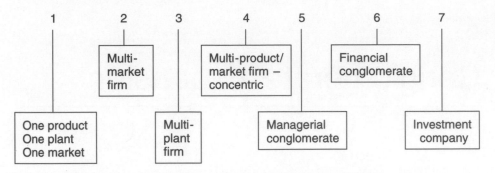

Figure 4.1   Categories of business firm (after Weston (1973))

The Nature of Conglomerate Firms

In order to analyse firms it is useful to identify the whole spectrum of types of firm in terms of the scope of their activities. Figure 4.1 illustrates seven categories of business firm. Category 1 represents the 'classic' firm of economic theory – one product produced in one plant. Category 2 represents geographical diversification into multi-regional, national or international markets, whilst category 3 represents multi-plant expansion; economies of scale play an important part in both these forms of expansion. Category 4 – 'concentric' expansion – is the multi-product firm in which there is some relationship between research, production or marketing functions for two or more products. This type of firm development involves a considerable potential 'carry over' of specific management functional capabilities.

Conglomerate firms are represented by categories 5 and 6. These are firms whose diversification, either internal or external, involves products whose engineering, design, production and marketing functional capabilities requirements overlap only to a very small degree (or not at all).

Category 5 – the 'managerial' conglomerate – is one in which a group of management specialists provides services to all of the operating entities. Category 6 – 'financial' conglomerates – is one in which the parent unit provides financial resources but does not interact with the management of the operating entity to any great extent except to hire or fire when performance falls short of some predetermined 'standard'. Investment companies – category 7 – have a financial stake in other operating entities but do not exercise any management control, i.e. they sell their investments if performance does not meet standards set. This framework is developed further below under the heading 'Motives for Diversification'.

The Extent of Diversification

Diversified firms, as has been noted, are characterized by the fact that they are engaged in a number of 'separate' activities, unlike a 'specialist' firm which is engaged in only one. Most techniques which measure diversification by counting products made by a firm or listing the number of industries the firm is engaged in are inevitably reliant upon the precision and width of the product and industry definitions employed. The problem of defining activities and markets was dealt with in chapter 2 where it was noted that demand definitions of markets need not correspond with supply definitions of industries generated from 'standard industrial classification' (SIC) data. If industries are defined narrowly, e.g. metal, glass and plastic containers, then expansion by a glass jar manufacturer into plastic containers might be regarded as concentric diversification. By contrast, if all of these items are encompassed within a broadly defined 'food packaging industry', then such expansion would be regarded simply as horizontal growth. In practice, most measures of diversification rely heavily upon disaggregated SIC data.

Number of business activities embraced and their relative importance

A related problem is that of measuring diversification itself. Two widely used measures are (1) the number of industries in which a firm is engaged and (2) the proportion of a firm's sales (or other size measure) undertaken outside the firm's primary or core industry. The first method indicates the number of industries in which the firm operates but can be misleading if the firm operates on only a small scale in many of its industries. The second method has the merit of highlighting the relative importance of a firm's primary versus secondary activities, but gives no indication of the range of secondary activities undertaken. For this reason, composite measures of diversification are to be preferred, such as that developed by Utton (1979). Figure 4.2 shows that 50 per cent of the firm's total sales is derived from its primary industry, a further 20 per cent from its next most important industry and so on. Utton derived a diversification index from the cumulative diversification curve which is a weighted average of the different industries in which the firm operates, each weighted by its relative importance as indicated by its rank. The index ranges upwards from 1 for a completely specialized firm, with larger numbers showing the extent to which the firm is diversified.

Another way of defining the extent of diversification is to examine the degree to which a firm specializes in particular products or activities. Rumelt (1974) uses the concept of the 'specialization ratio' (percentage

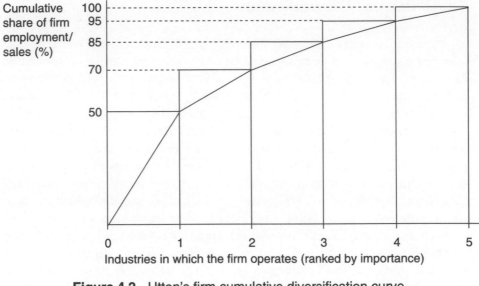

Figure 4.2 Utton's firm cumulative diversification curve
Source: Utton (1979)

of a firm's turnover attributable to a single product) and the 'related ratio' (percentage of a firm's turnover attributable to its largest group of related products) to identify four categories of firm:

1 *Single product firms* – firms which specialize almost entirely in one product.
2 *Dominant product firms* – firms which have diversified to a small degree but remain highly dependent on one particular product.
3 *Related product firms* – firms which have diversified by adding new products that are related to the original core skills of the firm.
4 *Unrelated product firms* – firms which have diversified into products which are not related to its original core skills.

Such a classification goes beyond mere counting of the number of SIC categories a firm operates in and attempts to analyse the breadth of the firm's product portfolio in strategic terms. Rumelt used this approach to analyse 250 large US firms between 1949 and 1969, classifying these firms into strategic categories and then examining their performance. He found that the highest profit performers were in the 'related product' category (see under the heading 'The Nature of Conglomerate Firms Revisited' below). However, this analysis requires the exercise of 'judgement' about the degree of relatedness of products in a firm's portfolio and the use of arbitrary percentages of total sales in order to distinguish the four categories outlined above. Thus, there is a danger that even this measure may not be a reliable one in so far as different analysts could place the same firms in different categories. Later attempts to refine this technique have experienced similar judgemental difficulties (see Luffman and Reed (1984)).

Propensity to diversify

Diversification measures of the kind indicated above are essentially cross-sectional, using SIC or company sales data for a particular year to measure degrees of diversification among a sample of firms. Although a comparison of successive 'snapshot' pictures of diversification indicate broad trends in diversification over time, they do not capture the full dynamic considerations which lead some firms to diversify and others not. In order to highlight the motivations which impel a firm to pursue diversification, it is necessary to concentrate upon the policies pursued by particular firms over time. For example, as box 4.1 indicates, Glaxo has remained a specialist pharmaceutical firm whilst Hanson has continued to pursue a pure diversification policy adding new activities to its product/market portfolio. Glaxo, it will be noted, has reduced its dependency on the UK market by developing an extensive international presence (see chapter 5). Thus, to understand why firms differ in their propensities to diversify it is necessary to explore the reasons for diversification.

Motives for Diversification

As noted earlier in chapter 1, a firm's controlling management group may pursue growth of the firm as a primary objective in order to further their own self-interest in terms of enhancing their remuneration, status, prestige etc. However, the single-minded pursuit of asset growth by managers has to be tempered by the need to maintain profits so that share prices remain at a level which avoids the firm becoming vulnerable to a take-over bid. In evaluating profit–growth mixes over the longer term managers must pay due regard to the risk–return opportunities involved. Growth which involves diversification may be more appealing to managers in this regard than horizontal or vertical growth since the firm is able to increase its sales and assets by expanding into a number of products and markets, thereby reducing the variability of profits and consequent take-over risk.

The main attraction of diversification as a growth strategy compared to horizontal expansion and vertical expansion is the ability to spread risks and broaden the firm's profit-earning potential. Specifically, a one-product/market firm is vulnerable not only to erratic, cyclical profit

Box 4.1   Examples of company specialization and diversification

Glaxo	Turnover (£ millions)		Trading Profit (£ millions)		Geographic breakdown of turnover (%)		
	1980	1991	1980	1991		1980	1991
Pharmaceuticals (including wholesaling)	599	3,397	65	1,283	UK	47	11
					Continental Europe	23	32
					Americas	8	43
Surgical and other products	19	–	1	–	Asia-Pacific	15	11
					Other	7	3
Total	618	3,397	66	1,283			

Hanson	Turnover (£ millions)		Trading Profit (£ millions)		Geographic breakdown of turnover (%)		
	1980	1991	1980	1991		1980	1991
Industrial services[1]	465	–	30	–	UK	37	47
Agriculture products	211	–	9	–	US	63	40
					Other	–	13
Consumer division[2]	–	3,325	–	347			
Industrial division[3]	–	2,321	–	450			
Building products division[4]	–	1,507	–	178			
	676	7,153	39	975			

[1] Includes bricks, stone, concrete, cement, textiles, yarns, threads, distribution of earthmoving and construction equipment, laboratory equipment, trade journal publications, brewing equipment, industrial components, machine tools, packaging materials, food service and vending machines, typewriters and accessories.
[2] Includes cigarettes and tobacco, batteries, torches and lamps, clocks, kitchen appliances, vacuum cleaners, leisure equipment (golf clubs, pool tables, electronic darts scoring machines etc.), toys.
[3] Includes gas meters and fires, office furniture, cranes, aircraft seating and fittings, accommodation units, coal and gold mining, construction services, bathroom and household products.
[4] Includes aggregates, stone, concrete, bricks, lighting products, windows and doors, industrial hand tools, pumps.

Source: Company reports

Box 4.2 Diversification by tobacco companies

Tobacco companies such as BAT, Gallaher (now owned by American Brands) and Imperial (now owned by Hanson) operate in a mature industry which is still highly profitable with a good cash flow but which is experiencing a steady decline in some key markets. Consequently, tobacco companies have looked to diversify their businesses in order to spread risks and to improve their long-run growth prospects. However, even where these companies possess similar 'core' skills and resources, their diversification strategies may differ widely:

- *BAT's* early diversification moves led it into a wide range of markets including paper and packaging (Wiggins Teape Appleton), department stores (Marshall Field etc.), catalogue retailing and food retailing (Argos), (International Stores), scientific instruments (VG Instruments), perfumes (Yardley etc.), and plastics (Eurotec). In the 1980s the company acquired a number of insurance companies, notably Eagle Star and Allied Dunbar in the UK and the Farmers Group in the US. In the 1990s BAT has 'refocused' its activities on tobacco and financial services, and has sold off or demerged all of its other businesses.
- *Gallaher* likewise has built up a broad portfolio of businesses by acquiring market leaders mainly in relatively mature markets such as kitchenware (Prestige), optical products and distribution (Dolland and Aitchison), office equipment (Ofrex), engineering and newsagents stores.
- *Imperial's* diversification was concentrated on the acquisition of fast-growing convenience food companies (Ross and Young frozen foods, Golden Wonder crisps) and the leisure industry (Courage brewing/retailing chain).

returns resulting from the business cycle, but worse still, its very survival may be threatened by a declining customer base as the firm's product moves into the final stages of its product life cycle. Diversification is thus the main way the firm can reduce its exposure to business risk and fluctuating profitability, whilst reorientating its activities away from mature and declining markets into new areas offering sustained growth and profit opportunities. (See box 4.2.)

Risk-spreading

Risk-spreading has a number of different facets. Where a firm specializes in a narrow range of products then it is dependent upon a single market area and vulnerable to short-term changes in technology or consumer tastes. It may, therefore, seek to 'pool' such risks by seeking to operate in a number of different product markets. This offers the firm a degree of 'insurance' against unexpected changes. Furthermore, where a firm operates in industries characterized by severe cyclical variations in demand over time it can increase the stability of its sales and profits by spreading its activities over industries which reach their peak sales at different phases of the business cycle. International expansion may also serve to enhance the stability of sales and profits to the extent that overseas markets experience the peaks and troughs of their business cycles at different times. Finally, the firm may seek to reduce its vulnerability to long-term product and market obsolescence in a world of increasing technical complexity and change by having a wide portfolio of products at different stages of their industry life cycles.

These various ways of spreading risk all help to reduce the risk of company failure and bankruptcy. Even if one of a firm's products incurs sustained losses this need not threaten the survival of a diversified firm since it is able to cover such losses from profits generated elsewhere in the business. Diversification also serves to reduce the variability of profits of the firm and by stabilizing earnings and dividends makes it easier for the firm to raise new equity capital and loans on advantageous terms. With a more stable rate of return on capital employed the firm is able to increase its capital-gearing, making greater use of borrowed funds because of the reduced risk of default for debt-holders. Loan capital offers certain tax advantages to the firm since loan interest is regarded as a charge against profits rather than as a distribution of profits and so is not subject to company taxation.

The analysis of risks and returns for investors can be formalized in terms of the 'capital asset pricing model' which seeks to show how short-term share prices are determined. The capital asset pricing model provides a method of computing the return on a share which specifically identifies and measures the risk factor within a share portfolio. The expected rate of return on a particular investment has two components:

1   the risk-free percentage return which could be obtained from, say, a gilt-edged, government financial security like a Treasury bill;
2   the risk return associated with the investment.

Risk itself can be split into *market* or *non-diversifiable risk* and *specific* or *diversifiable risk*. Market risk is the variation in share prices associated with general movements in share prices as measured by a share index such as the Financial Times All-Share Index or the Dow-Jones Index. It is not possible to diversify such risk away because however large the portfolio of shares an investor holds, they are all influenced by general market trends. By contrast, specific or diversifiable risk is the risk uniquely

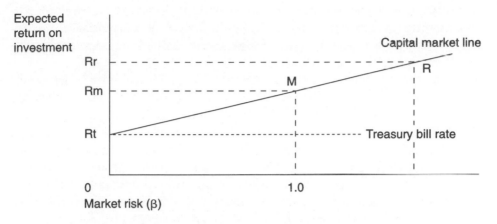

Figure 4.3   The capital asset pricing model

attributable to the holding of shares in a particular company. Such specific risk is entirely independent of general market variations and is associated with corporate decisions in matters such as dividend policy, changes in capital structure, and changes in the fortunes of the particular company. As a consequence, changes in a company's share price may be positive or negative depending upon the opinion of investors and occur randomly. In these circumstances, if an investor holds a sufficiently large and well-diversified portfolio of shares such variations in share prices will tend to cancel each other out, allowing the investor to eliminate specific risk by diversifying his/her portfolio.

The relationship between risk and return is shown in figure 4.3. The vertical axis of figure 4.3 shows the expected return on an investment. The horizontal axis shows the market or non-diversifiable risk factor, beta. The beta coefficient (β) shows the degree of responsiveness of the price of a particular share to changes in general share prices. For example, if a 10 per cent change in the price of share X is associated with a 10 per cent change in general share prices then the share and market are perfectly correlated ($\beta = 1$). Risky shares have a beta coefficient greater than 1 and their share prices can move much higher or much lower than share prices generally. The capital market line intercepts the vertical axis 0Rt and thereafter slopes upwards, reflecting the association between general share price movements and expected returns.

If investors are risk-averse they may concentrate their investment on completely risk-free gilt-edged securities like Treasury bills ($\beta = 0$) and accept a modest return on their investment, 0Rt. If investors are prepared to take some risks then they will invest in a diversified portfolio of company shares ($\beta = 1$), hoping to earn a higher return such as 0Rm, whilst accepting some variability in share prices and returns associated with general market movements. If investors are prepared to accept still greater risks, then they will invest in particular company shares which have a beta coefficient greater than 1 in the hope of earning higher returns such as 0Rr.

Investors can secure all the diversification they require by building up a portfolio of shares in specialized companies, and even small investors can obtain a diversified portfolio by investing in a unit trust. Hence, there is no immediate advantage to them in investing in diversified companies as such unless the expected rate of return is superior. However, unlike shareholders who can diversify their share portfolio to stabilize their incomes, company managers are unable to diversify their employment and stand to lose their jobs if the business in which they operate fails. Consequently it is in their interests as controllers of the company to diversify into a number of business areas in order to reduce the variability of overall company performance and so reduce their own unemployment risk. Where company diversification reduces risks but does not affect return on shares then shareholders would be unaffected by managers' diversification policies. However, where managers attempt to reduce risks by excessive diversification into unrelated businesses at the cost of a reduction in expected returns, managerial policies can adversely affect shareholders' interests. Thus, diversification can be seen as part of the 'agency costs' of having businesses controlled by salaried managers, although shareholders can monitor managers' policies and could remove managers if their interests were severely prejudiced.

The pursuit of growth

A firm may seek to diversify not only to reduce risks but also as an opportunity to secure growing profits, sales and assets over time. Growth-orientated companies would wish to avoid situations where their growth prospects are constrained by the slow overall growth of their existing markets. The imperative to seek new markets is likely to be heightened in situations where a firm already has a high share of a particular market, making it increasingly difficult to expand its market share further in the face of competition from other suppliers, or where the competition authorities of a country limit market dominance. Furthermore, where a market itself is characterized by a limited rate of growth of industry demand or involves a group of products in the mature phase of their product life cycles, few growth opportunities may present themselves from current operations. In such situations, a firm may still realize its growth objectives by pursuing *international* expansion to find new geographical markets for its existing products. Alternatively, a firm may seek to offer new products to its existing geographic markets, either products which are similar to those already supplied (concentric diversification) or

Products Markets	New products	
	Related technology	Unrelated technology
Same type	(1) Horizontal expansion of product range	
Firm its own customer	(2) Vertical integration	
Similar type	(3) Concentric diversification (market and technology related)	(4) Concentric diversification (market related)
New type	(5) Concentric diversification (technology related)	(6) Conglomerate diversification

Figure 4.4 Ansoff's diversification matrix
Source: Ansoff (1968)

products which are substantially different from its present products (pure diversification). Thus, as in box 4.1, Glaxo has concentrated on becoming a leading multinational supplier of pharmaceutical products by increasing the number of geographic markets it produces in or sells to. By contrast, ICI has developed a range of new product groups largely related to its core technology and expertise in the manufacture of chemicals, and has sought to develop these products on a worldwide basis by exporting, licensing and foreign direct investment (see chapter 5). Finally, it will be noted that Hanson has pursued growth through the addition largely of new, unrelated businesses to its product portfolio whilst restricting its geographical scope mainly to the US and the UK.

Growth directions A useful framework for examining the various growth vectors which a firm may pursue is provided by Ansoff's (1968) diversification matrix (see figure 4.4). The two main axes of the matrix are first, products, indicating the extent to which a firm's new products are related to its existing products in terms of technology; and second, markets, indicating the extent to which buyers are similar to existing buyers or different from them in terms of their buying requirements. Segment 1 involves the horizontal expansion of a firm's product range; segment 2 denotes vertical integration with the firm supplying itself with new products; segments 3, 4 and 5 represent varying degrees of concentric diversification offering products and servicing markets which are related to existing technology and markets. The final segment, 6, involves conglomerate diversification adding new products based on unrelated technology to the firm's product portfolio and servicing new markets. Such diversification is often seen as a high-risk strategy since it leads the firm far from its existing product and process technology and far from its knowledge of existing markets and distribution systems. For this reason, conglomerate diversification is often achieved by means of take-overs, mergers and joint ventures which afford an opportunity to acquire product and market know-how, rather than by means of internal growth. However, since the Ansoff matrix measures markets largely in terms of buyer type, it unfortunately tends to understate the importance of geographic market dimensions and thus does not emphasize the role of international expansion.

Alternative growth strategies   Companies seeking to grow through diversification can pursue different strategies to do so and the Ansoff matrix provides a means of classifying such strategies. For example, a firm may devote large amounts of resources to R & D and exploit new products and processes emerging from discoveries by its R & D function. Such R & D-driven growth is largely internal and would tend to be concentric in nature. By contrast, another firm may devote few resources to R & D but rather will 'buy' the technology and market knowledge it requires through mergers, take-overs, licensing etc. This might be concentric in nature but is more likely to involve widespread conglomerate diversification. The motives for this latter kind of expansion are grounded in financial considerations, the firm using the high market value of its shares and its advantageous access to loan capital based upon its high price–earnings ratio, as the means to buy other companies whose shares do not fully reflect the asset values of the companies.

Synergy

Synergy serves to create an overall return on a firm's resource which is greater than the sum of its parts (the so-called '2 + 2 = 5 effect'). Synergy often results from the exploitation of complementary activities or from the carry over of management capabilities, synchronizing activities in a way which achieves a better result overall than any of the activities by themselves. Such synergies have a number of facets. First, it might involve improving the utilization of physical, human and intangible assets. Second, synergy can result from the achievement of economies of scope or size which lower the costs of, say, raising capital or marketing products.

Improving asset utilization   Improving the utilization of the firm's assets could involve:

1   Improving the usage of indivisible plant and equipment by making new products with it in order to spread the fixed costs of the plant

and equipment over as many products as possible. This can be particularly beneficial where the demand or supply for certain products is seasonal and off-peak plant utilization can be improved by producing complementary seasonal products, e.g. as with freezing and canning of various fruit and vegetables harvested at different times of the year. In other cases the by-products generated as a firm produces its main products may provide opportunities for diversification by undertaking further processing of these by-products.

2   Enhancing marketing effectiveness by utilizing the goodwill which a firm has built up for its existing products to launch new products which capitalizes on the firm's established brand names. For example, a producer of a successful vacuum cleaner range could secure brand transference benefits by introducing a range of washing machines under the same brand name. Where the firm has accumulated considerable knowledge of particular markets and customers it may utilize this expertise more intensively be selling new products to these customers.

3   Improving distribution efficiency by using established physical distribution facilities more intensively by distributing additional products through the network; e.g. Unilever's use of its specialist freezer lorry and warehousing facilities to distribute a wide range of frozen products.

4   Improving the firm's profitability by deploying any retained cash which is surplus to its current expansion needs by investing such monies in new businesses rather than accepting a lower return on these liquid resources by leaving them, for example, on deposit with a bank.

5   The firm's R & D efforts may produce inventions and innovations which have applications beyond the firm's current product range. In this case, the firm may choose to sell off or license its inventions to other firms or develop them itself, the choice between these options depending upon such considerations as likely financial return, perceived ability to produce and sell the invention and the ability to protect the invention through patent rights.

6   Finally, an important factor in the decision to diversify is often the need to fully utilize human assets, in particular managerial experience and expertise. At senior management levels the organizational and business skills involved are rarely related solely to current products and operations, but can be generalized and employed in managing other products and processes to good effect. Penrose (1959) emphasizes this factor, pointing out how once managers have dealt with the early and complex problems of establishing new products and markets, and move down the 'experience curve', they are able to reduce many of these problems to simple and routine decision-making

rules for subordinates, and so they will be left with a degree of what she terms 'surplus management capacity' which then may be deployed elsewhere.

Economies of scale and scope A second major source of synergy derives from economies of scope or size. As the discussion in chapter 2 emphasized, single-product, single-plant firms pursuing horizontal growth may be able to achieve substantial economies of scale which lower their production and distribution costs. However, even multi-product, multi-plant firms can achieve certain economies of size or scope from the overall size of their operations, although plant level economies are unachievable where they operate on a small scale in many different markets. The economies of size and scope can take various forms including:

1 bulk-buying economies;
2 marketing economies achieved through the use of common market-ing and distribution channels and by 'cross-selling' related products (e.g. an insurance company selling other related financial services such as pensions, mortgages and personal equity plans through established sales offices);
3 R & D economies which arise from operating larger R & D facilities which allow the firm to pool research risks and to cross-fertilize ideas.

The extent to which these economies of size and scope are achievable depends upon the degree of relatedness of the various businesses involved. For example, bulk-buying economies can only be achieved where a diversified firm uses common raw materials in several of its businesses and thus is able to aggregate its purchases to secure better purchasing terms. Similarly, marketing economies are highly dependent upon the use of common marketing and distribution systems across a range of related products. Finally, R & D economies are only possible if a firm employs a group of related technologies between which cross-fertilization is possible.

A pure conglomerate operating in totally unrelated areas or businesses has no potential for achieving these kinds of economies. However, even a conglomerate operating in related businesses might not achieve such economies unless it organizes the company in such a way as to ensure affinity and coordination between related areas. For example, where a company operates a series of related businesses in a decentralized manner each with its own purchasing, marketing and R & D functions then no procurement economies, marketing economies or R & D economies can be secured. Moreover, even where the managers of related businesses operating within a conglomerate group are organized such as to maximize interchanges of information, ideas and facilities between them, synergy gains may still fail to materialize either because other links between the technologies themselves are weak or because they cannot be synthesized to produce a commercial product. The latter problem may be compounded on the marketing side where the firm operates different marketing and distribution arrangements for its related businesses without any interchange of marketing intelligence between them, thus making it more difficult to identify common or overlapping customer requirements. To the extent that such synergy gains are either non-existent or very difficult to achieve in practice, particular businesses within a conglomerate may have no advantages over their 'free-standing' rivals. Indeed, it could be the case that a well-managed business in a conglomerate could perform worse than its independent competitors if it is subject to excessive head office management control, a case of negative synergy resulting from too much coordination of the related businesses to the detriment of their autonomy.

Since conglomerate firms tend to have more stable earnings than more specialized firms they may be able to raise long-term capital on cheaper and more advantageous terms. This economy of size applies broadly to all diversified companies, although pure conglomerates with a very wide spread of businesses are likely to have more stable overall earnings than concentric companies operating a narrower range of businesses. A stable earnings record generally permits conglomerates to raise external finance partly in the form of fixed interest loans and debentures since its stable earnings reduces the risk of default on loans and generally provides a stable cash flow to meet payments. Diversified companies are thus able to raise a greater proportion of their long-term capital in the form of loans, increasing their capital-gearing. Loan finance is generally cheaper than equity finance since loan interest is deductible in calculating profits rather than being counted as a distribution of profit like dividends and is not therefore chargeable to company taxation. Furthermore, in periods of inflation the real interest cost of debt finance tends to fall as does the real value of the outstanding debt denominated in money terms.

The Nature of Conglomerate Firms Revisited

This chapter began by referring to various categories of business firms. The above discussion of the reasons for diversification can now be summarized in terms of the categorization of firms initially presented in figure 4.1, now extended as figure 4.5. All seven categories of firm exhibit some growth potential, although firms in category 1 are restricted by the specific nature of their product and market to the growth rate of that market and their share of the market. Multi-market and multi-plant

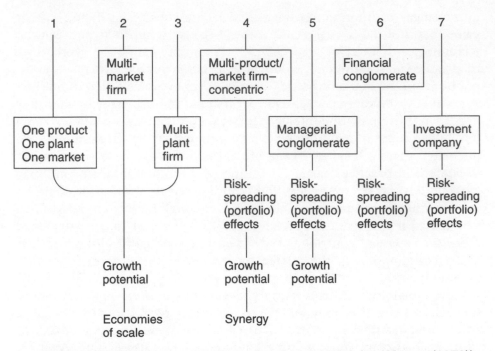

Figure 4.5   Categories of business firm (extended) (after Weston (1973))

firms are less locked into a particular product or geographic market and so have greater growth potential. Firms in categories 4 onwards consist of a more generalized 'bundle of resources' which can be deployed in a number of product and market areas and so offer increasingly high growth opportunities. Additionally, as conglomerates they offer risk-spreading (portfolio) advantages and opportunities for the exploitation of synergy.

Beneficial risk-spreading or portfolio effects are evidenced in category 7; investment companies through financial diversification can improve on return–risk trade-off; for a given return, risk can be reduced, or for a given risk, return can be increased, provided a sufficiently wide and varied portfolio is held to reduce variability in return.

For category 6, the financial conglomerate exercising financial responsibility and control, two extra elements are introduced. The risk reduction advantages of the portfolio can be retained. In addition, by utilizing the enhanced ability to raise funds which is conferred by its corporate form or by using funds internally generated by its mix of businesses, the conglomerate is in a position to financially support a loss-making individual operating business to avoid its short-term failure. The second potential benefit, compared with the pure financial conglomerate, is that management's skill in formulating effective financial plans and controls can improve the operations of the individual entities.

The managerial conglomerate, category 5, carries both of the attributes of the financial conglomerate further. By providing managerial advice from head office and interacting with managers of operating units on managerial decisions, there is potential improvement of the performance of operating units. In addition, where management quality differs between operating units within a managerial conglomerate, it may be possible to redeploy managers so that the superior managers are spread over both operating units, improving the performance of the weaker unit.

In the concentric firm, category 4, many of the same risk-spreading advantages of categories 5–7 can be enjoyed, although with a narrower spread of complementary activities the portfolio advantages may be diminished somewhat. However, in the concentric firm it is possible to achieve synergy effects through a high degree of carry over or cross-fertilization of production, marketing and management expertise such that the cost of operations, quality of product, etc. is superior to that which could be achieved by separate, independent operating units. Non-conglomerate firms in categories 1, 2 and 3 have the most opportunities to gain from close integration of their activities and, furthermore, may benefit considerably from economies of scale in production and marketing.

The Performance of Diversified Firms

As a strategy diversification has mixed fortunes. The evidence relating to the performance of diversified companies, whether related or unrelated, is inconclusive. One of the problems has been that researchers have used differing classification systems for describing and measuring diversity (see above under the heading 'The Nature of Conglomerate Firms Revisited'). The evidence seems to point to the fact that diversified companies grow faster than other forms (see box 4.3). Rumelt's 1974 study and Luffman and Reed (1984) found that US and UK unrelated diversifiers grew at twice the rate of single-product companies. In terms of earnings and profit growth both studies found a superior performance by unrelated companies; however, profitability as measured by rate of return on capital employed was found to be poorer than other forms.

An interesting footnote to this research is that the Luffman and Reed study looked at diversifying as a strategy whereas Rumelt only looked at diversified companies. The broad conclusion is that the *process* of diversification makes companies more profitable. However, diversification can fail to improve profitability where companies find themselves in industries they do not understand, or where they cannot transfer skills gained in other industries, or they have failed to spread the risk.

On the other hand, there are examples of successful diversification; indeed some companies owe their very success to diversification. It may

Box 4.3 Performance of differing organizational forms

	Organizational form as measured by product strategy			
	Single product	Dominant product	Related products	Unrelated products
Sales growth (%)				
R*	7.2	8.0	9.1	14.2
L & R[†]	1.0	1.5	1.3	2.1
Earnings growth (% p.a.)				
R	4.8	8.0	9.4	13.9
L & R	0.09	0.75	0.67	1.31
ROI R	10.8	9.6	11.5	9.5
ROCE L & R	18.1	19.1	16.9	16.7

* Rumelt (1974).
[†] Luffman and Reed (1984).

be that such companies have gained core skills in diversification including the management of a diversified portfolio. The ability to manage the portfolio is important for at root the rationale for diversification is that management, with all its costs, can produce better returns for shareholders than would normally be earned on a diversified portfolio of shares. Some would say that they have become bankers with the ability to dispose of poor performers whilst others point to the superior profit performance of some conglomerates. Evidence suggests that certain types of conglomerates outperform other forms of organization. It must be recognized that conglomerates can and do have significant earnings from asset disposals. The efficient market hypothesis would suggest that conglomerate organizations should have low specific risk and low returns. The fact that some conglomerates can achieve above-average profits may reflect their superior managerial and financial skills, in particular their ability to spot suitable companies for acquisition. Hanson, for example, has a set of 'guiding' principles for acquisitions, namely:

- capable of improvement by creation of a profit centre;
- manufacturing rather than service;
- large, well known;
- basic products – not high tech or high R & D.

Basically, Hanson acquires companies which have become strategically 'sleepy' and need turning round. Hanson has stuck to this strategy for some time and it may be argued that it is now part of the culture of the company.

The evidence on conglomerate performance is not conclusive. Many conglomerates appear to do well but their performance may well depend upon the prevailing economic climate. What is of continuing interest, however, is the degree to which their growth and development has caused commentators to look for new rationales and consequent skills for their creation and management.

Management 'Style' and 'Strategic Fit'

Whilst conglomerate expansion may, as noted above, secure the benefits of risk-spreading and synergy leading to enhanced growth and profit opportunities, these benefits can only be achieved and sustained over time by the effective management of internal resources and careful attention to the strategic direction of the firm over time. Key factors in the latter respect are internal investment allocation procedures and financial controls and the motivation of divisional managers. For example, a particular division might seemingly be 'underperforming', but this could be due not to managerial inadequacies but because of a lack of appropriate investment funding by head office limiting the division's ability to modernize its operations. By the same token, lack of management accountability may lead to an inefficient use of resources. To some extent these potential problems can be overcome by the use of organizational control procedures such as the establishment of a product group as a decentralized profit centre. Strategic direction or 'fit' considerations may also have an important bearing on managerial competencies and the efficient running of a conglomerate. Some observers point to the dangers of 'loss of focus' and 'spreading resources too thinly' as a conglomerate takes on more and more business activities. This, they suggest, can be particularly acute in the case of pure conglomerates, less so in the case of concentric conglomerates.

Broad-based conglomerates

Managing and growing a pure conglomerate requires the articulation of some well-defined corporate philosophy which knits the whole together. This will allow even 'opportunistic' acquisitions to be successfully absorbed into the conglomerate's corporate culture. The Hanson 'approach' provides one example of how to run a pure conglomerate successfully. Hanson's choice of the diverse portfolio of businesses which it owns can be explained in terms of their conformity to a strict set of management characteristics.

Hanson's best-known criteria are that the businesses it keeps should be in industries which are: relatively basic; have reliable demand patterns; enjoy a stable competitive environment; have relatively low technology and no great capital intensity. As Lord Hanson himself put it: 'we aim to invest in good basic businesses, producing essential products for which there is a clear continuing demand. We avoid areas of very high technology . . . [and] businesses which are highly capital intensive and where decision-making has to be centralised' (Goold and Campbell (1988)). The Hanson group buys firms either because it believes them to be under-managed, or because it believes the firms' existing managers have over-extended themselves. In dealing with the problem of under-management Hanson utilizes a particular style in 'parenting' its businesses which involves Hanson's head office managers fixing the sights of managers of 'strategic business units' on shareholder returns, rewarding or penalizing them as their performance varies and retaining tight financial control over operating units. This involves generous stock options and performance-related pay for managers of operating units. In turn, the managers of strategic business units are given considerable autonomy in running their divisions' day to day business, planning, budgeting etc. Nevertheless, a key requirement is that the monthly budget for operating units agreed with head office is met and any discrepancy between monthly results and budgets may become a cause for head office intervention.

Focused conglomerates

Whilst the Hanson style of management may be appropriate for managing businesses which are mature, low technology, and require relatively little capital investment, such a style may be less appropriate for high-technology, capital-hungry and volatile businesses. In these cases, the logic for a more focused approach is perhaps compelling. Lord Blakenham of the Pearson group has argued (*Observer*, 6 May 1990) that where a conglomerate concentrates on a limited number of related areas the central management team are capable of fully understanding the businesses in which they operate and thus are in a position to make a major contribution to their strategic development and provide them with encouragement to grow and undertake long-term investment decisions that the businesses might feel unable to take on their own. This long-term view and willingness to invest heavily where necessary takes the conglomerate further than a pure orientation to financial performance. As Lord Blakenham puts it: 'although conglomerates are composed of unrelated firms, the more successful ones need to have a coherence or culture that helps to bind the whole together, and that they need to restrict their activities to a number of manageable fields if they are to prosper in the longer run'.

Coherence may be achieved through limiting the number of disparate businesses managed or by clustering businesses with some commonality in technology, distribution or markets in a concentric group.

Endgame Strategy and Divestment

A conglomerate seeking to remain in operation over the long term will have to constantly adapt its portfolio of products to accommodate dynamic changes in the business environment. These changes can provide the conglomerate both with opportunities to establish or acquire new businesses and with threats to its current activities, necessitating the rationalization, closure or divestment of existing businesses. The latter considerations are particularly important for firms whose products have reached the mature phase of the industry life cycle or more acutely face a decline in industry sales.

Although an industry which has moved into the decline phase of the industry life cycle is characterized overall by falling demand and problems of excess capacity, it nonetheless may still offer attractive returns to firms possessing competitive advantages over rival suppliers. For others, immediate exit from the industry rather than hanging on may be appropriate to the situation. Thus, it is important to formulate a framework for analysing the nature and causes of decline in an industry and for identifying strategies most appropriate to the firm operating in such an environment.

Endgame strategies

A framework for 'endgame strategies' has been developed by Harrigan (1980) which recognizes that each industry differs in its make-up, so that an appraisal needs to be made of:

1 the particular reasons for decline, the rate at which demand is declining, whether demand declines at a constant rate or erratically, and whether there are any remaining buoyant market segments which the firm could target through niche marketing strategies;
2 the structure of the market in terms of levels of market concentration, buyer characteristics and factors influencing the intensity of competition. If a firm has well-established brands protected from competitive encroachment by product differentiation advantages then its sales are likely to decline more slowly than competitors and it may still be able to command a price premium. By contrast, in

commodity-type markets where competition is primarily price-driven, overcapacity is likely to precipitate ruinous price wars. Thus, the stability of prices and profits is crucial to endgame strategy and where the firm is forced by competition to price at or below costs it will be motivated to withdraw from the market.

A number of strategic possibilities will emerge from this evaluation, including:

1　holding or increasing the firm's investment in the market by, for example, merger/take-over to expand its market share and, simultaneously, rationalizing the industry by removing excess capacity from the market. This is a high-risk strategy but acceptable if the firm possesses competitive advantages (e.g. low costs or superior products) and the industry itself exhibits certain favourable endgame characteristics, e.g. a slow rate of decline in overall demand coupled with the existence of profitable market segments;
2　shrinking selectively – this strategy involves refocusing the firm by exiting from unprofitable sectors and remaining in profitable ones;
3　milking or harvesting the investment – the firm would continue its operations with a minimum of expenditure and make no effort to maintain its market position;
4　divesting now – selling the business to competitors wholly or in part, or liquidating it.

Which of these strategies is pursued will be influenced by the nature and height of the various barriers to exit which the firm may encounter, including the age of assets employed in the firm, their resale value, reinvestment requirements, extent of excess capacity and shared facilities. Whilst these factors will apply to all firms to a greater or lesser degree, conglomerate firms in general will have more latitude in withdrawing from industry than would a specialized, horizontal firm since for the conglomerate the removal of one of its activities does not mark the end of its existence as a company.

Strategic re-positioning and divestment

In addition to the need to react to adverse market conditions the conglomerate firm may also have pro-active reasons for adjusting its product/business portfolio, where some of its businesses are perceived to lack 'strategic fit'. In some cases this may be because the conglomerate has had a major re-think of the firm's strategic positioning involving either a change in direction in terms of the markets to be served or a retrenchment back to 'core' businesses. (See box 4.4.) In such circumstances the

---

Box 4.4 Divestment

Recent examples of companies reshaping their business portfolios through divestment include:

- *APV*, the UK food machinery group, sold its subsidiary, Vent-Axia, the ventilation and hand-dryer company, to Smiths Industries in 1992. APV's chief executive said: 'Vent-Axia is not part of APV's principal business and its disposal will provide the flexibility to address further structural issues.'
- *Lucas Industries*, the UK automotive components and aerospace group, sold its fluid-power systems business to Sophus Berendsen (of Denmark) in 1993. This business was considered by Lucas to be 'non-core'.
- *ICI*, the UK chemical group, sold Tribol, its industrial lubricants business, to Burmah Castrol, the international oil concern, in 1993. ICI described Tribol as a 'strong business with a good reputation' but the company's view was that it was not a 'strategic' business for its new Zeneca offshoot.

---

divestment of 'peripheral' businesses serves to release cash and managerial resources which, in opportunity cost terms, could be more effectively redeployed in the firm's other activities. In other cases where a conglomerate firm has sought to extend its position in its mainstream lines of business by acquisition it often finds that the companies taken over are themselves involved in activities which are unrelated to the main businesses of the acquirer. In this case the acquirer may wish to 'unbundle' the businesses of the acquired firm, retaining those which constitute its primary target and disposing of those which lack strategic fit. Occasionally, divestment may be required in order to avoid the opposition of the competition policy authorities, particularly in cases of merger and take-over. These kinds of strategic considerations often result in the disposal of a whole business or division rather than the removal of individual plants.

Means of market exit

There are a number of mechanisms which a firm can use to withdraw or partially withdraw from a market. These include:

1 *Rationalization*. This involves the reorganization of a firm to enable it to use its resources more efficiently, possibly involving some redundancies and a reduction of plant capacity to achieve a better balance between market demand and the firm's supply.

2   *Plant closure.* This involves permanently shutting down, temporarily
    shutting down ('mothballing') or selling as a going concern, redun-
    dant plant. Rationalization and plant closure are primarily a response
    to adverse market conditions.
3   *Disposal of whole businesses or divisions as going concerns.* Such disposals
    may be motivated by economic adversity or strategic considerations
    and disposals can take two main forms. First, disposals could involve
    divestment – the sale of a business or division to outside interests.
    Divestment provides an opportunity for former competitors to in-
    crease their market shares or presents an opportunity for the acquir-
    ing firm to diversify into a new business area. Second, disposal could
    take the form of a management buy-out involving the sale of the
    business to its existing managers and employees.

   A further means of accommodating a strategic re-think is a 'demerger'
which involves splitting a conglomerate into separate quoted companies,
with the conglomerate's existing shareholders being given shares in each
new company.

Implications of market withdrawal

Each of the mechanisms for withdrawing from a business activity can
have different implications for market competition, efficiency and resource allocation. Rationalization and plant closure by a firm often not
only serves to improve its own efficiency but by removing surplus capacity, also helps the industry achieve a better balance between supply
capacity and industry demand (provided that the plants are scrapped and
not merely mothballed). The effects of the sale by a firm of a plant or
business as a going concern upon competition and efficiency will depend
largely upon the nature and motives of the acquirers. If, for example, a
plant is acquired by an existing competitor, this may serve to increase
the market share of the acquirer, although it might also result in significant efficiency benefits if the acquirer takes the opportunity to close
some plants and concentrate production in fewer more modern plants in
order to achieve scale economies. On the other hand, if a plant or
business is acquired by a firm from an unrelated industry as a means of
diversification, no immediate change in market share or overall industry
supply may occur. However, the injection of new management by the
acquirer may result in a more efficient use of assets and the development
of new market opportunities, thus enhancing market efficiency.
   Inevitably efficiency improvements involve some rationalization of the
acquired business and the sale of surplus assets. In its most extreme
form this could involve opportunistic 'asset-stripping' by acquirers who
purchase companies whose share prices undervalue their company assets

and who dispose of certain of these assets at a profit, with little regard for the strategic logic of the remaining assets. However, even the activities of such 'corporate raiders' may have a salutary effect on market efficiency by prodding incumbent managements to make more intensive use of company assets. Similarly, a management buy-out may result in a more effective use of resources insofar as the new owner-managers have greater incentives and opportunities to develop the business once released from head office constraints.

Conglomerates and Market Power

Compared with horizontal expansion (growth by a firm in its existing market), conglomerate expansion involving the growth of a firm into unrelated or loosely related markets would appear to have few detrimental effects on competitive processes in the markets entered. In the former case, horizontal growth could result in a firm expanding its market share to the point where it becomes a dominant or monopoly supplier. By contrast, in the case of a conglomerate firm entering a new market through organic growth, the establishment of a new greenfield supplier increases the number of competitors in the market. Where the conglomerate enters a new market by merging with, or taking over, an existing supplier this would appear to have only a 'neutral' effect on competition insofar as the number of firms supplying the market remains the same. Thus, whereas horizontal expansion often results in increasing levels of market concentration, conglomerate expansion may well leave market concentration levels unchanged or even serve to deconcentrate a market.

Positive effects on competitive processes

Conglomerate expansion can have various positive effects on competitive processes and resource allocation efficiency. Where entry barriers into a market are very high, then small specialized firms may be unable to enter and only a conglomerate, with its larger financial resources and alternative profit sources from which to draw, would be able to undertake the necessary greenfield capital investment and withstand the initial losses before getting established in the market. An important consideration in this regard is the conglomerate's ability to raise capital on equal or more advantageous terms than existing firms in the target market. As an alternative to acting as a 'barrier breaker', the conglomerate firm can effect market entry by taking over an established supplier and this, too, can be beneficial. The injection of new management expertise and capital by a conglomerate into an acquired firm can improve the firm's operating efficiency and make it a more effective competitor in its market.

The impact of 'cross-entry' by take-over needs to be looked at in relation to the current market position of the acquired firm. Where the conglomerate takes over a relatively small or middle-sized firm then it may help the firm to mount a more effective challenge to the dominant suppliers in the market. On the other hand, where the conglomerate shows a preference for acquiring market leaders, then the conglomerate's 'financial muscle' may simply serve to reinforce the dominant market position of the acquired firm. However, 'aggressive' diversification by a conglomerate which has a wider perception of the market's capabilities than the established firms may do much to alter the accepted ways of doing business by, for example, identifying new market niches, introducing new distribution systems etc. On the other hand, the conglomerate may do little to change the way in which its acquired firm operates in the market, minimizing disturbance to the existing relationship between the firm and its competitors by, for example, maintaining existing tacit price/output agreements.

Possible adverse effects on market processes

Public policy interest in diversification has largely centred on the extent to which conglomerate firms may employ a variety of predatory techniques to suppress or eliminate competition in a market. Where one firm in a market is part of a wider conglomerate group whilst its competitors only supply this market, then the conglomerate firm may be in a position to apply pressure on competitors by making use of its 'deep pocket' advantages. Specifically, diversified firms are in a position to cross-subsidize temporary losses in a particular market with profits earned elsewhere. This allows the diversified firm to practise predatory pricing in the market to drive out competitors or discipline them, so raising prices to monopoly levels in the long run. The same financial power and cross-subsidizing capabilities of the diversified firm can be used to bear the short-run costs of deterring new entrants into one of its markets, thereby raising entry barriers. This could be achieved by, for example, selective price-cutting or by financing advertising and R & D to enhance product differentiation advantages.

Other 'alleged' anti-competitive practices attributed to conglomerates are less convincing or untenable. For example, where a diversified firm produces several related products it can attempt to 'tie' the sale of one product to that of another insisting, for example, that distributors buy the full range offered and not just one or two items. If this is done on an 'exclusive dealing' basis, competition may be impaired since rival suppliers are denied access to distribution channels. However, a critical consideration is the degree of dominance possessed in the relevant market irrespective of the degree of firm diversification. A specialized dominant firm can just as easily deprive competitors of access to distribution outlets as can a dominant firm which is part of a conglomerate group.

Where diversified companies face each other in a number of markets then they may adopt a less competitive stance, each firm avoiding taking competitive action in markets where it is strong, for fear of risking retaliatory action by diversified rivals in other markets where it is weak. Here companies may develop 'spheres of influence', adopting live-and-let-live policies by dominating in certain of their markets and recognizing the domination of rivals in other markets. In addition to establishing spheres of influence in national markets, multinational companies may also recognize international spheres of influence. The result of such behaviour is a lack of vigorous competition with higher prices to the detriment of consumers.

The interdependence of diversified companies as buyers and sellers may also distort competition. Where firm A is both an important supplier to firm B for one product and an important customer of firm B for another product, they may engaged in reciprocal dealing, buying from firms that are good customers rather than alternative suppliers. The practice allows diversified companies to increase their market shares and increase obstacles to new entry.

Summary

Firms diversify for a number of reasons, including spreading risk, taking advantage of growth opportunities and possible exploitation of synergy. Although there is a great deal of common ground concerning why firms diversify, the chosen *direction* of growth may differ widely, reflecting differences between companies in terms of their core resources and strategic perception of how the business should be developed. In developing and managing a conglomerate the firm must decide which new areas to move into, how many diverse activities the firm should embrace and what management 'style' is appropriate to running the firm, in particular the degree of centralization employed.

Questions

1 Define and discuss the concept of a 'conglomerate' firm.
2 What are the factors likely to affect the *extent* of a firm's diversification (i.e. the number of business activities embraced by the firm)?
3 Discuss the main reasons why firms seek to diversify.
4 What are the possible disadvantages of diversification for a firm?
5 Discuss the main reasons why a firm may wish to divest a business division.
6 Examine the nature and significance of 'endgame strategies'.

References

Ansoff, H. I., 1968. *Corporate Strategy*, Penguin.

Blakenham, Lord, 6 May 1990. 'Conglomerates', *Observer*.

Goold, E. and Campbell, A., 1988. *Strategies and Styles*, Blackwell.

Harrigan, K. R. 1980. *Strategies for Declining Industries*, D.C. Heath & Co.

Penrose, E. 1959. *The Theory of the Growth of the Firm*, Oxford University Press.

Reed, R. and Luffman, G., 1984. *The Strategy and Performance of British Industry, 1970–80*, Macmillan.

Rumelt, R. P., 1974. *Strategy, Structure and Economic Performance*, Harvard Business School.

Utton, M. A., 1979. *Diversification and Competition*, Cambridge University Press.

Weston, J. F., 1973. 'The Nature and Significance of Conglomerate Firms' in B. S. Yamey (ed.), *Economics of Industrial Structure*, Penguin.

Further Reading

George, K. D., Joll, C. and Lynk, E. L., chapters 3 and 4, *Industrial Organization*, Routledge, 4th edn, 1992.

Grant, R. M., chapters 12 and 13, *Contemporary Strategy Analysis*, Blackwell, 1991.

Hay D. A. and D. J. Morris, chapters 10, 14 and 15, *Industrial Economics and Organization*, Oxford University Press, 2nd edn, 1991.

Luffman, G., Sanderson, S., Lea, E. and Kenny, B., chapters 9 and 11, *Business Policy*, Blackwell, 2nd edn, 1991.

Thompson, J. L., chapters 17, 18 and 19, *Strategic Management*, Chapman and Hall, 1990.

5

International Expansion

The internationalization of its operations provides a firm with an opportunity to expand its sales and profits and to establish and maintain competitive advantage. This is important when the domestic market is small, or where domestic sales have reached maturity, or are declining. Horizontal global expansion can be an alternative to domestic conglomerate expansion in sustaining firm growth, although some firms may wish to pursue horizontal, vertical and conglomerate expansion in a global context because of various cost and marketing advantages bestowed by international operations. The present chapter explores the international growth of firms and the advantages to firms of operating on a global basis; shows how firms may seek to become international in scope; and looks at the particular problems of managing firms which operate across national boundaries.

For many firms a first step in 'going international' is exporting, supplying overseas markets from their established 'home'-country production base. For others, exporting is undertaken alongside licensing and foreign direct investment (FDI). FDI is what distinguishes the 'multinational' company (MNC) from the 'national' company. The hallmark of an MNC is the *ownership* of income-generating assets in two or more countries. The very largest MNCs (or 'transnational' companies as they are often referred to) such as IBM, General Motors of the US, ICI and Pilkington of the UK, Hoescht and Volkswagen of Germany, Sony and Toyota of Japan, have an FDI presence in the major 'triad' economies of North America, Western Europe and the Pacific Basin.

MNCs may operate each of their overseas businesses on a 'stand alone' basis or these businesses may be linked together as part of a complex global sourcing and market servicing operation. In the former case the MNC's manufacturing plants in a number of countries may, for example, run basically as separate units but with some profits being

---

Box 5.1   Market servicing modes

Glaxo, the UK multinational pharmaceutical firm, services the 'small' Swedish market with its anti-ulcer drug 'Zantac' by exports from its UK manufacturing plant. In the case of the US, the world's largest drugs market, Zantac is manufactured at Glaxo's US plant, but using 'active ingredients' (the core patented technology) exported from the UK plant. Originally, 'Zantac' had been sold in the US market via a co-marketing arrangement with Hoffman La Roche, the Swiss multinational, which had an established US distribution network, the complete product being exported from Glaxo's UK plant. Likewise, Labatt, the Canadian brewer, has licensed a number of UK brewers to produce its lager in the UK using a specially formulated yeast ingredient exported from its Canadian brewery.

---

repatriated to the controlling parent company. In the latter case an MNC may, for example, use a subsidiary company making components in country A as an input source for a manufacturing plant operated by it in country B. Likewise, an MNC manufacturing a product in country C may choose to market the product in other countries (D, E etc.) through its own sales subsidiaries rather than through independent distributors.

Foreign Market Servicing and Sourcing: The Strategic Options

There are three main generic strategies which may be deployed by firms in supplying their products to overseas markets and in sourcing materials and products from overseas markets:

1   Exporting (and importing).
2   Strategic alliances with foreign partners based on contractual arrangements (knowledge agreements such as licensing, co-marketing of products, co-production, and technical cooperation).
3   FDI (joint venture investments with foreign partners and wholly owned investment in production, sales and research operations).

Each of these strategies has specific attractions (and drawbacks) in enhancing the firm's competitiveness and its ability successfully to enter and develop a profitable position in targeted foreign markets. In practice, firms tend to use combinations of these three modes both to service *different* foreign markets and *within* particular markets (see box 5.1).

Exporting

Exporting is the most traditional and well-established form of operating internationally and is often the first choice for the firm. Exporting requires decisions to be made about:

- the selection of products for specific markets abroad;
- the marketing mix (i.e. product, price, promotion, place) to employ; and
- the choice of distribution channels to use (via agents, brokers, distributors and trading companies operating on an exclusive or a non-exclusive basis).

Exporting can be serviced, in a foreign country, through a local investment presence (for example, local sales office, marketing subsidiary); or through collaboration agreements via export agencies (goods are sold by the firm in the home country to another firm that undertakes to sell them abroad); or through an import agent/distributor (a firm in a foreign territory which undertakes to represent exporters); or through some other types of cooperative product sales agreement (e.g. a consortium).

Exporting from an established 'home' production plant is a relatively inexpensive and low-risk way of servicing a foreign market (i.e. it obviates the need to invest in overseas plants). It often uses existing spare capacity at home, and so involves minimal commitment of additional resources. Maximum advantage can be taken of centralized production to secure economies of scale and thus lower unit costs and may enable the firm to control product quality more effectively compared with decentralized manufacture abroad.

Using local agents and distributors to handle the firm's products in overseas markets may enable the firm rapidly to gain extensive market coverage with low capital investment in marketing and distribution. In addition, agents and distributors are likely to have well-developed customer contacts and distribution networks in target overseas markets and local knowledge of these markets.

On the other hand, the firm could be put at a competitive disadvantage if host governments impose import restrictions such as tariffs and quotas, if exchange rates become unfavourable, or if the firm loses touch with changing host-country market conditions. Furthermore, where the firm makes use of agents or distributors then it can exercise little control over the marketing and distribution of its products, and in some cases its ability to penetrate the market may be impaired by the fact that its distributors are also handling competitors' products.

Contractual strategic alliances

Strategic alliances based on contracts can cover a wide variety of arrangements between alliance partners. Broadly, they fall into two categories:
(1) knowledge-sharing arrangements which involve mainly the transfer
of basic know-how and (2) cooperative arrangements covering marketing,
production etc. which are often characterized by a more comprehensive
association between the partners.

Knowledge-sharing arrangements can take a variety of forms: e.g. licensing, franchising, management contracts, contract manufacture, technical
assistance agreements and construction contracts. They have in common
that they normally do not involve the movement of goods, and that
the proprietor of the know-how (which is often patent-protected) will
not have a substantial investment abroad. To illustrate: licensing is a
contract between two firms in different countries, whereby one firm (the
licensor) provides technical information (including the right to use its
patents, brands and trademarks) to another firm (the licensee) in return
for an agreed lump-sum fee or royalty on sales. The licensee takes responsibility for investing in production facilities which embody the licensed
technology or for marketing a licensed brand. For an innovating firm
with limited financial resources for investment abroad, licensing offers a
means of obtaining extensive international sales and a quick return on
its know-how or brands. Licensing also provides a means of obtaining
market entry where exporting is difficult or impossible because of trade
restrictions such as tariffs and quotas and inaccessible distribution systems,
and FDI is prevented by host-country restrictions on inward investment.
However, it has potential disadvantages. The production and/or marketing
standards of the licensee may be difficult to control so that inadequate
licensees may undermine the value of the licensor's know-how or brands.
Licensing may involve the under-exploitation of profit potential (i.e. the
royalties obtained may be much smaller than the profits which the firm
could have generated by its own investment). Finally, there is a danger
that the firm, by providing actual and potential (long-run) competitors
with its know-how and brands, will lose control of core technology and
products to rivals, with licensees turning into competitors.

Cooperative arrangements in respect of production and marketing require firms to specify, through detailed contracts, the precise contribution
each firm will make to the production, distribution or marketing of a
product. Such agreements allow partners to achieve synergistic effects
through contributing particular mixes of resources and skills to a degree
unavailable to each partner separately, e.g. enabling foreign firms to take
advantage of host-country firms' local market knowledge and distribution channels. Strategic alliances, however, need careful handling to
optimize results – lack of commitment, disagreements over operational

---

Box 5.2 International alliances: some examples

- *New product development.* In 1993 Honda, the Japanese producer of cars and motorcycles, established a technical collaborative agreement with Piaggio, the Italian motorcycle and scooter manufacturer, to develop a range of new small and medium-sized motorcycles; BSN, France's largest food company, and Unilever, the Anglo-Dutch food and consumer products group, established a joint venture in 1993 to develop a range of new products combining ice-cream and yoghurt.
- *Co-distribution.* In 1993 Alcatel, the French-based world number one supplier of telecommunications equipment, and Sprint, the third largest US long-distance telephone company, established a joint venture which will distribute each partner's products and provide both companies with the complete range for their own distribution.
- *Sourcing.* In 1991, Tioxide, a division of ICI of the UK and Kronos of the US established a joint venture to manufacture chloride titanium pigment, providing Tioxide with a reliable source of input supplies and Kronos, likewise, a 'captive' customer.
- *Co-marketing.* Wellcome, the UK pharmaceutical company, has set up a number of co-marketing agreements involving the marketing of its anti-viral drug Zovirak by Hoechst in Germany, Sigma Tau in Italy and Sumitomo in Japan.
- *Licensing.* Molson, the Canadian brewer, has concluded licensing agreements with the UK brewers, Allied and Vaux, involving local production and distribution of its main draught lager product.
- *Franchising.* In 1991, Mothercare, the UK babywear company, established a franchise agreement with Negoro, a Japanese wholesaler, under which Negoro is to open 20 Mothercare stores selling products which are sourced in the UK.

---

matters and strategic direction may blunt the seizing of competitive opportunities. Box 5.2 cites some examples of international alliances.

Foreign Direct Investment (FDI)

FDI involves the establishment of the firm's own raw materials, production, distribution or selling facilities in a target overseas country.

Some advantages of FDI Such investment may be undertaken by setting up new, greenfield, component and manufacturing plants, distribution networks and sales subsidiaries, or by taking over, or merging with, established businesses in target countries. Foreign investment can be undertaken on a joint venture basis involving two or more firms, or it can be a wholly owned investment.

FDI occurs because of its potentially greater cost-effectiveness and profitability in sourcing inputs and servicing markets through a direct *presence* in a number of locations, rather than relying solely on a single 'home' base and on imports and exports as the basis of its international operations. For example, with FDI a firm is able to supply 'just-in-time' from in-market plants and provide better back-up services such as maintenance and repair.

A firm may possess various competitive advantages over rival suppliers in the form of patented process technology, know-how and skills, or a unique branded product which it can better exploit and protect by establishing overseas production or sales subsidiaries. A production facility in an overseas market may enable a firm to reduce its distribution costs and keep in touch more closely with local market conditions – changes in customer tastes, competitors' actions and new government regulations etc. Moreover, direct investment enables a firm to avoid governmental restrictions on market access such as tariffs and quotas and the problems of currency variation.

For example, the growth of protectionism by the European Community and the rising value of the yen have been important factors leading to increased Japanese investment in the EC, in particular in the UK. By the same token, firms may be able to benefit from the availability of grants and other subsidies given by 'host' governments to encourage inward investment. Again, Japanese investment such as Nissan's car manufacturing plant at Washington has been attracted into the UK by the availability of regional selective assistance.

In the case of sourcing, direct investment allows the MNC to take advantage of some countries' lower labour costs or provides it with access to superior technological know-how, thereby enhancing its international competitiveness. Moreover, direct investment by internalizing input sourcing and market servicing within the one organization enables the MNC to avoid various transaction costs of using the market, i.e. the costs of finding suppliers of inputs and distributors and negotiating contracts with them; and the costs associated with imperfect market situations, e.g. monopoly surcharges imposed by input suppliers, unreliable sources of supply and restrictions on access to distribution channels. In addition, the MNC is able to take advantage of the internal transfer of resources at prices which allow it to minimize its tax bill or practise price discrimination between markets.

In some cases, a multinational company may favour 'offshore' production, producing components overseas which are then exported to be incorporated into the final product; or producing final products overseas to be marketed through the firm's local sales subsidiaries. 'Offshore' production is undertaken primarily to enable the firm to maintain its international competitiveness by taking advantage of the lower labour costs of host countries and the financial subsidies offered by their governments.

Finally, in the case of some products (e.g. flat glass, metal cans, cement), decentralized local production rather than exporting is the only viable way an MNC can supply an overseas market because of the prohibitively high costs of transporting a bulky product or one which, for competitive reasons, has to be marketed at a low price.

Box 5.3 cites some examples of the motives underlying FDI.

Possible disadvantages of FDI   A main potential disadvantage of wholly owned FDI is that it can be expensive (despite, occasionally, the availability of host-country government subsidies) particularly in industries which require large investments in plant and equipment in order to achieve economies of scale (e.g. a petrochemical complex). This investment may be exposed to more risk than an equivalent investment in the domestic market because of the extra commercial risks of operating in a less familiar 'foreign' market, characterized by different business practices, consumer preferences, language and culture; and the extra political risks of expropriation, profit and dividend repatriation limitations, price controls etc. encountered in some countries.

In part, these disadvantages can be overcome by joint venture investment arrangements which share investment expenditures between partners and which pool the commercial and political risks involved. Indeed, where the joint venture involves an alliance with a *local* partner rather than another overseas partner, then these commercial and political risks can be reduced by capitalizing on the partner's local identity. However, as with contractual alliances, problems can arise in respect of communication difficulties and differences in the objectives and commitment of partners.

Another way of reducing the risk attendant on moving into a 'foreign' market is to enter that market by merging with, or taking over, a local firm with established business connections rather than establishing a greenfield operation. This helps overcome the cultural problem of 'learning' the ways of doing business in an unfamiliar market. This also facilitates more rapid entry into the market by 'buying' market share and providing a vehicle for the acquiring company to establish its *own* products in that market. On the other hand, mergers and take-overs of foreign companies may pose significant 'inheritance' problems because of differences in objectives, management style and organization structure between headquarters and foreign subsidiaries.

Choice of servicing mode

Which of these strategies a firm will choose to use, either singly or in combination, will be dependent on an amalgam of considerations, in particular:

Box 5.3 Motives for FDI: some examples

- *Cost reduction.* Thomson Consumer Electronics, the leading French manufacturer of audio and video equipment, switched production of its cheapest video cassette recorders from Berlin to its plant in Singapore in 1992 in order to take advantage of lower labour costs in Southeast Asia. Similarly BMW, the German luxury-car-maker, has established a manufacturing plant in the US, its biggest market, partly because of the high costs of production in Germany compared to the US.
- *Market presence.* ICI announced in 1993 that it is to establish a new greenfield manufacturing plant in Belgium to produce a meat substitute product specifically to service mainly European markets. In 1993 the UK frozen food group, Iceland, entered the French market by purchasing Au Gel, a frozen food store group, thereby obtaining a base for expansion through established cold storage facilities and shops. In 1992 Pepsico and General Mills, the US food groups, merged their subsidiaries in Belgium, France, the Netherlands, Greece, Portugal and Spain, to form the second largest snack food business in the European Community.
- *Market access.* Nissan, the Japanese car producer, established a greenfield manufacturing plant in the UK in 1986 and followed this by establishing a manufacturing plant in Spain. These investments were undertaken partly in response to the EC's 'protectionist' stance on Japanese car imports, in particular the limitations imposed by the EC–Japanese export restraint agreement. Similarly, Toyota opened a greenfield plant in the UK in 1992 to produce models for the European market.
- *Control of distribution.* In 1991 Nissan Motor, the Japanese car producer, acquired its French importer and distributor, Richard Nissan, which had been selling the company's cars since 1971. In the UK, Nissan has replaced its independent distributor by a greenfield company-owned distribution subsidiary.
- *Access to technology.* In 1992, Toray, the Japanese synthetic fibre company and Shimadzu, a precision-equipment-maker, jointly acquired Therma-Wave, a US company which produces measuring and inspection equipment for the semiconductor industry. The acquisition has enabled the Japanese companies to gain access to Therma-Wave's patented technology.
- *Brand acquisition.* In 1991 Grand Met, the UK drinks company, acquired Kaloyannis of Greece which makes Ouzo 12, a leading aniseed-flavoured aperitif; and Sankyo of Japan took over Daks Simpson, the fashion house 'with an internationally-recognised brand name'. In 1992, Grolsch, the Dutch lager brewer, took over Ruddles, the UK real ale brewer, to expand its product portfolio.

1   *firm-specific factors:* e.g. the nature and 'uniqueness' of the firm's products *vis-à-vis* competitors' products, the need to protect proprietary technology and products and the resources (management and capital, in particular) available to it;

2   *industry-specific factors* in target markets: e.g. the level of market concentration, the degree of market segmentation and the extent of barriers to entry; and

3   *location/country-specific factors:* e.g. 'presence' and 'closeness to customer' considerations in meeting local demand, host-government policies in respect of tariffs and inward investment and differences between countries in factor endowments and cost structures.

Allowing for these factors there is generally no one 'optimal' foreign market-servicing strategy which can be applied 'across the board' in all of a firm's overseas markets; rather firms must be prepared to be pragmatic and flexible in servicing *particular* foreign markets, 'customizing' their approaches according to present circumstances and modifying the mix in the light of changing firm, market and macroeconomic conditions (Buckley, Pass and Prescott (1992)). For example, if governments seek to limit imports by raising tariffs, the firm may switch to in-market direct investment from exporting.

Some Analyses of the FDI Decision

Several conceptual models have been developed which examine exporting, strategic alliances and FDI as modes of foreign market servicing:

Cost-Minimization

Hirsch's (1976) analysis is based on cost-minimization, and he derives the following inequalities to give firms in country A simple decision rules on the best way to service the foreign market B, either from source country A by export, or by direct investment in country B. (Subscripts $_a$ and $_b$ indicate location.) Therefore for firms in A:

Export to B if	$P_a + M < P_b + K$	(1)
and	$P_a + M < P_b + C$	(2)
Invest in B if	$P_b + C < P_b + K$	(3)
and	$P_b + C < P_b + M$	(4)

Where P_a and P_b are production costs in the two countries, M is the difference between export and domestic marketing costs, C represents the extra costs of controlling a foreign rather than a domestic operation, and K represents firm-specific know-how and other intangible income-producing assets. All quantities are present values of costs covering the life span of a specific investment project. The meaning of inequalities (1) and (2) is that exports should be undertaken if costs of domestic production and export marketing costs are below costs of doing business abroad. Inequalities (3) and (4) suggest that investment should be undertaken when total costs of production abroad (including control costs) are below costs of utilizing the firm-specific advantages (K) in production abroad and below the costs of exporting from the parent country A. This analysis is limited, however, since it ignores the influence of demand, market imperfections and dynamic change. Other writers such as Horst (1971) emphasize market imperfections as a major factor underlying FDI. Thus, where exporting is made more costly by the imposition, for example, of governmental tariffs, or where exporting is made physically more difficult by, for example, government quotas or control of distribution by local suppliers, then an FDI presence will be required.

Dynamic adjustment

Product life cycle influences on the pattern of international trade and investment have been analysed by Vernon (1966). In the 'new product' phase, innovating firms have a monopolistic advantage both domestically and internationally, which they seek to capitalize on by exporting. In the 'maturing product' phase, competition increases with the emergence of new suppliers, both locally and internationally. Exporting is still viable but may have to be augmented by FDI to overcome market imperfections and domestic competitors in host countries. In the 'standardized product' phase, the product is highly uniform and ability to compete on price may become paramount. FDI in host countries may become imperative as well as 'offshore' production in low-labour-cost countries to keep prices competitive in key markets.

More recently the dynamics of FDI have been modelled by Aliber (1970) and Buckley and Casson (1985). Aliber examines the dynamics of foreign expansion by reference to the capitalization of returns from the firm's alternatives: exporting, licensing and foreign investment. Aliber assumes that the firm possesses a 'patent' or monopolistic advantage. He argues that the costs of doing business abroad prevent investment from being the preferred strategy until a certain market size. Only at a particular size of market will the higher capitalization ratio which applies to source-country firms, overcome the cost advantage of a local producer (which can be exploited via licensing the 'patent' to a local 'firm'). In Aliber's system, the source-country firm will always be a higher cost producer than the host-country firm, provided the latter has access to

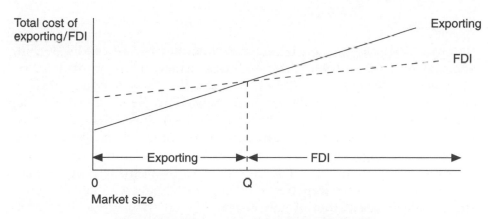

Figure 5.1 The switch from exporting to FDI
Source: Buckley and Casson (1985)

the patent at competitive rates. This limits the analysis by ruling out those situations where the source-country firm (through familiarity with the technology, firm-wide economies of scale, etc.) has compensating advantages *vis-à-vis* host-country competitors.

The dynamics of the 'switch' from exporting to licensing and then to FDI are thus dependent, according to Aliber, on the host-country market size and the differentials in capitalization ratios between assets denominated in different currencies. The latter is determined by the currency premium in the capital market – the compensation investors require so that they will bear uncertainty concerning fluctuations in exchange rates. Tariffs are easily incorporated into this framework – an increase in the host-country tariff will bias the foreign plant owner towards use of the patent in the host country; the choice between its use in licensing or internally via FDI remains unchanged, the choice depending on whether host-market size allows the capitalization factor to outweigh the cost of doing business abroad.

Buckley and Casson's model specifies the optimal *timing* of a 'switch' to direct investment by reference to the costs of servicing the foreign market, demand conditions in that market and host-market growth.

A simple 'break-even' model of a firm facing a significant overseas market is illustrated in figure 5.1. This model specifies two kinds of relevant or incremental costs, fixed and variable, and two forms of foreign market servicing: exporting which has low fixed but high variable costs, and FDI which has high fixed but low variable costs. Should foreign market size become greater than 0Q then the firm will switch its mode of market servicing to direct investment. (The linear model, of course, assumes sufficient domestic capacity to meet export demand.)

Internalization

'Internalization' as an explanation of FDI has been advanced by Buckley and Casson (1976). Internalization, in particular, offers an explanation of how firms seek to capitalize on firm-specific know-how and skills in an (external) world of market imperfections. The theory thus builds on the Hymer–Kindleberger (Kindleberger (1969)) thesis that to succeed internationally firms must possess some firm-specific advantage over rival suppliers, but suggests that this is best exploited (in an imperfect world) by FDI rather than arm's-length exporting or licensing. The classic example of a market imperfection leading to the creation of a firm-specific advantage is that of knowledge. The creation of knowledge requires investment in R & D. The firm incurs the 'private' costs in developing new technologies and products, but once they are established they then become 'public' goods. The originating firm may be able to 'protect' its invention by obtaining patent protection (but this offers, at best, only transient, protection) or through acting as sole supplier of the product: the 'internal' market of a firm permits production of final products which use knowledge as an intermediate input, and the monopoly use of the knowledge advantage permits the firm to appropriate a return for its initial outlays on research generation. The MNC can exploit its property rights to knowledge by either exporting to nations that do not impose trade barriers, or setting up subsidiaries in nations that do. Moreover, FDI is preferable to licensing since with licensing there is a risk of dissemination of information and the 'capture' of knowledge by rival suppliers.

Pathways to Internationalization

Figure 5.2 outlines one typical path to internationalization by a firm moving into foreign markets for the first time.

'Incrementalist' approach

In this internationalization process, the firm regards foreign markets as risky, since these markets are unknown to it. To avoid or reduce information costs and risk, the firm's strategy is to go abroad at a slow and cautious pace, often using the services of specialists in international trade outside the firm. Over time, familiarity with the foreign environment will reduce the information costs and help to alleviate the perceived risks of foreign investment.

Initially, the firm may seek to avoid the risk of foreign investment by arranging a licensing deal (this strategy being most suitable for a

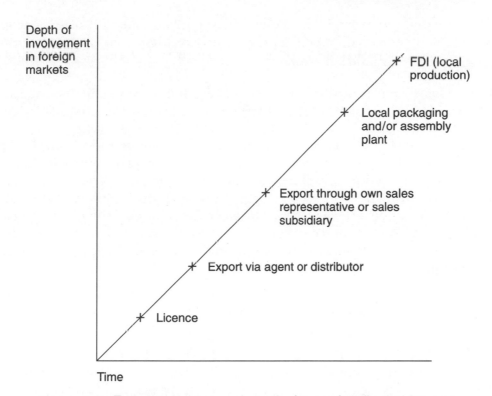

Figure 5.2 Entry into foreign markets: the internationalization process
Source: Rugman et al. (1988)

standardized product where there is no risk of dissipation of the firm's technological advantage). However, when it is important for the firm to retain its firm-specific advantage in technology, licensing will come as the last mode of entry.

Other types of foreign entry for a firm are:

1 export via agent or distributor;
2 as foreign sales build up, the firm may export through its own local sales representative or establish a sales subsidiary;
3 as the firm becomes more familiar with the foreign market, it may begin to move into foreign production, by engaging in local assembly and packaging;
4 the final stage of foreign involvement (i.e. FDI in production or manufacturing facilities) comes when the firm has generated sufficient knowledge of the host country to overcome its perceptions of risk. It now produces the entire product line in the host nation, and either sells its output there, or it may even re-export back to the home country. These decisions depend on the relative country-specific

costs. For example, if labour is inexpensive in the host country (e.g. Southeast Asia), then this country may be used as an export platform to service other markets.

Considerable empirical support has been found for the 'incrementalist' or 'gradualistic' approach to international expansion (see e.g. Buckley, Newbould and Thurwell (1978)). However, there is no set 'formula', and in many cases firms may find it advantageous to move from no or little international presence to FDI in order to exploit innovative technology or products, especially if the firm's preferred growth mode is joint venture or acquisition as opposed to greenfield. Joint ventures and other forms of strategic alliance between firms, in particular, have accelerated of late in the context of exploiting market opportunities in the European Community (the '1992' initiative) and the opening up of Eastern Europe.

Maintaining competitive advantage

Flexibility in the selection of an appropriate foreign market servicing mode can be important in securing and maintaining competitive advantage in foreign markets, as revealed in a recent study of the foreign servicing strategies of a sample of UK companies in pharmaceuticals, scientific instruments, paint and financial services (Buckley, Pass and Prescott, 1992). Table 5.1 summarizes the findings for five pharmaceutical firms. The major producers of patented drugs were predominantly concerned with a switch from either exporting or licensing to some form of local presence, usually a manufacturing presence. For these large firms, determined entry into key markets has an important impact on corporate performance. For some companies, it will be noted, production of the 'active ingredients' of their drugs (the patented element of the drug) is centralized in the UK in order to protect key proprietary know-how. Active ingredients are then exported to overseas production plants undertaking secondary manufacturing operations and packaging, often involving the customization of products to suit local preferences and prescription requirements.

MNCs' Advantages over National Firms

The MNC, as distinct from firms which undertake their international operations exclusively from a single 'home' country, may be in a position to enhance its competitive position and profitability in four main ways.

First, the MNC can take advantage of differences in country-specific circumstances. Given a world economy that consists of a spectrum of countries at different stages of economic evolution (some industrially advanced, others mainly primary producers), certain general country advantages may have knock-on effects in terms of creating or augmenting firm-level competitive advantages which the MNC can exploit on a global basis. For example, the MNC may locate its R & D establishments in a more technologically advanced country in order to draw on that country's embodied scientific and technological infrastructure and skills to develop innovative new processes and products. Similarly, MNCs may locate their production plants in a less developed country in order to take advantage of lower input costs, in particular the availability of cheap labour. Alternatively, the MNC may choose to continue to produce its outputs in its 'home' country but seek to remain competitive by sourcing key components from subsidiary plants based 'offshore', again taking advantage of lower labour costs.

Second, MNCs benefit from the flexibility of being able to choose an appropriate mode of servicing a particular market as between exporting, licensing or direct investment. For example, exporting may provide an entry path into a low-price commodity-type market, with the MNC taking advantage of marginal pricing and the absence of set-up costs; licensing may be an appropriate mode if market size is limited or market niches are being targeted. Direct investment in production and sales subsidiaries may be a more effective way of capturing a large market share where 'closeness' to customers is an important consideration, or market access via exporting is limited by impositions such as tariffs. Through these various routes, MNCs are able to pursue a complex global market servicing strategy. For example, Ford makes car engines in its British plants and gearboxes in its German factories which are then shipped (along with other parts) to Spain for assembly into complete cars. These, in turn, are then exported to other European markets.

Third, 'internalization' of the MNC's operations across countries by direct investment provides a unique opportunity for the firm to maximize its global profits by the use of various transfer-pricing policies. Whilst a national vertically integrated firm needs to establish transfer prices for components and finished products being transferred between component and assembly plants and between assembly plants and sales subsidiaries, the greater scale and cross-frontier nature of such transactions by MNCs makes these transfer prices more significant.

Finally, an international network of production plants and sales subsidiaries enables an MNC to introduce a new product simultaneously in a large number of markets (an important consideration in the case of products having a relatively short life cycle span and/or patent protection) in order to maximize sales potential. Equally importantly, it spreads the risk of consumer rejection across a diversified portfolio of overseas markets so that failure in one market may be offset or perhaps more than

Table 5.1 Pharmaceutical firms: foreign market servicing mode of five firms

Firm and market	Competitive advantages	Previous foreign market servicing mode	Current foreign market servicing mode	Impact of current foreign market servicing mode on competitiveness (defined in terms of profitable market share)	Likely change in foreign market servicing mode to improve performance
1 Japan	Patented drugs, R & D	Licensing of major indigenous manufacturer	50/50 joint venture with former licensee (local manufacturing and marketing); 'active ingredients' exported from UK	Strongly positive	Possibly a wholly owned subsidiary to capitalize on their 'learning experiences' of the market
Australia		Exports of patented drugs through distributor	Acquired a generic manufacturing company (1974)	Poor, due to government price controls	Likely to pull out, unless government becomes more 'sympathetic'
2 France	Patented drugs, R & D	Direct exporting	Greenfield manufacturing/ sales subsidiary (1989); 'active ingredients' exported from UK	Strongly positive	Proposes a major re-think of the location of its manufacturing/ sales subsidiaries in the light of the Single European Market 1992 initiative

	Products	Exporting method	Foreign market development	Attitude	Future intentions
3 Various countries	Generics, specialist low costs/prices		'Incidental' exporting	Very marginal	Intends to put exporting on a firm footing in the light of the Single European Market initiative, possibly using agents or sales subsidiaries (but financial constraints are a problem)
4 US	Patented drugs, R & D	Exports through agents augmented by co-marketing with European producer's US sales subsidiary	Take-over of small manufacturing company ('1974') as a prelude to establishment of major greenfield manufacturing/ sales facility; 'active ingredients' exported from UK	Strongly positive	
Japan		Exports through agent	Established 50/50 sales subsidiary with major Japanese manufacturer (1968) followed by greenfield manufacturing plant; 'active ingredients' exported from UK	Strongly positive, but 'could do better' with more effective marketing	
5 US	Patented drugs and generics. Development rather than basic research		Exports through a number of distributors selected to service particular market segments	Positive (but slow progress)	FDI operation (but financial constraints)

Source: Buckley, Pass and Prescott (1992)

compensated by rapid acceptance in another. In this respect, transnational product development is an important component of a risk management policy. Additionally, it enables the MNC to develop a 'global brand' identity (as with, for example, Coca Cola and Foster's lager) or, alternatively, more effectively 'customize' a product to suit local demand preferences.

Managing MNCs

All companies need to ensure that resources are rationally allocated within the organization; coordinate the activities of different sub-units and functions in the company; provide an early warning of things going wrong with operations; assist with evaluating the performance of various sub-units or subsidiaries; help with evaluating the performance of individual managers; and provide a means of motivating managers. Decentralization adds to the difficulties of coordinating the activities of sub-units in order to achieve overall company goals. In delegating responsibility to subordinates, top management needs to define the various responsibility centres that have control over costs, revenues and profits. These management tasks become more complex where a company operates across national frontiers. Geographic distance may preclude frequent personal contacts between headquarters managers and sub-unit managers, and can even slow down the transmission of formal written communications, so that prompt feedback about sub-unit performance is hindered. Cultural distance arises from cultural differences and language difficulties between parent company managers and local sub-unit managers. Institutional backgrounds also differ with differences in national economic systems and policies, distribution arrangements and financial institutions.

Customization

Even companies whose international operations are confined to exporting need to make some adjustments to their products and packaging to allow for the linguistic and technical requirements of their various export markets, along with differing consumer or user preferences. In practice there are few true 'global brands' which can be produced and marketed in identical form in all countries. Instead most products need to be 'customized' to varying degrees to meet local conditions. Where there are marked differences between countries in terms of consumer preferences and technical standards, firms may need to produce a wide range of products to meet these differing requirements and may need to market them in quite different ways using various combinations of marketing mix elements as appropriate. In such circumstances a critical factor in securing and maintaining competitive advantage is the employment of indigenous managers who are most familiar with the languages and cultures of their local communities. Where domestic buyers are strongly chauvinistic an MNC may reject the option of greenfield development (even one staffed by local personnel) in favour of take-over of an established local concern which is left largely unchanged in order to preserve its national character and so retain consumer loyalty to the subsidiary and its brands.

Networking

When companies decide to service their markets by FDI through either partial or total ownership of overseas production or sales companies, then they need to address the question of whether to allow each of these companies to operate as an autonomous business unit responsible for controlling its own costs, revenues and investments; or, alternatively, operate them as a network of coordinated business units subject to strong central control. In practice most MNCs favour the latter, co-ordinated managerial philosophy since the more pro-active management of subsidiaries allows various synergy and efficiency gains to be generated. By networking its various subsidiaries the MNC can reduce the real costs of servicing markets by choosing the most effective locations for production and marketing units and taking maximum advantage of various financial incentives offered by host-country governments and the benefits of liberal tax regimes.

Tax-planning and transfer-pricing

In their tax-planning, multinational companies can aim to incur most of their expenditure in countries with high tax rates and generous depreciation and expenses allowances in order to gain maximum tax relief on expenditures. At the same time companies can aim to generate most of their revenues and profits in low-tax countries where they attract little tax. Following this principle, multinationals may locate their expensive plants and R & D facilities in high-tax countries to take advantage of investment allowances there. In addition they may siphon off profits earned in high-tax countries to low-tax countries through inflated interest payments between group companies, high royalty payments between group companies and high intra-group management charges and consultancy fees. Furthermore, where subsidiaries supply components, goods and services to one another or supply/are supplied by the parent company, the parent company will have an incentive to adjust the transfer prices at which such transfers are invoiced. By charging a low transfer price for components, goods or services shipped from a subsidiary located in a high-tax country to another subsidiary located in a low-tax country, taxable profits in the first subsidiary will be reduced and those of the second subsidiary increased, acting to increase post-tax profits of the group as a whole.

To take maximum benefit from such opportunities MNCs may also use tax havens. These are countries which often have few natural resources and which seek to foster commercial development by offering permanent tax inducements. Examples include the Bahamas and the Cayman Islands which have no taxes at all, and Gibraltar and the Virgin Islands which have very low tax rates. Such countries generally have few tax treaties with other countries, so they are not obliged to furnish information about companies to other governments; they operate few exchange controls making it easy for companies to move funds into or out of these countries; and they generally have liberal incorporation laws making it easy to set up new companies there.

Establishing a foreign holding company or major subsidiary company domiciled in a tax-haven country enables a multinational group to use this shell company to receive tax-free the profits earned by operating subsidiaries. Recycling of funds can allow operating subsidiaries to be financed through loans from the tax-haven country, so that interest payments reduce the taxable income of subsidiaries in high-tax countries. In similar fashion, group patents can be assigned to the haven company allowing it to collect royalties from operating subsidiaries in high-tax countries, whilst management charges and fees could also be levied upon operating subsidiaries and invoiced to the haven company.

In pursuing the taxation and other fiscal benefits to be derived from their multi-country, multi-currency operations, the MNC can distort the profitability and capital base of subsidiaries by shifting profits or capital from one subsidiary to another. Such considerations make it difficult to evaluate how well a subsidiary is doing as an economic entity. These distortions can mask the underlying real cost-effectiveness of the different operating subsidiaries. In addition, these distortions can have significant effects on management motivation in operating units and thus upon the efficiency of these units. In principle, managers should only be held responsible for cost and revenue items which they can control. Yet, where sub-unit managers must buy or sell to other subsidiaries at predetermined transfer prices, evaluating and rewarding these sub-unit managers according to the reported profits of their unit is inconsistent. Some distinction between the financial performance of the sub-unit and the performance of the managers is thus needed, and managers should be evaluated purely in terms of costs and revenues which they can control, otherwise X-inefficiency within operating units will tend to creep in.

Table 5.2 The contribution of foreign-controlled enterprises to UK manufacturing industries (1990)

	Number of enterprises	Employment (thousands)	Net output (£ millions)	Net investment (£ millions)
All establishments	132,940	4,808	138,984	14,258
Foreign-controlled as percentage of all	1.1	16.1	22.4	27.0

Source: Census of Production, 1990

Government Policy towards FDI and MNCs

FDI by MNCs has implications for countries' balance of payments and domestic economies. If outward investment flows exceed inward investment flows then this may lead to a foreign currency drain if the 'gap' is financed by capital transfers rather than overseas equity issues and borrowings. On the other hand, the balance of payments may benefit from *net* overseas investment in the form of repatriated profits and dividends. In 1991, for example, direct investment contributed net earnings of £8 billion to the UK's invisible surplus. Inward investment can add to domestic capital formation, bringing with it job creation, and can contribute to improving a country's economic efficiency and growth potential by increasing competition and by the introduction of new technology and products. A good example of this is provided by the revitalization of the UK motor car industry with the greenfield entry of the Japanese firms Nissan and Toyota and the former joint venture between Rover and Honda. More generally, as table 5.2 shows, although only 1 per cent of the enterprises in UK manufacturing industry are foreign-controlled they employ 16 per cent of the labour force and are responsible for 22 per cent of the output of the manufacturing sector. These figures indicate that foreign-controlled firms are larger than the average UK enterprise, and that they operate at higher levels of labour productivity. They are also, on average, more capital-intensive than their UK counterparts, as indicated by their contribution to net capital formation, totalling 27 per cent. Thus inward investment has had a significant impact on UK investment, employment and output.

For some critics, however, inward investment brings with it problems of loss of sovereignty and local autonomy when segments of domestic industry fall under the control of foreign-owned businesses. Such problems arise essentially from the international nature of MNCs with policies towards any one subsidiary reflecting the pursuit of some global objective of the MNC (i.e. pursuit of its 'private' interest) which may not necessarily correspond with the economic policies and priorities of the host or source country. For example, MNCs may use transfer-pricing to minimize their tax bills. Or they may limit the extent of technology transfer so that subsidiaries become technologically dependent on their overseas parents and are confined solely to assembly operations with very few 'spin-offs' into the local economy. For this reason many host-country governments insist on joint ventures and other forms of strategic alliances between local firms and MNCs with a commitment to technology transfer rather than exclusive foreign ownership. MNCs' sourcing policies are often constrained by countries' 'local content rules' which stipulate that to qualify as an 'authentic' domestic product it must be manufactured predominantly from locally supplied as opposed to imported components. Local content rules are used by governments mainly to prevent the operation of so-called 'screwdriver' plants (plants producing final products from mainly imported components) established to circumvent tariffs etc. imposed on imported final products. Such content rules attempt to ensure that any inward investment is more than 'token' investment and involves the establishment of significant business units. Countries may, for example, stipulate that, say, 80 per cent of the value added of a product must be produced locally, thereby securing the involvement of local component suppliers, so helping to generate jobs and providing opportunities for technology transfer.

Repatriation of profits by MNCs or their transfer-pricing policies may also be constrained by rules imposed by host countries. Some countries impose restrictions on the repatriation of profits by restricting interest and dividend payments made by domestically based subsidiaries to their overseas parent companies. Again, host countries may impose withholding taxes on interest and dividend payments made by subsidiaries as a means of taxing these cash flows before they move out of their national jurisdiction. Finally, where countries' tax authorities feel that the transfer prices have been artificially manipulated so as to understate the profits earned by domestic subsidiaries, they may attempt to substitute their own transfer prices as a means of adequately taxing the subsidiaries' profits.

In many cases, governments have adopted an 'open door' policy on FDI. There are no restrictions, for example, on inward investment in the UK, where the Invest in Britain Bureau serves to act as a catalyst for such investment, nor are there restrictions on repatriation of profits and capital. Foreign investors in Pakistan, for example, can own up to 100 per cent of equity in any venture; dividends and original investments can be remitted abroad at any time; foreign companies can negotiate their own terms and conditions of foreign exchange credits and can also determine freely the mode and level of transfer of technology. Likewise, Taiwan has recently introduced a liberal set of rules for foreign investment: foreign companies are permitted to invest up to 100 per cent in most sectors; have rights to repatriate profits and enjoy a host of tax-breaks and other incentives; and to streamline decision-making, the State Committee for Cooperation and Investment handles virtually all investment approvals.

Summary

Companies can service foreign markets in a variety of ways: exporting (through market intermediaries such as agents and distributors and company-owned sales offices); strategic alliances (licensing/cross-licensing and joint ventures with indigenous firms); and by a direct presence in overseas markets (through wholly owned manufacturing plants and sales/marketing subsidiaries). Which of these modes will be selected, either singly or in combination, for any *particular* foreign market will depend upon an amalgam of factors (e.g. nature of the product, locational advantages, distribution arrangements etc.) impinging upon the firm's cost structure and marketing effectiveness, and hence its ability to compete successfully in the market.

FDI may enable the firm to secure cost advantages by, for example, locating production in low-wage economies; gain access to advanced technology by establishing R & D facilities in technologically sophisticated countries; and enhance its marketing effectiveness and differentiation opportunities by getting closer to the customer through investment in production/distribution/sales operations in target markets. Thus, FDI is an important means of maintaining the *real* competitiveness of firms. In addition, by coordinating its plant location, investment financing and transfer-pricing decisions, an MNC can secure various *fiscal* benefits from its multi-currency, multi-country operations such as tax-savings and investment grants.

Finally, even where firms have a well-defined approach to foreign market servicing the need for a long-termist and flexible outlook is considered to be particularly important. The former underpins learning curve effects and encourages the firm to seek long-term rather than short-term profit returns; the latter emphasizes (given the different nuances and characteristics of different markets) the need to approach each market separately – looking to the optimum mode of servicing individual markets rather than attempting a holistic, global strategy.

Questions

1 Define and discuss the concept of 'internationalization'.
2 Discuss the relative merits of servicing a foreign market through exporting, strategic alliances and FDI.

3 Examine some of the main considerations which affect the sourcing of inputs by a multinational company.
4 Discuss the possible advantages which multinational companies may possess over firms which operate purely on a domestic basis.
5 What are the main implications of internationalization for the management of a firm?
6 Discuss the possible impact of inward investment on host-country economies.

References

Aliber, R. Z., 1970. A Theory of Foreign Direct Investment', in C. P. Kindleberger (ed.), *The International Firm*, MIT Press.

Buckley, P. J. and Casson, M., 1976. *The Future of the Multinational Enterprise*, Macmillan.

Buckley, P. J. and Casson, M., 1985. *The Economic Theory of the Multinational Enterprise: Selected Readings*, Macmillan.

Buckley, P. J., Newbould, G. D. and Thurwell, J., 1978. *Going International – The Experience of Smaller Companies*, Associated Business Press.

Buckley, P. J., Pass, C. L. and Prescott, K., 1992. 'Foreign Market Servicing Strategies and Competitiveness', *Journal of General Management*, vol. 17, no. 2, Winter.

Census of Production, 1990. Business Monitor PA 1002, HMSO, 1992.

Hirsch, S., 1976. 'An International Trade and Investment Theory of the Firm', *Oxford Economic Papers*, vol. 28.

Horst, T. O., 1971. 'The Theory of the Multinational Firm – Optimal Behaviour under Different Tariff and Tax Rates', *Journal of Political Economy*, vol. 79.

Kindleberger, C. P., 1969. *American Business Abroad*, Yale University Press.

Rugman, A. M., Lecraw, D. I. and Booth, L. D., 1988. *International Business: Firm and Environment*, McGraw-Hill.

Vernon, R., 1966. 'International Investment and International Trade in the Product Cycle', *Quarterly Journal of Economics*, vol. 80.

Further Reading

Buckley, P. J., Pass, C. L. and Prescott, K., *Servicing International Markets*, Blackwell, 1992.

Luffman, G., Sanderson, S., Lea, E. and Kenny, B., chapter 10, *Business Policy*, Blackwell, 2nd edn, 1991.

Porter, M. E. (ed.), *Competition in Global Industries*, Harvard University Press, 1986.

Young, S., Hamill, J., Wheeler, C. and Davies, J. R., *International Market Entry and Development: Strategies and Management*, Harvester Wheatsheaf, 1989.

6

Competitive Strategy and Industrial Economics: Background

Markets constitute the particular arenas in which companies 'do business'. No matter how few or how many business activities a company undertakes, its corporate prosperity will depend fundamentally on how well it succeeds in the individual product markets making up its business. It is thus important for companies to understand the underlying characteristics of the markets in which they operate (or are likely to enter) and the forces driving competition in these markets in order to become 'corporate winners', achieving above-average profit returns on their investments.

The present chapter draws on established conceptual frameworks in the area of industrial economics as a means of describing how markets 'work' and how the interaction of *market structure* and the behaviour of firms in the market (*market conduct*) affects *market performance*. The market structure–conduct–performance schema provides a useful starting point in formulating competitive strategy for firms. Market structure and conduct patterns enable an analysis to be made of the nature and intensity of competition in the market, whilst observed market performance gives an indication of the general 'attractiveness' of the market in terms of growth and profit potential.

Market Structure–Conduct–Performance Schema

Conventional market economics is concerned with the effectiveness of market processes in achieving economic efficiency. It examines the way in which certain basic demand and supply elements operating in a market combine with the *structure* of the market and the *conduct* of suppliers and buyers to produce certain market *performance* results (figure 6.1).

Although, for expository convenience, the following sections of this

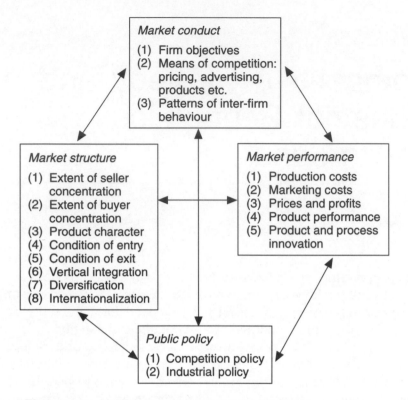

Figure 6.1   Market structure–conduct–performance schema

chapter will deal with the elements of market structure, conduct and performance separately, it is important to emphasize, as highlighted by the arrows in figure 6.1, that these elements are highly *interrelated*. Thus, although market structure may lead to certain patterns of market conduct (e.g. high seller concentration may encourage firms to form cartels so as to avoid mutually ruinous price competition); firms' conduct may itself cause structural change (e.g. firms may merge, thereby leading to an increase in seller concentration). By the same token, market structure and conduct may combine to produce certain performance results (e.g. high seller concentration and price collusion may lead to 'excessive' market price and profit levels), but these high profits, in turn, may encourage new suppliers to enter the market, leading both to a reduction in seller concentration and an increase in price competition.

The market structure–conduct–performance schema provides a useful analytical framework both for firms seeking to formulate appropriate competitive strategies to ensure corporate success and for public policy-makers designing appropriate industrial and competition policies aimed at promoting market efficiency. For example, structure and conduct enable an analysis to be made of the 'forces driving competition' in a market, which, together with observation of market performance results, enables a firm to assess the 'attractiveness' of the market in terms of growth and profit potential (see chapter 8). Some established firms may be high-cost producers because of their failure to exploit economies of scale, or because they neglect potentially lucrative market niches. Consideration of such factors may allow a new firm to successfully enter this market by establishing an optimal scale plant (giving it cost advantages over some existing suppliers) and by segmenting the market (focusing on under-exploited segments of the market). The schema is also relevant to public policy agencies in applying remedial measures to rectify poor market performance. For example, structural initiatives involving mergers and rationalization may be the preferred means of reorganizing markets to eliminate excess capacity; alternatively, mergers between the leading firms in a market may be vetoed because they would lead to an undesirable degree of monopolization. Likewise, conduct measures may be used to improve cost-efficiency and lower excessive market price and profit levels by, for example, the prohibition of price-fixing cartels and anti-competitive practices such as exclusive dealing and tie-in sales.

Market Structure

The structure of a market refers to the way in which it is organized. There are, of course, many facets to market structure; theoretical and empirical analysis is usually limited to those elements of market structure which appear to have a *strategic* influence on the character of market conduct and market performance.

Key elements of market structure include:

1   the number of suppliers and their relative size distribution, indicating the extent of seller concentration in the market;
2   the number of buyers and their relative size distribution, indicating the extent of buyer concentration in the market;
3   the nature of the product, whether it is a standardized good or service or differentiated in a variety of ways;
4   the condition of entry to the market, i.e. the extent and severity of barriers to entry;
5   the condition of exit, i.e. the extent and severity of barriers to exit;
6   the degree of vertical integration, i.e. the extent to which suppliers produce their own input requirements, or, own distribution outlets for their products;
7   the extent to which firms are diversified and so operate in several different markets;
8   the extent to which firms operate on an international basis.

The degree of seller concentration

Seller concentration refers to the extent to which the supply of a good or service is controlled by the leading suppliers of the product. The number and size distribution of sellers in a market can be measured by various concentration indices (see chapter 2). Some markets are characterized by a very high degree of seller concentration. The UK sugar market, for example, is dominated by British Sugar (52 per cent market share) and Tate and Lyle (40 per cent market share) and the UK detergents market by Proctor and Gamble (45 per cent market share) and Unilever (44 per cent market share), while Nestlé accounts for 56 per cent of the UK coffee market.

High concentration levels arise for a number of reasons. In many markets, economies of scale in production, marketing and R & D are so important that in order to lower their costs, enhance their marketing effectiveness and be able to develop new products, firms must supply on a large-scale basis. In other cases, a desire to promote more 'orderly' market conditions or an outright desire to 'monopolize' a market have been factors encouraging firms to merge or take over competitors, thereby increasing concentration levels. Ultimately, the persistence of high seller concentration over time depends on the exclusion of new competitors from the market. Even seemingly entrenched dominant firms may be vulnerable to new entry. For example, Rank Xerox's share of the UK photocopying market fell from 90 per cent in 1975 to around 30 per cent in 1991 in the face of powerful international competitors such as Canon and Kodak. The significance of seller concentration for market analysis and competitive strategy lies in its effect on the nature and intensity of competition. Structurally, as the level of concentration in a market progressively increases, 'competition between the many' becomes 'competition between the few' until, at the extreme, the market is totally monopolized by a single supplier. (See Technical Appendix: 'Theory of Markets', at the end of the book.) In terms of market conduct, as supply becomes more concentrated in fewer and fewer hands so that suppliers' fortunes become more and more interdependent, they may seek to avoid certain actions which are potentially ruinous (e.g. price competition), preferring instead to channel their main efforts into advertising and product innovation, activities which offer a more profitable and effective way of establishing competitive advantages over rival suppliers.

The degree of buyer concentration

Buyer concentration refers to the extent to which the purchase of a good or service is dominated by the leading buyers of the product. Buyer concentration is usually negligible or non-existent in most 'final' (i.e.

consumer good) markets since purchases by individual consumers are small scale. Many 'intermediate' (i.e. producer good markets and retailing) are, however, themselves heavily concentrated and in a position to exercise buyer power to obtain favourable price discounts and other concessions from supplying firms. Thus, for example, BT is the preponderant buyer of telecommunications equipment in the UK, both as a user itself and as the UK's main distributor of such equipment to other users. The emergence of multiple retail chains such as Sainsbury and Tesco in the UK has been a particularly potent source of buyer power and these groups have been able to secure favourable bulk-buying discounts from supplying firms.

Product characteristics

Markets can consist of products that are homogeneous (standardized) or differentiated. In the former case, competing suppliers offer products that are physically identical or nearly identical. Standardized or homogeneous products are usually found in 'intermediary' goods markets (raw materials, components etc.) and often are supplied according to an industry- or government-imposed 'grading' system as is the case for iron ore, timber etc. or to a common technical specification such as the British Standard Specification which covers such things as electric meters, valves, gauges etc. Some 'final' products may also be supplied in a standardized format; e.g. petrol retailed according to a 'star' code (two star, four star) as well as in unleaded and diesel form. Even such products, however, may be subjected to attempts by suppliers to apply branding and other differentiation techniques to reduce their 'sameness'; e.g. Esso petrol, it is suggested, 'puts a tiger in your tank', implying 'superior performance' compared to rival brands.

Where products are regarded by buyers as homogeneous (i.e. virtually identical) and as such closely substitutable one for another, buyers will have no particular 'preferences' for the products of any particular supplier and will be strongly influenced to switch from one supplier's product to another's by a price differential. Thus, in markets where products are highly standardized, market competition is typically price-driven and the prices offered by rival suppliers are likely to be the same (i.e. 'parallel') as a *result* of competitive pressures rather than because suppliers have deliberately set out to eliminate price competition (i.e. 'rig' the market price through collusion).

In many markets suppliers attempt to *differentiate* their own product from that of competitors. This can be done in a number of ways. On the 'supply side' products may be differentiated according to differences in quality, performance, innovatory or novelty features, design, styling, packaging etc. On the 'demand side', 'imaginary' differences may be cultivated between products by the use of advertising and sales promotion techniques emphasizing imputed or subjective qualities; 'better than', 'cleaner and whiter than' etc. The more ignorant buyers are of the relative performance, qualities, etc. of the competing brands, the more susceptible they are to persuasive advertising and the like.

Product differentiation is an important means of market segmentation, targeting particular products at particular buyer groups, and aims to establish strong customer loyalties to the firm's brands, thereby enabling suppliers to command premium prices whilst reducing the likelihood of buyers switching to competitors' brands. Thus, differentiation widens the parameters of competitive action from one largely based on price to the deployment of various other marketing mix variables such as advertising.

Condition of entry

Market entry refers to a situation where a new supplier comes into a market. An entrant may be a 'greenfield' (start-up) business which establishes a new supply source or the entrant could be an existing business which chooses to effect entry by merger with, or take-over of, an established producer in the market. The 'condition of entry' refers to the ease or difficulty new suppliers face in entering a market.

Market entry occurs largely in response to the perceived long-run profit potential of the target market, which in turn is importantly influenced by the size of the market and its perceived growth potential, both with respect to the expansion of total primary demand and particular market segments. Successful new entry requires the firm to overcome any initial *'barriers to entry'*. In some markets entry is relatively simple – the establishment of a new hairdressing business, for example, can require little capital outlay (premises can be rented and second-hand, rather than new, hair dryers etc. can be purchased) and little training or experience may be required. By contrast, entering the petrochemical market requires the outlay of millions of pounds on complex plant and equipment and specialized know-how. Entry in some markets may be impossible (e.g. the government may have established a state monopoly) or temporarily prevented by, for example, exclusive patent rights granted to established firms.

Some potential barriers to entry can be regarded as a 'natural' consequence of the economics of the market; e.g. lower unit cost advantages to established firms through economies of scale. Others, however, may be 'artificial' and designed to hamper competition; e.g. exclusive dealing contracts. Moreover, entrants must be mindful of the likely reactions of established firms both to the 'threat' of entry and to actual entry. In the former case established firms may deliberately attempt to forestall entry not only by erecting 'artificial' barriers as noted above but also engaging in 'limit-pricing' strategies to reduce the attractiveness of entry. (These issues are discussed in chapter 7.)

The significance of market entry lies in its role as a 'regulator' of the competitive behaviour of established firms insofar as they must consider not only the effect of their pricing, advertising etc. strategies on other existing rivals but the likely effects of their pricing etc. in inducing market entry by new rivals. Where entry is impeded, new firms are unable to enter the market and in the process eliminate any tendency for established firms to restrict market output and earn 'excessive' profits.

Condition of exit

Market exit refers to a situation where an established supplier leaves a market. Market exit may involve the closure of the firm's plants or their sale either to other suppliers operating in the market or to an 'outside' firm wishing to enter the market. In the case of the sale of the firm's capacity to an established supplier, this provides an opportunity for that firm to increase its market share, and, where appropriate, rationalize its own capacity to take advantage of economies of large-scale production. Market exit often occurs in response to a sustained loss-making situation or poor profit rate, or low perceived growth potential. Spillers, for example, pulled out of the UK bread-making industry following protracted losses; Hitachi, Sharp and Sanyo have recently exited the UK portable radio market, again because of poor profit and growth potential. In some cases, market exit occurs not so much because of poor underlying market conditions but rather because the firm (specifically, a diversified firm) has undertaken a 'strategic' re-think: the wish to shed 'peripheral' businesses in order to release cash and management resources or a retrenchment back to 'core' businesses.

The 'condition of exit' refers to the ease or difficulty with which an established firm can leave a market. Various 'barriers to exit' may impede the withdrawal of a supplier from the market. Where, for example, a firm owns rather than leases its plant, where this plant is relatively modern, where this plant has only one specific use and where this plant has little resale value, then the firm will find it difficult and expensive to leave the market. (These issues are discussed in chapter 7.)

The significance of market exit, like that of market entry, is the 'regulatory' role it plays. Thus, if there is overcapacity in the market and suppliers are experiencing low profitability or losses, then the departure of some firms (the more inefficient ones especially) from the market will, by reducing supply, enable a closer 'balancing' of supply and demand to be achieved and the establishment of market prices which provide the remaining firms with a 'fair' profit return. However, where exit is impeded this is not conducive to the achievement of the desired result.

Vertical integration

Vertical integration involves the combining of two or more vertically related production and distribution activities in one firm. The firm may integrate backward towards its component and raw material sources, or forward into further production operations or distribution. Vertical integration may serve to improve production and distribution efficiency by a better coordination of successive operations and by eliminating various costs of using markets. On the other hand, it may adversely affect the competitive process if integrated firms are able to deprive non-integrated rivals of inputs or access to market outlets. (See chapter 3.)

Diversification

A diversified firm is one which operates in a number of markets rather than a single market. Diversification can affect the competitive process both positively and negatively. On the one hand, diversified firms can use profits earned in one market to finance entry into a new market thereby increasing competition in the market entered. On the other hand, a diversified firm may be able to undercut competitors' prices and force them to exit the market by underwriting losses from profits earned elsewhere. (See chapter 4.)

Internationalization

Finally, the internationalization of markets exposes domestic suppliers to greater international competition both from imports and from the establishment of production plants in the local market by multinational companies. Multinational companies can often achieve cost or marketing advantages over purely national producers by, for example, developing cheaper offshore sources of supply. (See chapter 5.)

Market Conduct

The second major influence on market performance is market conduct which itself, as has been noted in the previous section, is significantly affected by various structural variables. Market conduct refers to the behavioural characteristics of suppliers and buyers as they interact in the market. Key elements of market conduct emphasized in market analysis are:

1   firm objectives;
2   the means of competition; and
3   patterns of inter-firm behaviour.

Firm objectives

As noted in chapter 1, the strategies pursued by firms and their pricing, output etc. policies will depend upon their objectives, and these objectives can differ from one firm to another. In conventional market analysis, certain uniform assumptions are made with respect to firms' motivation in order to facilitate the comparison of markets with different structures. *All* firms, whatever the structure of the market in which they operate, are assumed to have as their sole objective the maximization of profits.

Alternative objectives to profit maximization range from sales maximization and asset growth maximization on the one hand, to 'quiet life' and long-run survival considerations on the other. Particular attention has been paid to firms where there is a 'divorce of ownership from control', i.e. where effective control is in the hands of the firm's management rather than its shareholders. In the 'managerial' theories of the firm, the desire for large size is regarded as an important part of the 'managerial preference function' because of its association with managerial salaries, power, status and prestige. In the managerial theories the firm has some 'satisfactory' or 'acceptable' profit goal in mind but profits are seen as contributing to the attainment of some other objective rather than as an end in themselves.

The significance of these managerial models in the context of market analysis lies in their prediction of higher market output levels and lower market prices in comparison with the profit-maximizing model.

Means of competition

Competition refers to the process of active rivalry between the firms operating in a market as they seek to win and retain buyer demand for their brands. Competition can take a number of forms and three of these methods of competition are discussed below – price competition; advertising and promotional competition; and new product competition. A fourth, related, aspect of competition, cost-effectiveness, represents an essential way of strengthening the market position of a supplier. The ability to reduce costs is a vital means of underpinning price competition, or, alternatively, because it increases profit margins at existing prices it provides extra financial resources for the firm to increase its advertising expenditure or spend more on the development of new products. The nature and intensity of competitive relationships in a market, in turn, depends on various factors such as product and buyer characteristics, the extent of market concentration, and cost and demand considerations.

Price competition   The range in which a supplier is free to set its price is limited by the price-sensitivity of buyers, its own costs, its profit requirement, the prices set by rivals, and the prices of close substitute products. Suppliers may attempt to secure buyer support by putting their product on offer at a lower price than that of rivals. They must bear in mind, however, that given the sensitivity of demand, a low price may result in smaller, not greater, profits. Moreover, in response to a price cut, rivals may simply lower their prices also with the result that all firms finish up with lower profits. In general, suppliers (particularly oligopolistic firms operating in concentrated markets) will try to avoid 'aggressive' price competition because 'price wars' are mutually ruinous. Instead, 'orderly' price levels tend to be preferred with firms adhering to price leadership conventions or collusion to control prices (see below under the heading 'Patterns of inter-firm behaviour'). Moreover, in many markets segmentation and product differentiation have 'blurred' the traditional notion of price competition since they involve firms in selecting a *price structure* which reflects differences, for example, in product type and qualities. Thus, firms compete by offering customers various 'value for money' combinations across a broad product range. By contrast, in the case of 'standardized' products their commodity-like nature tends to result in a heavy emphasis on price as a selling feature, but again the intensity of this is often tempered by a desire to avoid destructive price-discounting.

In terms of its wider impact on market processes, price competition is seen by market analysis as being particularly conducive to the promotion of economic efficiency. Specifically, price competition serves to eliminate inefficient, high-cost producers, and removes any tendency for firms to secure 'excess' profits, thereby ensuring that consumers are charged 'fair' prices (i.e. a market price which is consistent with the real economic costs of supplying the product including a so-called 'normal' profit return to suppliers).

Product differentiation competition   Product differentiation is used by suppliers to distinguish their own products from those offered by competitors. There are two basic ways in which products can be differentiated, and these are as follows:

• They can be differentiated by variations in the physical appearance and attributes of the product based on differences in design, styling, colouring and packaging and differences in quality.
• Broadly similar products may be differentiated in the minds of buyers by the use of advertising and sales promotion techniques (free trial offers, money-off coupons etc.) which emphasize imputed or subjective aspects of the product.

The purpose of product differentiation is to create and sustain a demand for the firm's products by nurturing consumer brand loyalty.
Product differentiation is an important means of establishing competitive advantage over rival suppliers, and in some markets, most notably
those characterized by high levels of seller concentration, it is often
regarded as constituting a more effective competitive strategy than price
competition. The attraction of product differentiation competition over
price competition lies in the fact that whereas price cuts, for example,
can be quickly and completely matched by competitors, a successful
advertising campaign is less easily imitated. Moreover, whereas price
competition lowers firm's profitability, product differentiation tends to
preserve and even enhance profit returns. In particular, the establishment of product uniqueness may allow firms to command premium
prices over competitors' offerings. Moreover, in some cases the 'costs' of
advertising etc. can be built into the final prices paid by customers
so it is they rather than the supplier who 'finances' this form of competition. Finally, product differentiation may serve as a barrier to
entry, thereby protecting existing market shares against competitive
encroachment.

A key point to emphasize, however, is that the ultimate 'success' of
advertising and sales promotion in stimulating demand cannot be div-
orced from the intrinsic qualities and properties of the brand itself. It is
these factors which are of crucial importance in determining customers'
satisfaction with the brand and hence their willingness to repeat purchase
it. Thus, 'slick' advertising may induce some buyers to purchase a brand
once, but if the brand fails to live up to expectations because, for example, its quality or performance is 'poor', then existing buyers will defect
and adverse word-of-mouth publicity will further kill off sales.

In terms of its impact on resource allocation processes in a market,
advertising has been variously criticized on the grounds that it increases
supply costs, raises market entry barriers and distorts 'rational' decision-
making by buyers. Equally, however, advertising by facilitating mass
production and distribution of a product may lower supply costs through
scale economies and facilitate new product launches. (See Technical
Appendix at the end of this book.)

New product development   In technologically dynamic markets the ability
to develop new innovative products is often a critical factor in establishing
competitive advantage over rival suppliers. Although it may be possible
to buy in research ideas and products from other firms through licensing
deals, this may represent a poor substitute in competitive terms for the
establishment of the firm's own internal pool of R & D skills and
competencies; i.e. it is the difference between the firm being able to
assume the position of market leader and it becoming a 'me-too' follower.

New products can be used both to enhance the firm's position in established market sectors or to develop new market segments, thereby securing 'first-mover' advantages. How permanent or transient these advantages are will depend on the degree of product uniqueness, whether the product can be 'protected' by patents and marketing back-up.

New product development requires firms to commit resources both to scientific research aimed at *inventing* new products and to *innovation*, i.e. the refinement and modification of research ideas and prototypes aimed at the ultimate development of commercially viable products. R & D is usually very resource-intensive and the substantial capital outlays required to pursue development work, coupled with a high risk of failing to come up with a marketable product, tend to favour the larger business which is able to cross-subsidize R & D out of profits from existing products and also pool risks.

In strategic terms, firms in most markets need to pursue a *sustained* new product development programme in order to maintain competitive advantage. Ideally, given product life cycle tendencies and new product competition, firms need to possess a product portfolio consisting of mature products, growth products and new products, together with embryonic products in the R & D pipeline. From a wider resource allocation perspective, new product competition is beneficial insofar as it widens consumer choice and leads to the introduction of superior products, although the proliferation of 'me-too' copy-cats may make this spurious.

Patterns of inter-firm behaviour

In some markets it may be possible for a firm to formulate its marketing strategy without having to take account of the possible reactions and counter-moves of competitors to its own strategies. This is most obviously the case in markets where a single firm totally monopolizes the supply of a product, and may also occur in commodity markets where each firm supplies only a tiny fraction of industry output and so has a minimum impact on other suppliers. It is more usually the case, however, that firms are mutually interdependent such that any alteration in one firm's prices, advertising etc. is likely to have a discernible effect on the market position of its competitors, thereby inviting retaliatory action. Thus, each firm in setting its own price, arranging advertising etc. must *explicitly* take into account the effect of its action on competitors and their likely response. Where firms recognize their interdependency they will be strongly disposed towards avoiding actions that are mutually ruinous. This can lead firms to pursue marketing strategies which are broadly parallel (e.g. charging similar prices) even when they act without any agreement with competitors as they all seek to promote 'orderly' and profitable trading conditions.

Alternatively, firms may seek to collude in formulating their marketing strategies. Collusion implies something more than mere parallel action. In essence, it refers to a conduct pattern in which firms arrive at an 'understanding' or agreement covering their market actions. In some cases this collusion may simply be a defensive response to poor trading conditions or, more aggressively, firms may seek to monopolize a market by various collusive conduct arrangements such as price leadership systems, information agreements and cartels.

Price leadership conventions may be used to coordinate firms' prices with suppliers accepting one of their number as the 'lead' firm in changing market prices (see 'Oligopoly' – Technical Appendix). An information agreement is an 'informal' arrangement between rival suppliers which involves them in furnishing each other with details of their prices, discount terms, output and sales figures etc. Disclosing such information to competitors helps to facilitate coordination/collusion between firms over their marketing strategies. Cartels can take a number of forms. For example, suppliers may set up a sole selling agency which buys up their individual output at an agreed price and arranges for the marketing of these products on a coordinated basis. Another form is where suppliers operate an agreement which, for example, sets uniform selling prices for their products, thereby suppressing price competition, but with suppliers then competing for market share through product differentiation strategies. A more comprehensive version of a cartel is the application not only of common selling prices and joint marketing, but also of restrictions on production involving the assignment of specific output quotas to individual participants and the coordination of capacity adjustments to ensure market supply is kept broadly in line with market demand. (See Oligopoly – Technical Appendix.)

Where firms match rivals' marketing strategies or seek to coordinate their own marketing strategies with those of rivals, competition is likely to be less intense, with adverse effects on market performance; e.g. inefficient firms remain in the market and consumers do not receive the full benefits of price competition.

Market Performance

Market structure and market conduct interact to produce certain patterns of market performance. Market performance refers to the effectiveness of suppliers in a market in utilizing economic resources to their maximum efficiency and to the ultimate benefit of consumers. Important elements of market performance include:

1 production costs – the production of the market's output at the lowest possible cost;
2 selling costs – the utilization of cost-effective advertising and promotional techniques;
3 prices and profits – the setting of 'fair' prices so that buyers are charged prices which are fully consistent with the real costs of supplying the product, including a 'reasonable' (i.e. 'normal') profit return for supplying capital and risk-taking;
4 product performance – the satisfaction of consumer demands for product variety (choice) and sophistication; and
5 technological progressiveness – the invention and introduction of new technologies and new products which enable supply costs to be reduced and which provide consumers with superior products over time.

In practice, evaluating market performance is difficult since there are no 'absolutes' to indicate an optimal position. What is a 'fair' price or a 'normal' profit return? If market profit levels are on the low side this might suggest that suppliers have charged consumers reasonable prices. Equally, however, it may reflect the fact that firms are grossly inefficient and although prices appear to be fair they are in fact unnecessarily high because of higher costs.

Production costs

Ideally, the market's output should be produced at the lowest possible cost. A number of factors affect the level of production costs. First, as discussed in chapter 2, the extent to which firms are able to exploit available economies of large-scale production is one important consideration. If firms operate plants of optimal scale, they have the potential to minimize production costs. If, however, plant sizes are sub-optimal then actual supply costs will be higher than attainable costs. The balance of market supply and demand is also a significant factor. If a market suffers from overcapacity, either because of over-investment in new capacity or because of a fall in demand, then capacity utilization rates may be insufficient to achieve full efficiency. This can be a severe problem in industries where fixed costs represent a significant proportion of total costs, and hence 'break-even' throughput may be as high as 80–90 per cent of installed capacity. Thus, if optimal-sized plants are under-utilized because of a lack of demand then, again, actual production costs will be higher than attainable costs.

Another factor affecting cost levels is the incidence of 'X-inefficiency' (see chapter 9). X-inefficiency represents various *internal* inefficiencies in a firm – the poor deployment, utilization and management of resources within the firm arising from, for example, bureaucratic rigidities and restrictive labour practices. This can result in increased costs at *all* levels of output, and is likely to be particularly a problem, it is suggested, in large monopolistic firms which lack effective competition 'to keep them on their toes'.

In addition, cost reductions may accrue over time through 'learning/experience effects' (see chapter 9). Learning effects refer to the process whereby managers and operators learn from experience how to operate new technologies and production methods more effectively over time such that a growing familiarity with, and the repetitive operation of, a new technology etc. enables unit costs of production to be progressively reduced.

Selling costs

Selling costs refer to expenditures on advertising and sales promotion incurred by firms in building and sustaining demand for their brands. If these are 'excessive' then supply costs and prices may be raised and new entry prevented, thus enabling established firms to earn above-normal profits.

In many markets, particularly those characterized by high levels of seller concentration and differentiated products, advertising and sales promotion are used extensively to maintain and expand firm market shares. Thus, as seen by the firms operating in a market, advertising etc. is a key way in which they compete against each other, i.e. advertising etc. is pro-competitive. Conventional market analysis, however, views this issue differently, typically portraying advertising as a *substitute* for price competition (as discussed earlier). From a resource allocation perspective this distinction is crucial – price competition serves to *lower* market prices whereas advertising and promotional competition tends to increase supply costs and prices since the 'extra' costs incurred in these activities are simply 'passed on' to customers. This negative view of advertising, however, needs to be qualified by the role advertising plays in maintaining firms' market shares and, in particular, ensuring that firms' sales volumes continue to remain at levels which enable them to fully exploit economies of large-scale production. In this case, advertising and promotion, far from increasing supply costs, may contribute to the achievement of lower *overall* market supply costs and prices (see 'Oligopoly' – Technical Appendix).

Conventional market analysis also suggests that advertising by established firms acts as a barrier to entry enabling them to secure above-normal profits. The potential entrant is depicted as being at a disadvantage because it has an 'unknown' product and in order to penetrate the market the entrant must 'buy' itself sales by incurring 'extra' expenditures on promotion compared to established firms to encourage brand-switching. An alternative view of advertising in this respect, however, emphasizes its supporting role in underpinning *actual* entry – advertising is an 'entry facilitator' playing an essential part in launching, building and maintaining demand for a new brand.

Prices and profit levels

Production, advertising and promotion costs are important factors affecting the *supply side* efficiency of a market. Price and profit levels provide the 'bridgehead' into the *demand side* of the market. Ideally, market prices and profit levels should be consistent with the real economic costs of supplying the product including a 'normal' profit return to suppliers. In practice, the concept of normal profit is somewhat elusive since it must be looked at in the light of a market's risk profile, investment requirements and R & D propensities – and these, of course, can differ markedly from market to market. Thus, the 'reasonableness' or otherwise of prices and profit levels need to be looked at in the particular context in which they arise. This in itself can be difficult to discern. If, for example, profits are on the low side this may suggest firms are pursuing 'conservative' pricing policies or it may reflect the fact that firms are grossly inefficient. On the other hand, high profits may not result from superior efficiency but instead may be due to monopolistic exploitation.

Conventional market analysis focuses particularly on this aspect of performance and emphasizes the critical role of seller concentration as a determinant of differences in price and profit levels between markets. Competitive markets, specifically perfectly competitive markets, are shown to yield 'normal' prices and profits, whilst oligopolistic and monopoly markets are characterized by 'above-normal' profits (see Technical Appendix). Empirical support is to be found for the proposition that highly concentrated markets tend to earn higher rates of profit than less concentrated markets (for a review, see Hay and Morris (1991) and George, Joll and Lynk (1992)). However, it is important to bear in mind a number of qualifications when considering this issue. For example, profit rates between industries are affected by factors other than concentration levels. As stated above, the degree of risk is one such factor. Firm efficiencies are also important since studies also reveal wide variations in the profitability of oligopolistic firms supplying the *same* market. The 'trade-off' between high profitability in the short run and investment in plant modernization and the funding of R & D over the longer term is another consideration. Thus, to the extent that society benefits from new technology and new products, paid for by current profits, a wider evaluation of performance results should be undertaken.

Product performance

'Product performance' refers to the variety and quality of existing products and firms' efforts to improve existing products and innovate new products over time. Conventional market analysis emphasizes the important role played by 'choice' in the enhancement of consumer welfare. Product diversity which offers buyers a range of brands incorporating different mixes of product attributes and sophistication rather than a single homogenous 'no frills' item enables consumers to select a product which best accords with their own individual preferences.

The extent of choice in a market is a function of the number of suppliers, the comprehensiveness of their product lines and the degree of market segmentation. The greater the number of individual suppliers in a market, the greater the number of *alternative* supply sources available for buyers to turn to. However, even if suppliers are few they may offer a wide variety of brands both within particular market segments and across market segments. Again, the more a market is segmented, the greater the degree of perceived product variety. In some cases suppliers may offer a variety of brands in all segments of the market, whilst in other cases they may choose to adopt a niche approach.

There can be a number of drawbacks to providing product diversity. Choice spectrums may be superficial with the brands on offer being largely 'me-too' copy-cats rather than representing genuine product differences. Product 'proliferation' is a characteristic feature of many markets, and whilst the availability of a wide choice of brands may indicate that competition is strong, the *overall* effect of such activity may be perverse. In particular, small production runs and the fact that each brand requires its own marketing effort to support it may well serve to increase supply costs.

Over time, product improvements and new product development serve to enhance consumers' welfare by providing them with superior products and 'better-value-for-money' in terms of price/quality trade-offs.

Technological progressiveness

Technological progressiveness is an important dynamic element of market performance, technical advance enabling market supply costs and prices to be reduced and consumers to be provided with better products. The scope for process and product inventions and innovations varies considerably between industries depending upon their technological profiles and the nature of the product. In some markets, e.g. computers and consumer electronics, the pace of technical change has been rapid and spectacular, whilst in more 'traditional' industries, e.g. brewing and textiles, changes tend to be more gradual and incremental.

In a dynamic market environment where changes in technology and short product life cycles can rapidly make a firm's costs uncompetitive and its products obsolete, suppliers are under considerable pressure to invest in R & D and improve operational efficiencies. The competitive advantage framework developed by Porter (1980, 1985) highlights the importance of 'first-mover' advantages in introducing new technologies ahead of competitors to establish/maintain cost leadership and product innovation to nurture product differentiation advantages over rivals.

There is no one 'optimal' form of market structure in respect of technological progressiveness. In some industries, small firms contribute as much to *invention* (the act of discovering new techniques and products) as do the R & D departments of large firms. *Innovation* (the commercial exploitation of inventions) is much more resource-intensive and the balance of advantage tends to lie with larger firms, particularly oligopolists and monopolists which have the profits to finance expensive and risky new product development and some degree of 'protection' accorded by their high market shares. The fact that some degree of monopolistic protection may be conducive to the stimulation of invention and innovation has been recognized in many countries which have patent systems giving limited monopoly rights (usually 20 years) to inventors.

Market Performance and Market Structure

The effects of market structure and conduct on performance have been formalized within the 'theory of markets'. A comparison of markets with different structural characteristics indicates that markets supplied by numerous small firms yield performance results superior to those markets characterized by high seller concentration and monopoly elements (see Technical Appendix). Specifically, traditional market theory demonstrates that a monopoly market results in a poorer market performance (lower outputs and higher costs and prices) than a perfectly competitive market. The conclusion that perfectly competitive markets yield superior performance results has, however, been brought increasingly into question. First, large firms and market concentration may be required in order to fully exploit available economies of large-scale production and distribution. To the extent that supply costs are *lower* at higher levels of output the concentrated market is a technically *more* efficient entity than its atomistic counterpart. Second, the traditional analysis neglects *dynamic* aspects of the market system. Major improvements in consumer welfare occur largely as a result of technological innovation – i.e. the introduction of new cost-reducing techniques and new products over time rather than adjustments to provide maximum efficiency at a given (static) point of time. To the extent that such innovative effort is frequently centred in the large oligopolistic firm, a comparison of concentrated markets with perfect competition at a fixed technological position systematically understates the technological performance of firms in concentrated markets.

Furthermore, as has been seen earlier, there are many aspects of market performance all of which need to be considered simultaneously in evaluating the performance of any particular market. In so far as the elements of performance are often interrelated, trade-offs between them need to be considered. For example, profitability needs to be considered alongside the financial requirement for firms to invest in R & D to maintain their competitiveness which, in turn, will have an impact on the pace of technological advance in the market. Moreover, judging the 'reasonableness' or otherwise of any one element of performance itself poses problems. For example, if profit rates in a market are on the low side this may be indicative of effective price competition amongst efficient producers, or it may reflect the fact that firms are grossly inefficient. On the other hand, high profits may not result from superior efficiency but instead may be due to monopolistic exploitation.

Public Policy and the Operation of Markets

Unregulated markets may fail to achieve an efficient allocation of resources: supply costs, for example, may be unnecessarily high due to the operation of sub-optimal-sized plants or the failure to adjust supply to falling demand leaving persistent excess capacity; or market prices and profit levels may be unnecessarily high because dominant forms have 'abused' their monopoly power. Alternatively, market inertia may have led to a situation where firms have failed to invest sufficiently in new technologies and in expanding capacity to take full advantage of new opportunities. For these reasons, governments may intervene in markets to correct instances of 'market failure' through competition, industrial, labour and regional policies.

Competition policy

Competition policy can cover a number of areas, including the monopolization of a market by a single supplier (dominant firm), the creation of monopoly positions by mergers and take-overs, collusion between sellers (cartels and restrictive trade agreements) and anti-competitive practices (exclusive dealing, tie-in sales etc.).

Competition policy is implemented mainly through the control of market structure and market conduct but also, on occasions, through the direct control of market performance itself (by, for example, the stipulation of maximum levels of profit).

There are two basic approaches to the control of market structure and conduct: the non-discretionary approach and the discretionary approach. The non-discretionary approach lays down 'acceptable' standards of structure and conduct and prohibits outright any transgression of these standards. Typical ingredients of the non-discretionary approach include:

1   The stipulation of maximum permitted market share limits (say, no more than 20 per cent of the market) in order to limit the degree of seller concentration and prevent the emergence of a monopoly supplier. Thus, for example, under this ruling any proposed merger or take-over which would take the combined group's market share above the permitted limit would be automatically prohibited.
2   The outright prohibition of all forms of 'shared monopoly' involving price-fixing, market-sharing etc.
3   The outright prohibition of specific practices designed to reduce or eliminate competition.

Thus, the non-discretionary approach attempts to preserve competitive conditions by a direct attack on the possession and exercise of monopoly power as such.

By contrast, the discretionary approach takes a more pragmatic line, recognizing that often high levels of seller concentration and certain agreements between firms may serve to improve economic efficiency rather than impair it. It is the essence of the discretionary approach that each situation be judged on its own merits rather than automatically condemned. Thus, under the discretionary approach, mergers, restrictive agreements and specific practices of the kind noted above are evaluated in terms of their possible benefits and detriments. If, on balance, they would appear to be detrimental, then and only then are they prohibited.

The US and the European Community by and large operate the non-discretionary approach; the UK has a history of preferring the discretionary approach.

Industrial policy

Industrial policy can take several forms depending upon the extent to which governments pursue interventionist policies. In its most comprehensive form industrial policy is used as an arm of central planning, with governments 'directing' resources into particular areas of the economy. By contrast, in free enterprise economies the government relies largely on market forces to allocate resources, intervening on a more limited basis. In such economies, governments may employ across-the-board measures to stimulate efficiency and the adoption of new technologies, such as investment grants and taxation incentives applied at a uniform rate for *all* industries. Alternatively, governments can employ more narrowly focused industrial policies involving selective intervention in particular industries or support for particular projects and firms. Industrial policy in most countries is both reactive (responding, for example, to cases of market failure by acting to restructure and rationalize declining industries or support failing, 'lame duck' firms) and pro-active (acting as a catalyst for change by encouraging, for example, the establishment of new businesss, the development of new technologies and strategic mergers in industries where suppliers are currently too small to compete on an effective scale).

In some countries (most notably the UK), industrial policy has developed on a piecemeal basis and has varied in the degree of enthusiasm accorded to it by the government of the day. In others, e.g. France, industrial policy has been seen as an arm of indicative planning and has been applied on a continuous and coordinated basis.

In addition, industrial policies may incorporate regional policies to stimulate employment opportunities by, for example, encouraging new firms and industries to invest in areas of high unemployment to replace declining industries. Finally, it is possible for the government to improve the functioning of resource markets by, for example, attacking restrictive labour practices and reducing the monopoly power of trade unions.

These various public policy strands can act as constraints upon firms' expansion plans, for example, by limiting the horizontal or vertical growth of a firm which has a dominant or near-dominant position in its market. Alternatively, public policy may provide opportunities for firms seeking to compete with dominant suppliers or to access government financial incentives to rationalize their operations or expand into new markets.

References

George, K. D., Joll, C. and Lynk, E. L., 1992. *Industrial Organization*, Routledge, 4th edn.

Hay, D. A. and Morris, D. J., 1991. *Industrial Economics and Organization*, Oxford University Press, 2nd edn.

Porter, M. E., 1980. *Competitive Strategy*, Free Press.

Porter, M. E., 1985. *Competitive Advantage*, Free Press.

7

Market Entry and Exit

Market entry and market exit constitute major business strategy decisions reflecting a strategic initiative on the part of a firm to develop, or reshape, its product/market positioning.

Market entry occurs in response to the perceived 'attractiveness' of a target market expressed in terms of its long-run profit potential, which in turn is influenced by the size of the market and its growth potential. By the same token, market exit often occurs in response to a deterioration in the attractiveness of a market.

Successful new entry requires the firm not only to overcome any initial 'barriers to entry', but also to develop a long-term strategy for establishing and sustaining competitive advantage over rival suppliers. This strategy will depend upon the resources and capabilities the firm has to serve that market. Likewise, successful exit requires the firm to overcome any 'barriers to exit'.

Market Entry

Market entry considerations constitute an integral component of the conceptual frameworks both of microeconomics and business strategy. However, there are important differences in emphasis between the two approaches (see the list below, showing the characteristics of traditional entry (microeconomics) and 'strategic' entry (business strategy).

Microeconomics focuses on resource allocation processes at the level of the '*market*' with the firm being treated as a 'robotic' input–output agent; business strategy formulations shift the focus of the analysis to the '*firm*' itself, emphasizing its strategic dynamics, in particular the ability of the firm to deploy its own (internalized) resources *between* markets. A particular focus of microeconomic analysis is the identification of barriers to entry and how these might then be exploited by incumbent firms

Traditional entry	*'Strategic' entry*
Nature of entrant	
• new supplier ('first-time' business)	• new supplier ('first-time' business) • established firm undertaking 'cross-entry' by *vertical* integration, local and international *diversification*, international *horizontal* expansion
• single-market operator • entrepreneur (owner) – controlled	• multi-market operator • entrepreneur (owner) – controlled, but more likely to be management-controlled
Motivation	
• profit maximizer (short-run/ static market) – new firms will enter the market as long as the post-entry price exceeds long-run average cost	• long-run growth of sales and profit 'targets' (which requires expanding market) – will accept lower return for lower risk (hence product and market spread)
Modes of entry	
• greenfield	• greenfield • merger/take-over, joint ventures • additionally, in the case of international entry exporting, licensing
Barriers to entry	
• 'fixed' and static including relative cost disadvantages (economies of scale, product differentiation), absolute cost disadvantages (access to inputs/ outlets), and capital requirements. Established firms may practise entry-deterrence (limit-pricing, excess capacity, patenting)	• 'variable' and dynamic entry opportunities are created by changing market conditions (new input sources, new technology, new products, new distribution channels, expanding primary demand, new market niches) and the inability or inertia of established firms to exploit these to the full

to *deter entry*, with consequent adverse effects on *market performance*. In business strategy analyses, market entry (and exit) is presented as a strategic issue from the firm's point of view as it attempts to expand and orientate its activities towards markets exhibiting growth and profit potential, and thus enhance *corporate performance*. A particular emphasis of this approach is the attempt to identify and establish positions of competitive advantage in the firm's target markets, i.e. the focus is on ways of successfully *entering a market*.

Analytically, these distinctions are fundamental. A key factor is the potency of barriers to entry. In the traditional schema barriers to entry are 'fixed' and incumbent firms are assumed to possess advantages over potential entrants which they can exploit to deter actual entry. By contrast, in the strategic approach barriers to entry tend to be more transient and given the 'right' circumstances (exploitation of new technology, new products, expanding primary demand, market niches etc.) competitive advantage may well lie with the entrant.

The Nature of Barriers to Entry

Barriers to entry are obstacles in the way of firms attempting to enter a market, which may operate to give established firms particular advantages over newcomers. A number of potential barriers to entry can be identified, including:

- *Economies of scale* – where unit costs of production, marketing, distribution and R & D decline with the volume produced and sold, the minimum efficient scale of operation may require entry on a large scale, otherwise entrants would be put at a relative cost disadvantage.
- *Product differentiation* – entrants with 'unknown' and 'untried' products may be unable to win a viable share of the market because of customer loyalty to existing brands built up by established firms through cumulative investment in advertising and sales promotion.
- *Capital requirements* – the cost of financing investment in plant, product differentiation and R & D, and meeting initial operating losses, may be prohibitively high. This barrier may be particularly potent in risky areas like R & D and brand-building rather than in machinery and stock which have a salvage value.
- *Vertical restrictions* – key raw materials and components sources, and distribution channels, may be controlled by established firms, thereby limiting access to inputs and market outlets. Where access to inputs or distribution channels cannot be secured on competitive terms, or these are foreclosed by established firms through vertical integration, exclusive licensing etc., the entrant may need to develop new material sources or set up new distribution channels.

- *Switching costs* – where the cost of switching from one input supplier to another, or one distributor to another, is high this can constitute an entry barrier. Switching costs can include re-training costs and changes in organizational routines for purchasing or distribution and the loss of technical help previously received from suppliers or distributors. Where existing firms have long-term contracts with suppliers or distributors it may be difficult to persuade these firms to bear the switching costs involved in moving to a new supplier or distributor unless substantial cost or performance gains are offered.
- *Cost disadvantages independent of scale* – entrants' costs may be higher than those of established firms at comparable output levels because they are, for example, denied access to 'best state-of-the-art technology' because of patent rights accruing to established firms and are thus forced to adopt inferior, higher cost methods of production etc.
- *Government policy* – various discriminatory government controls and impositions may limit entry opportunities. These could include restrictions on the number of licenses granted by government to produce or distribute particular products and tariffs. (See box 7.1.)

Entry-forestalling Behaviour by Incumbent Firms

In addition to the various barriers of entry of the kind outlined above, potential entrants must consider the defensive reactions which existing suppliers may employ to make entry more difficult and unattractive. Incumbents' policies to deter entry can include the use of so-called 'limit-pricing', investment in product differentiation, product innovation and a deliberate increase in their output potential to create 'excess capacity'.

Limit-pricing

In conventional market analysis established firms can actively prevent entry by selecting an entry-forestalling price. Whether or not entry into a market occurs depends upon the profits that the potential entrant expects to earn. This will depend on the entrant's own cost position and upon the post-entry price and demand conditions anticipated by it. These factors, in turn, will depend on the anticipated reaction of established suppliers to the threat of entry.

Originally the theory of entry was largely based on the assumption that potential entrants anticipate that established firms will maintain their outputs at the pre-entry level following actual entry (see Bain, Sylos, Labini, and Modigliani; for a review of these and other studies see Hay and Morris (1991) and George, Joll and Lynk (1992)). This

Box 7.1   Barriers to entry

1   *Plasterboard*
Until 1987 BPB was the sole UK producer of plasterboard accounting for 96 per cent of market supply, the remainder being accounted for by imports from mainland Europe. Evidence to the Monopolies and Mergers Commission identified a number of potential barriers to the entry of new suppliers:

> Technology represented a major obstacle to a would-be entrant with no existing plasterboard experience. While plasterboard plants could be purchased 'off the shelf', there were often significant technical problems in operation, and, as manufacture was computer-controlled, the ranges of board size increased the complexity of programming.

> The capital investment required was large and there were additional costs for the entrant not previously involved in plasterboard manufacture.

> A new entrant had to source its raw materials from outside the UK because most UK-based supplies (crucially, gypsum) were controlled by BPB.

> There were significant economies of scale in marketing, distribution, R & D and administration.

> BPB's strong market presence and its brand 'Gyproc' had been established for many years and would be formidable factors to overcome.

> Despite these barriers, two new firms established manufacturing plants in the UK in 1987 and 1988. (See box 7.2.)

2   *Coffee*
In the case of consumer products such as coffee, the need for entrants to develop innovatory new brands and invest in advertising and sales promotion may act as barriers to entry. These may be overcome, however, by 'deep pocket' entrants and by multinational entrants who 'transfer' established brands into new markets. More limited entry may occur, with new suppliers targeting niche segments of the market or producing 'own-label' brands for established retail groups. In the UK coffee market Nestlé's dominant position ('Nescafé' etc.) has been put under threat by the entry of the US concern General Foods ('Maxwell House') and a UK 'cross entrant', the Allied-Lyon's subsidiary Brooke Bond ('Red Mountain') as well as a multitude of 'own label' brands ('Tesco', 'Sainsbury' etc.). (See box 7.2.)

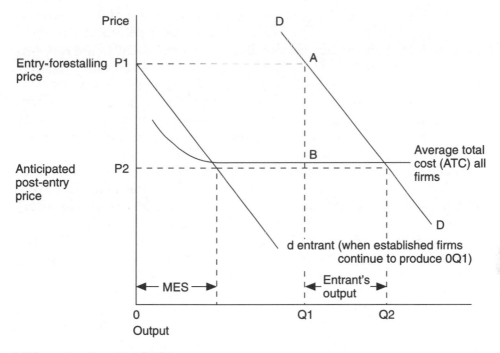

MES = entrant's output Q1Q2

Figure 7.1 Scale economies and limit-pricing

proposition is shown in figure 7.1 where the entry barrier is assumed to be one of scale economies. In the figure, given the above assumption, established firms produce output 0Q1 before, and would continue to do so *after*, entry. The entrant's demand curve is thus 'd entrant'. The potential entrant is assumed to have access to the same average cost curve as that of established firms (i.e. there are no absolute cost advantages accruing to established firms). Economies of scale, however, are important such that to operate a minimum efficient scale of plant (MES) the entrant would need to supply an output of Q1Q2. It will be noted that as a result of the addition of the entrant's output to established firms' output (0Q1) the market price is lowered to 0P2. Hence the price that is relevant to entry decisions is the anticipated post-entry price, not the existing pre-entry price (0P1). The existence of substantial scale economies is not in itself sufficient to prevent entry. Entry will occur if the post-entry price is *above* the entrant's cost curve, but entry will be deterred if 0P2, as in figure 7.1, is below the entrant's ATC curve. Thus, the greater the importance of scale economies, the greater is the amount by which established firms can raise prices above ATC (i.e. make above-normal profits) without inducing entry. The entry-forestalling price is 0P1 and the size of unit 'excess' profits is AB.

Market entry theory has been developed in a number of directions but with a common focus on the strategic interplay between incumbents' policies and their impact on potential entrants. Initially, interest was directed at the 'trade-off' between short-run and long-run profitability implied by limit- and non-limit-pricing policies, and how various non-price parameters, particularly product differentiation investments, might serve to limit entry. More recently, consideration has been given to the possibility that established firms might deliberately *increase* their output potential by creating 'excess capacity' in order to forestall entry.

If entry barriers are severe, established firms may be in a position to prevent entry whilst securing 'excess' profits over the long run. More usually, however, established firms will be faced with the choice of (1) setting a price which yields short-run profit maximization (SRPM) *but* which induces entry or (2) setting a limit price below the SRPM level. Whilst limit-pricing will result in lower short-run profits than the SRPM policy, it would be the more attractive of the two strategies if it produced a higher level of discounted profits over the longer term. Thus, in selecting a price policy, established firms must weigh the initially lower but more persistent profits of the limit price policy against the initially higher but eventually lower profits of the SRPM policy. This decision will depend upon various factors including, the differences in short-run profits arising from the respective strategies, the rate of profit erosion due to entry under the SRPM policy and the rate of growth of market demand.

These two strategies represent the broad options. According to some writers the optimal policy might consist of some combination of the two. For example, established firms might set prices initially above the limit price level, thereby inviting actual entry, but would then 'control' the rate at which they lost market share to newcomers by price-shading and by increasing expenditure on product differentiation.

However, a passive response to entry by incumbent firms may not be appropriate if such a passive response is interpreted by other potential entrants as a sign of weakness. Consequently, incumbents may decide to initiate a 'price war' against early entrants if further future entry is predicted, so as to establish a 'reputation' for aggression. However, in so far as price wars destroy the profitability of the market, established firms may prefer to attempt to deter entry by other 'visible' means, particularly investment in product differentiation.

Product differentiation and entry

Cumulative expenditures on advertising and sales promotion and product proliferation may act as a barrier to entry by building buyer loyalty to the brands of established firms. Such expenditures could be used, as noted above, to reinforce a limit price policy, or deployed in their own right to limit entry (see Comanor and Wilson, Schmalensee, Cubbins etc. in Hay and Morris (1991)).

In differentiated oligopolistic markets firms incur advertising and promotional expenditures in order to maintain and increase the market shares of their existing brands, and also to launch new brands in competition with established rivals. The attraction of such differentiation investments is that whereas price competition (and limit-pricing) reduces industry profitability, often differentiation expenditures can be 'passed on' to consumers which, together with their entry-deterring effects, helps preserve a high level of industry profitability over the long run.

Whether or not established firms *deliberately* incur higher differentiation expenditure than would otherwise be perceived necessary to maintain their market position against established rivals cannot be readily determined. However, the escalation of differentiation costs as part of oligopolists' 'preferred' way of competing against each other does have the additional advantage for them of making entry more difficult. In particular, the potential entrant is conventionally depicted to be at a disadvantage because it has an 'unknown', 'untried' product. In order to penetrate the market the entrant must 'buy' itself market share (in static analysis, at the expense of established firms), which involves incurring initial penetration costs which in unit terms are *greater* than the equivalent costs of supporting an existing brand. Entrants may face higher penetration costs either because they are unable to match the economies of scale in advertising enjoyed by established firms, or even though they may have the financial resources to reach the minimum efficient scale of advertising, 'extra' expenditures are still required to break down customer loyalty to existing brands.

The conventional view is thus that advertising by established firms may well act to keep potential entrants out of the market. Other studies, however, draw attention to the supportive role played by advertising in underpinning *actual* entry. Successful new entry by greenfield suppliers is fundamentally linked to their ability to offer consumers a new innovative brand (see below) that performs better or is in some way more distinctive than established brands. Advertising is an adjunct to this process; it is an essential means of launching, building and maintaining demand for the new brand.

Product innovation

Product innovation may be used to buttress the market dominance of established firms. Clearly, cumulative investments by established firms in R & D facilities and personnel can provide an on-going pool of 'internalized' skills and expertise which firms currently outside the industry may find difficult to acquire and imitate. The power of incumbent firms to capitalize on their knowledge base and technological advantages is often enhanced by the patent system and the possible strategic use of 'pre-emptive' patenting against other actual and potential competitors. Again, there is the problem of distinguishing the entry-deterring effects of product innovations that are merely the by-product of firms' desire to keep abreast of technological opportunities from that stemming from pre-emption motives. The incidence of the latter, however, is likely to be small. Patent protection is of limited duration, is costly, and the competition authorities discourage 'sleeping' patents, i.e. patents that are neither used by the patentor nor licensed to others.

Excess capacity

Established firms may undertake strategic investment in excess capacity with the expectation that excess capacity will be seen by potential entrants either as a signal of aggressive intent, or as a credible threat. Basically, the proposition is that the creation of excess capacity puts established firms in the position of being able to retaliate effectively against actual entry by *increasing* their outputs thereby reducing post-entry prices to unprofitable levels. This, it is argued, alters the risk–return perceptions of potential entrants such as to divert their investments into other industries.

The matter, however, is complicated by the fact that excess capacity may arise for a number of reasons other than entry-forestalling motives. For example, in industries characterized by pronounced cyclical demand movements additional capacity may be held in reserve to meet peaks in demand. Also, where investments are 'lumpy' requiring large-scale capacity increases excess capacity may be temporarily created in anticipation of a long-term growth in industry demand; in contrast, excess capacity may reflect a long-term decline in demand, necessitating industry restructuring.

To date, little empirical support has been found for the use of excess capacity as an entry-forestalling technique and, as discussed below, there are doubts surrounding both its feasibility and rationality.

Problems with entry-forestalling tactics

Entry-deterring behaviour has been criticized on a number of counts both with respect to the assumptions upon which it is based and as an explanation of actual market behaviour. First, there is the question of awareness and identification. Such behaviour requires established firms be fully alert to the 'threat' posed by potential entrants. There is no strong evidence, however, that firms do in fact monitor their environment to this extent, and lack of information may make it difficult in any case to identify potential newcomers and the seriousness of their intentions. In some instances potential entrants can be readily located on the fringes of the market, e.g. suppliers who might be tempted to integrate forwards, or firms currently operating in adjacent markets; in other cases, less obviously the main threat of entry may come from foreign suppliers and from firms undertaking 'pure' diversification.

Second, assuming that established firms do actively seek to prevent entry by, for example, limit-pricing and excess capacity there is the problem of agreeing upon appropriate industry price and capacity levels. Conventional market analysis suggests that the more monopolistic the market the more easily this can be achieved. Where the market is comprised of a number of oligopolistic suppliers each with different costs and market shares, a great deal of 'group' cohesion or even formal collusion may be required to secure a coordinated policy. For example, a price cut initiated by one firm in the interests of limit-pricing may be seen, mistakenly, as an 'aggressive' in-market move by its rivals and precipitate a price war, thereby ruining the profitability of the market. Similarly, excess capacity must be seen by established firms unambiguously as a 'strike' weapon against potential entrants. However, excess capacity may simply intensify price competition between established suppliers as they strive to fill their order books. Again, although this makes entry less attractive, such a strategy lacks credibility because it destroys the profitability of the market for established firms too.

Market Dynamics and Opportunities for Entry

In dynamic market conditions technology, products and primary demand all tend to change and these changes can affect the potency of any entry barriers. Thus, unless established firms are cost-effective, active innovators and sensitive to changing consumer demand, opportunities for entry may arise. In dynamic terms certain factors which in the short run can act as barriers to entry now become *variables* which can be exploited as a means of achieving successful entry. These include:

Leads and lags in the adoption of new technology

A greenfield entrant may install *new* technology in a *new* vintage plant; established firms, however, operating older vintage plant are required to remove old equipment, machinery etc. before installing new, and rationalization and modernization together represent a far more difficult operation than either do separately. Where new technology brings with it significant operating cost reductions, the entrant is *more* cost-effective than established firms. In figure 7.2 at the post-entry price, established firms secure only

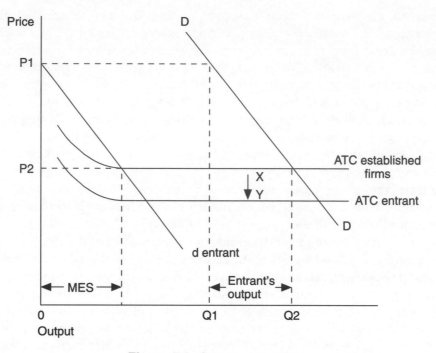

Figure 7.2   Lower cost entry

normal profits while the entrant obtains above-normal profits (**XY**). Alternatively, lower costs may be used to underpin an entry strategy based on 'penetration-pricing' (i.e. a level of prices which undercuts the limit price of established firms) aimed at securing an initial large share of the market.

Product innovation and differentiation

Product differentiation – the ability to offer a product which is significantly *superior to or more distinctive* than those currently offered by established firms – is often a more decisive element in successful new entry than price. In figure 7.3 the entrant comes in leaving the pre-entry price P1 undisturbed. Total industry output remains the *same* but the entrant's superior product enables it to win a large market share at the expense of established firms.

Expanding demand

A third factor associated with successful new entry is the ability to expand primary market demand by product differentiation and market segmentation strategies. The significance of an expanding total and

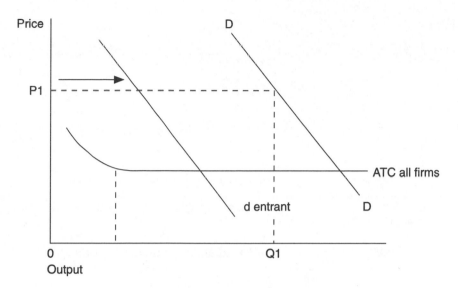

Figure 7.3 Superior product entry

segmented demand is that the newcomer is able to enter the market *without* necessarily undermining the position of established firms. In a static market, new entrants can only obtain viable market shares by attracting sales away from established sellers – one firm's gain is some other firm's loss. By contrast, a growing market, and the development of market segments, permits absorption of the entrant's output while at the same time enabling established firms to maintain (or even increase) their own sales and profits. In these circumstances established firms may take no positive action either to deter potential entrants or to retaliate aggressively against actual entry. In figure 7.4 the entrant's output is 'absorbed' by an expansion in the overall size of the market, again maintaining the existing pre-entry price 0P1.

Further factors which facilitate entry include:

Changing input technology

The innovation of substitute raw materials and components may encourage input suppliers to integrate forward into assembly operations. For example, some chemical companies entered the textile fabrication market in order to exploit their advantages in synthetic fibre technology against natural textile fibres such as wool and cotton.

Changing distribution channels

These may provide entrants with market access opportunities by circumventing traditional distribution networks, including outlets either owned

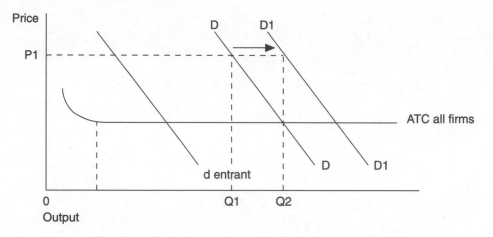

Figure 7.4 Entry based on expanding total market demand

or 'tied' to established firms. For example, in the UK small 'specialist' retailers have declined in the face of competition from supermarket chains and this has afforded entry opportunities to many firms as suppliers of store own label brands as well as their main branded items.

In sum, conventional market analysis assumes that established firms have some specific advantages over potential entrants; dynamic analysis, by contrast, suggests that given the right circumstances *competitive advantage may lie with the entrant*. To the extent that established firms are fully efficient and innovative, however, the scope for new entry is limited. Thus often the *real* opportunity for successful entry arises due to the *weaknesses of established firms*. (See box 7.2.)

Contestable Markets

The conventional analysis of entry barriers seems to imply that with the exception of competitive markets with *no* entry barriers virtually all markets which show modest degrees of market concentration are likely to be protected by entry barriers and thus foreclosed to potential entrants. However, as the analysis of dynamically mobile entry barriers, outlined above, suggests, markets may be more 'contestable' than traditionally allowed for. For example, Baumol et al. (1982) have argued that providing there are no 'sunk costs' constraints on market exit, so that any investment in plant or equipment is recoverable on exit, and that new firms have access to the same technology and cost structures as those of established firms, then the market will be contestable. In such circumstances even in markets characterized by considerable economies of scale

Box 7.2   Market entry

1   *Plasterboard Report, Monopolies and Mergers Report, 1990*
The UK plasterboard market has been transformed by the entry in 1987 and 1988, respectively, of two new businesses, RPL (a joint venture company 51 per cent owned by an established UK building materials group Redland and 49 per cent by CSR, an Australian producer of plasterboard), and Knauf, a German producer of plasterboard. Previously BPB was the sole UK producer of the product, accounting for 96 per cent of market supply, protected by a number of entry barriers (see box 7.1).

In the event, these factors were not sufficient in themselves to prevent RPL and Knauf from entering the market. RPL entered the market because it 'believed that, given the existing high margins, unpopular monopoly conditions and prospects for future growth, there would be considerable potential for a second supplier to establish a sound and profitable business in the market'.

Initially RPL imported plasterboard while it constructed its first (of two) UK plants which came on-stream in September 1989. CSR provided the technology and know how needed to build the plant, whilst Redland provided the market expertise and distribution contacts. RPL secured access to supplies of two key raw materials: liner paper by purchasing a 51 per cent interest in a Swedish paper concern and gypsum by importing it at competitive prices from Spain. Knauf's first UK plant came on-stream in April 1989, similarly sourcing inputs from abroad. In 1990 RPL's share of the UK market was 12 per cent and Knauf's 6 per cent. BPB's share had fallen to 76 per cent.

2   *Soluble Coffee Report, Monopolies and Mergers Report, 1991*
In the UK coffee market significant new entry has occurred in the main market sectors (General Foods, Brooke Bond and a multitude of 'own label' brands) as well as various niche segments (see box 7.1). In its 1990 investigation of the continuing dominance of Nestlé in this market the Monopolies and Mergers Commission concluded: 'The increasing success of its brands, particularly of Nescafé (38% market share), given the extent of choice available (over 200 brands, most selling at prices below those of Nestlé's brands) reflects Nestlé's success as a competitor in offering a reliable product of a quality and price in accordance with consumer performance' (paragraph 7.66). Whilst it cannot be denied that advertising expenses (national launches typically cost upwards of £5 million) might act as some deterrent to entry, a more formidable obstacle is represented by the need to offer innovatory products. Both the entry of General Foods and Brooke Bond into the mass market were facilitated by their 'deep pocket' ability to finance initial entry expenses, including advertising. However, their subsequent failure to undermine Nestlé's market position *despite higher* advertising–sales ratios indicates that it is product quality which represents the core competitive advantage in this market.

incumbent firms might not be able to effectively prevent entry. The high initial capital costs in such markets are only a deterrent if they are specific to the venture concerned and not readily transferable into the production of another good. Where capital is not specific a potential entrant can practise 'hit and run' entry, moving into a market to grab market share by cutting prices fractionally and then exiting the market without loss, to use its non-specific capital elsewhere should incumbents retaliate fiercely. Here the threat of entry may be sufficient to deter incumbents from exercising market power to charge prices which yield above-normal profits. However, for the threat of potential entry to be really effective in reducing monopoly power potential competitors may need to actually enter the market from time to time.

The notion of contestability may be particularly appropriate in explaining the potency of potential foreign competition. In the international context, entering a foreign market through exporting allows a firm to exploit competitive price and other advantages over local firms, and also to exit the market with no or little penalty in the form of sunk costs. Specifically, exports can be supplied to a particular market from a production base *outside* that market at marginal cost compared to local producers who are required to supply (long term) at average cost. Should a firm's price advantage narrow or disappear due to, for example, increases in transportation costs or tariff impositions, then a direct investment presence in the market may be effected to exploit other competitive advantages such as innovative products.

In practice, in markets where competition largely takes the form of price and cost competition based upon large-scale production with firms having a large element of sunk costs, they are unlikely to be subject to hit and run tactics from entrants because of these sunk costs. Furthermore, in markets where competition takes the form mainly of product differentiation competition, potential entrants would find it difficult to secure a significant market share within a short time in competition with the established brands of incumbents, even where potential entrants have flexible production equipment which they could deploy in that market. Similarly, in markets where competition primarily takes the form of new product development, the R & D and know-how advantages of established firms makes them less vulnerable to short-termist entrants.

Strategies for Market Entry and Their Consequences

The foregoing analysis is based on the traditional assumption that a market entrant is likely to be a start-up business which establishes a new supply source by greenfield entry and thus increases the number of competitors in the market. In practice, the new entrant is just as likely to be a 'cross-entrant', i.e. an established firm in other markets which effects a form of diversifying entry into the target market either by setting up a greenfield operation or by merging with, or taking over, an incumbent supplier. The list below summarizes some of the main advantages and disadvantages of the major forms of market entry. Which particular form of entry the firm chooses will depend on a number of factors but four are of crucial importance, namely, the relative investment costs of each entry mode, the relative risks of each mode, potential growth rate of company sales and control and communication aspects. It is possible to compare different forms of market entry in terms of these characteristics:

	Advantages	*Disadvantages*
1 Greenfield entry	• scale of operation can be matched to firm's resources and to the market – expansion can proceed in accordance with the company's progress and market penetration • operation 'fits' the firm's established 'culture' (i.e. no 'inheritance' problems as in take-over) • availability of fiscal inducements to investment (tax, profit write-offs, grants, subsidies etc.)	• up-front investment commitment (which may be substantial to achieve economies of scale) • risk – problem of winning viable customer base to support investment made • slow market penetration
2 Entry via merger/ take-over	• long-run – may be cheaper/less risky than greenfield • more rapid entry – existing production facilities, customer base, local contacts with suppliers etc., i.e. 'buy' an on-going profitable business • overcomes the culture problem of 'learning' the ways of doing business in an 'unfamiliar' market	• suitability and price of the assets acquired • 'inheritance' problems – conflict of management objectives and organizational 'style', technology and products may need modernization/ rationalization

3　Entry via strategic
　　alliances

(a) joint ventures	• shared investment and risks • 'synergy', e.g. partner provides complementary resources and capabilities	• dilution of control • 'communication' difficulties • differences in corporate objectives and commitment
(b) licensing	• extra sales/profits for limited capital investment – important for 'capital-constrained' smaller firms • market access particularly to protected foreign markets	• technical and marketing limitations of licensee • under-exploitation of profit potential (that is, competitive advantage 'sold off' on the cheap) • 'loss' of technology etc. to actual (and potential) competitors

Investment cost considerations

Entry via take-over may involve the firm in considerable financial investment since it will generally have to pay a goodwill premium over the cost of assets acquired for an established firm. In comparison, greenfield entry on a similar scale will generally involve a smaller investment since the firm will pay only for the assets it needs to establish itself in the market. However, even this investment will usually be larger than the investment required in a joint venture arrangement (again, for a similar scale of operation).

Risk considerations

Greenfield entry is generally risky since the firm may fail to obtain a big enough market share for its 'unknown' product to ensure long-term viability. By contrast, entry via take-over or merger gives the firm immediate access to established products and distribution channels and so is less risky. Strategic alliances allow either the sharing of risks with partners (through a joint venture) or the reduction of risks by licensing processes or products to others.

Growth rates

Greenfield entry will tend to offer only modest growth prospects for a firm since it will take some time for the firm to build up distribution channels and establish customer loyalty to its products. Take-over and merger entry, by contrast, gives the firm an immediate growth in sales since it is able to 'buy' the market share of established producers. Entry via strategic alliances will tend to facilitate faster growth than greenfield entry insofar as joint venture and licensing arrangements give the firm access to capital, brands, distribution outlets and know-how.

Control and communication

Entry via take-overs and mergers often involve initial problems of combining different management styles and operating systems which may blunt efficiency and competitiveness. Greenfield entry, on the other hand, generally carries over the firm's established 'corporate culture' and control systems to the new business activity. Entry via strategic alliances requires particular attention to the reconciliation of differences in objectives between joint venture partners and communications between them, or clarification of contract terms between licensor and licensee if the alliance is to be effective.

Consequences of market entry

Whichever entry strategy is adopted, the consequences of market entry will depend upon the extent to which entry 'disturbs' the existing pattern of competition in that market. In the last case of merger/take-over entry the number of suppliers remains unchanged which makes it easier for a diversified entrant to be quickly assimilated into the established *modus operandi* of the market without disturbing the existing relationship between the other incumbents. In the cases of both start-up and greenfield entry by a diversified firm the addition of a new supplier is likely to cause some disruption to the market behaviour of established firms insofar as newcomers need to win market share so that the market must now be divided between an enlarged number of suppliers.

The extent to which the intensity of competition in a market changes with the entry of new firms depends upon the structure of the market and the behaviour of entrants. Entrants may choose to behave 'passively' upon entry, matching the pricing and promotional strategies of established firms and seeking to minimize any disruption to current market practices caused by their entry. Alternatively, the entrant may behave 'aggressively', seeking to pursue different ways of doing business than the accepted ways of incumbents. The extent to which entrants are likely to behave aggressively will depend upon whether they have a wider perception of the opportunities afforded by the market than the incumbents and whether they have the managerial or financial resources to pursue these opportunities. (See box 7.3.)

Box 7.3   Retaliatory action against entrants

1   *Plasterboard Report, Monopolies and Mergers Report, 1990*
It was noted in box 7.2 that two new companies, RPL (a UK–Australian joint venture) and Knauf (of Germany) had entered the UK plasterboard market in 1987 and 1988. RPL complained to the Monopolies and Mergers Commission (MMC) that BPB had responded to the new entry by increasing the prices of plasterboard products not sold by the new entrants, such as specialist boards and plasters, and reducing the net prices on products readily available from the new entrants. BPB had also offered additional discounts and rebates to encourage buyers to remain loyal and had cross-subsidized its delivery charges in some areas to undercut RPL.

Knauf told the MMC that BPB's principal response to its entry had been the lowering of BPB's plasterboard prices in Germany very significantly (by around 30 per cent over a period of one year). Knauf believed that BPB was attempting thereby to cut Knauf's cash flow with a view to preventing it from building a second UK plant. BPB had also simultaneously lowered the price of plaster in Germany and raised plaster prices in the UK, and had modified its discounts to certain customers by 'verbal agreements' which discouraged these customers from placing business with Knauf.

Overall the entry of Knauf and RPL had led to a fall in UK plasterboard prices by around 25 per cent in real terms in the eighteen months from August 1988 to February 1990. Knauf told the MMC that it had expected prices to drop when it entered the market 'and its business plan in the short to medium term took this expectation into account'. Even so, Knauf was trading profitably and expected prices to firm over the longer term. RPL, however, had incurred losses during its start-up period, but was 'optimistic' that BPB could not sustain the lower prices over the longer term and would raise prices to more realistic levels.

2   *Soluble Coffee Report, Monopolies and Mergers Report, 1991*
In the UK coffee market (see box 7.2) Nestlé responded to the entry of General Foods ('Maxwell House') and Brooke Bond ('Red Mountain') and a host of cheap 'own label' brands by meticulous attention to product improvement to maintain its quality lead over competitors. Despite the fact that the company's main brand, 'Nescafé' is sold at a higher price than competitors' brands, it has increased its market share in recent years. In 1978 'Nescafé's share of the coffee market was 24 per cent; by 1990 this had increased to 38 per cent. Over the same period the market share of its main branded rival, 'Maxwell House', fell from 19 per cent to 9 per cent, whilst combined 'own label' brands' share of the market fell from 30 per cent to 24 per cent. Thus, as observed by the MMC in its report on the market: 'we believe that Nestlé has been able to achieve its current market share and present profitability in a competitive market by developing products and brands that offer consumers good value for money' (paragraph 1.4). Product 'uniqueness' is the core competitive advantage in this market.

In this regard diversifying entrants are often catalytic forces for intensifying competition and changing methods of supply. For example, the Imperial Tobacco Group's entry into the UK crisps market served to considerably widen the nature of the crisps market, which traditionally comprised sales of crisps to male adults through public houses, by adding new market segments, in particular family snack sales of crisps sold through supermarkets. In addition to this broader vision of the potential of the crisps market, Imperial was able to finance the introduction of new superior production and packaging technology and undertake sustained advertising to establish its brands.

Strategic Groups and Mobility Barriers

Some firms within a market are persistently more profitable than others because competing firms follow different strategies. These differences may be along a variety of dimensions such as degree of specialization, brand identification, channel selection, product quality, technological leadership, vertical integration, price policy, service and so on. The significant competitors within a market can be broadly characterized in terms of the above list of dimensions. The firms may then be slotted into what Porter (1985) terms 'strategic groups' of firms following a similar strategy along the above strategic dimensions. The profitability of each firm *within* a group will differ primarily according to their differential abilities in implementing a common strategy. The profit potential may well vary, however, *between* different strategic groups – having adopted (either by choice or necessity) a different orientation in dealing with competitive forces. (See chapter 8.)

Mobility barriers

Some of the entry barriers described above, deterring new entrants, will protect *all* firms in the market. However, some barriers will apply only to *certain* strategic groups. Entry barriers not only protect firms in a strategic group from entry from outside the market, but also provide barriers to shifting strategic position from one group to another. In this context Porter terms these 'mobility barriers'.

Mobility barriers are the obstacles which protect a strategic group within an industry and deter firms from moving from one strategic group to another. These mobility barriers parallel and reinforce the more general entry barriers which deter potential industry entrants and so protect all firms in the industry, but serve to give additional protection to particular strategic groups. Thus, for example, whilst lack of access to brewing technology might deter any potential entrant to brewing, the need for large-scale distribution in order to operate as a national brewer would also deter smaller scale local brewers from attempting to become national brewers. Mobility barriers can be developed by incumbent firms in a strategic group which is achieving above-average profits to prevent competitive encroachment.

It is the existence of mobility barriers which often explains why the success of some firms in a market is not simply imitated by other firms in the same market. In this regard, mobility barriers serve to reduce competitive threats and they provide an explanation of the stable market share of strategic groups in some markets.

It is important not only to identify the presence of inter-group mobility barriers, but also to examine how, and to what extent, these barriers influence competitive activity. Four main factors determine how strongly strategic groups interact:

1   Extent to which their target customers overlap.
2   Product differentiation achieved by the group.
3   Number of groups and their relative size.
4   Extent to which group strategies diverge.

All four factors interrelate to determine the pattern of rivalry between strategic groups in a market. The least interaction and rivalry between groups would occur where a few large groups serve distinctly separate customer segments with differentiated products and pursue strategies that differ markedly.

An example of strategic groups: UK brewing industry

An illustration of strategic group analysis is provided by the UK brewing industry. The industry can be divided into four broad strategic groups as indicated in table 7.1. Non-integrated national brewers without tied estates include such companies as Carlsberg and Guinness which, through the distinctive nature of their beers, occupy particular product niches in the market. Integrated national brewers, such as Bass and Whitbread, produce a full range of beers which they distribute primarily through their tied estates. Regional brewers, such as Wolverhampton and Dudley, are focused upon a specific geographic area of the UK with their own tied estates to serve these areas. Finally, local brewers are very small scale concerns which usually sell a limited product range. These strategic groups in the industry have been reinforced by barriers that make it difficult for firms in one strategic group to move to another. National brewers have certain advantages:

Table 7.1 Characteristics of strategic groups in the UK brewing industry

Characteristic	Strategic group			
	Non-integrated nationals	Integrated nationals	Regionals	Local brewers
Vertical integration	limited	full	full	full
Scale	large	large	medium	small
Product line	specialized	full	full	specialized
Advertising/sales	high	high	medium	low
Markets	national	national	reglonal	local
Distribution channels	mainly free trade	tied and free trade	mainly tied trade	tied trade
Diversification	limited	wide	limited	none
Growth	internal	merger	mainly merger	internal
National market share of typical firm	5%	8% to 20%	2%	small

Source: Bloor and Cockerill (1989)

1 They have economies of scale in production and an extensive network of tied houses which facilitatcs national distribution; regional brewers have not been able to compete on costs and distribution to the same extent, particularly in the expanding lager section of the market.
2 Heavy expenditure on advertising national brand names has enabled the national brewers to build larger market shares; regional brewers have less-well-established brands which they find more difficult to market outside their own tied estates. In the case of some products, particularly lager, they have to buy in the brands of the majors. On the other hand, regional and local brewers are protected to some extent from encroachment by the national brewers by regional differences in preferences for beer and their lower marketing and distribution costs.

Strategic groups provide a richer means of analysing market entry dynamics insofar as they augment the traditional approach to entry based upon entry by outsiders. In particular, they allow for more specific analysis

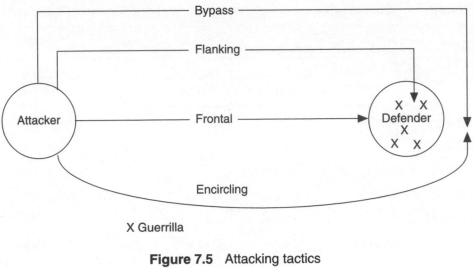

Figure 7.5   Attacking tactics
Source: James (1984)

of target market segments rather than considering the whole market as a basis for entry, and consider the possibility of entry into a particular market segment by a firm currently serving other segments of the market. In the last analysis, the potency of entry barriers depends upon the possession of financial and managerial resources. Where market niches are too small for large-scale, low-cost producers to pick up, then small-scale firms with limited financial resources can survive by emphasizing product differentiation and services which consumers value sufficiently to pay for. However, where such market niches develop to the point where they become sufficiently attractive to the large-scale, efficient producers then such producers are in a position to enter these market segments with very little incremental investment and imitate or overwhelm smaller firms within these market segments.

Attacking and Defending Tactics

Much of this chapter has been devoted to the means and techniques available to a firm wishing to keep other firms out of its markets or wishing to enter new or related markets itself. Some authors (James (1984), for example) have seen the 'battle' to attack and defend markets as akin to military strategy. Figure 7.5 indicates a number of possible 'attacking' configurations.

Attacking tactics

- *Frontal.* A frontal or direct attack is perhaps the most dangerous tactic to use as confrontation can pose severe potential risks, particularly for smaller or weaker attackers. To be successful the attacker should possess absolute or relative competitive advantage over the defender. Such an advantage could, of course, be a weakness in the defender which is exploitable. When the commercial banks entered the mortgage market, capturing a 20 per cent market share in one year, the building societies seemed powerless to react. Where a defender is seen to be too powerful, then a variation on frontal attack could be to build in smaller markets in an isolated strategy until the attacker is strong enough.
- *Bypass.* Here the attacker bypasses the existing competition by satisfying consumer demand with a substitute product. As was the case with digital watches, these new products can be based on new technology or, as is the case with some personal financial products, a repackaging and refocusing of existing products can take place.
- *Flanking.* This tactic involves the attacker building strength where the defender is weak either geographically or through marketing or technology. Examples of geographic flanking moves are dominance of a small part of a larger market by a company offering a product or service which others find difficult to emulate, e.g. airports. People may prefer airports because of ease of transit notwithstanding other inconveniences not encountered in others. Marketing examples would include the entry of lower price and margin foreign supermarkets into the UK food retailing industry. Aldi and Netto are not as yet taking on established layers in a direct confrontational manner. In terms of technological advantage, the production by Michelin of radial tyres is an example of a company attacking large and well-established companies via a technological advantage.
- *Encircling.* Firms which offer a full product range have the ability to compete in all segments of the market-place and thus build up large sales. The strategy clearly depends upon the firm's ability to fund such a strategy for any weakness can be attacked particularly by focusers who concentrate on particular market segments. The advantage for the attacker is that they are omnipresent in the market-place, attacking everybody by encircling competitors' products. This is a strategy which Boeing have employed for some time but which now appears to be emulated by Airbus Industrie.
- *Guerrilla.* This strategy is mainly concerned with winning small battles so as to upset the defenders and force them to lose heart or retire. It can lead to companies 'learning' about the market in order to

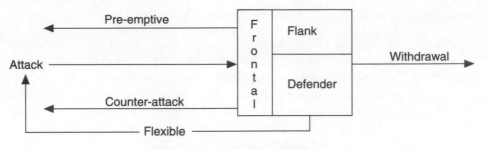

Figure 7.6 Defending tactics
Source: Adapted from James (1984)

build, say, bigger market shares from smaller markets. Examples are short-term price deals to gain share and upset the opposition.

Attacking is not solely confined to market entry; it is also a prime method of building market share. However, the above methods can be and are utilized in order to enter markets. Their success depends in part on others' ability to defend (see below).

Defending tactics

Figure 7.6 shows various 'defensive' postures.

- *Defending frontal attacks (having a position)*. Many firms worry about having a defensible position in their chosen markets from which they can defend frontal attacks. Strong positions would include elements of strategy such as patents and exclusive dealerships, but these tend to be the exception. Common defence systems are differentiation of service, products, design, distribution, image etc. Alternatively, defences can be built up around low costs. Firms seek to build ramparts or towers of particular strengths around which companies can mount defensive strategies.
- *Flank defence*. As was pointed out above, a common form of attack is to find weaknesses in defenders and then exploit them. Firms thus have to fill these potential or actual gaps in their defences by, for example, entering into alliances with others or by specializing in specific areas where they have strength. An example of this latter strategy would be Virgin Airlines which has built a reputation in one of the most competitive routes in the world, the North Atlantic, by offering a package which is attractive and valued by a certain sector of the public.
- *Pre-emptive defence*. Perhaps the most famous example of this form of defence was the decision of the BBC to launch its 'Breakfast TV'

programme in advance of the much publicized Independent Television version. The rationale for this strategy is to weaken and confuse
the attacker who is known to be about to attack. It can take many
forms including distribution strategies, financial manoeuvres and
lobbying regulatory authorities. This latter strategy is heavily utilized
in the airline industry.

- *Counter-offensive* – 'You attack me, I attack you'. This is probably the
  most common form of defence. It can take many forms including
  product enhancement, promotion battles, the formation of strategic
  alliances or any combination of these. There are numerous examples
  of these strategies from the efforts of the Swiss watch industry in
  combating the digital revolution with 'Swatch' to Rover's alliance
  with Honda to improve its products.
- *Flexible*. In a sense this is akin to guerrilla defence. Rapid product
  innovation is a good example of this type of defensive strategy. This
  policy can shorten product life cycles or 'cannibalize' existing products, but it may be a price worth paying in order to defend one's
  position. This form of defence can be readily seen in the consumer
  electronics industry which is characterized by rapid and constant
  product innovation.
- *Withdrawal or retreat*. Often firms have to withdraw from a market
  which may involve surrender or regrouping. Products can be withdrawn to be refurbished prior to re-launch in the same or new markets. Withdrawal is essentially a preservation strategy allowing for the
  best possible maintenance of strategic resources.

Defending strategies depend ultimately upon the strengths and weaknesses of the firm. Further, firms have to decide what is worth fighting
for. Defence for its own sake is worthless and potentially expensive.
Moreover, it can soak up resources. For example, defence of a weak
product can result in reduced resources for new product development –
a form of Pyrrhic victory.

Market Exit

Market entry occurs as a response to growing market demand and/or
above-normal profit opportunities where firms are able to surmount
entry barriers. By the same token, firms will be motivated to exit from
a market where demand is static or declining and suppliers are earning
a below-normal return on capital provided they are able to overcome
exit barriers which hinder departure from the market. In addition, firms
may decide to leave a market even though the market remains attractive
because they feel that this business no longer 'fits' with their other,
mainstream businesses.

Conventional views of the industry life cycle suggest that in declining industries the number of competitors is reduced; there will be a reduction in the number of products and market segments – a movement to a commodity-type product; and companies will compete on price and will reduce marketing and R & D expenditures.

However, this rather simplistic view does not allow for certain distinct characteristics observed in declining industries:

- There are different ways of marketing declining products to different types of customers.
- Technological differences will also differentiate industries.
- The competitive situation in the industry and the various responses to the declining demand situation have to be taken into account.
- There are different rates of decline.

Harrigan (1980) suggests a number of key variables that determine the attractiveness of a firm's market environment: condition of demand, exit barriers and rivalry.

Condition of demand

Table 7.2 lists the major demand conditions determining environmental attractiveness. Demand in an industry can decline for a number of reasons, including a shrinking consumer base caused by demographic changes, changes in consumers' life styles and tastes, changes in the costs of inputs or complementary products and technological advances which foster substitute products. It is important for the firm to understand which of these causes is the main force because this will shape its perceptions of future demand and the profitability of serving the diminished market. The variables outlined in table 7.2 are studied more closely below:

1   The rate and pattern of decline in demand in a market can have a significant effect upon a firm's decision to stay in or leave a market. Where the decline in demand is slow and steady, as is the case for example with cigarettes in the UK, firms can continue to supply the market profitably. By contrast, rapid and erratic decline in demand makes it difficult to adjust production to changing demand by withdrawing capacity and exacerbates the volatility of competition.

2   Uncertainty about the rate of decline in demand can also be important in influencing both competition and the timing of exit. Where all companies are fairly confident about the rate at which demand will continue to fall, reductions in capacity are likely to be orderly,

Table 7.2 Environmental attractiveness (condition of demand)

Condition of demand	Hospitable	Inhospitable
1 Speed of decline	very slow	rapid or erratic
2 Certainty of decline	100% certain, predictable patterns	great uncertainty, erratic patterns
3 Pockets of enduring demand	several or major ones	no niches
4 Product differentiation	brand loyalty	commodity-like products
5 Price stability	stable, price premiums attainable	very unstable, pricing below costs

Source: Adapted from Harrigan (1980)

whereas if some firms believe that demand will revitalize or level off they may attempt to hold onto their positions, perpetuating over-capacity and intense competition.

3   In many cases buoyant market segments provide opportunities for firms to remain profitable despite a shrinking overall market demand. On the other hand, where products are relatively homogeneous and there are no substantial market niches the potential for profit amongst remaining suppliers is poor.

4   Product differentiation may also serve to protect firms from falling overall demand insofar as consumer loyalty to their established brands will help them to maintain sales volume and market share, whereas firms selling commodity-like products will find sales of their products falling rapidly as industry demand contracts.

5   Where firms compete primarily on non-price factors, then they may find that prices remain stable and that they are able to command premium prices even in the face of declining overall demand. On the other hand, in markets where competition is primarily price-driven, declining demand may lead to rapidly falling prices as firms seek to boost their sales and cover their fixed production and distribution costs.

Exit barriers

Exit barriers are obstacles in the way of a firm contemplating leaving a market which serve to keep the firm in the market despite falling sales and profitability. These barriers can be substantial and serve to keep a firm in a market possibly for long periods of time, despite the fact that

Table 7.3   Environmental attractiveness (exit barriers)

Exit barriers	Hospitable	Inhospitable
1 Reinvestment requirements	none	high, often mandatory and involving capital assets
2 Asset age	mostly old assets	sizeable new assets and old ones not retired
3 Resale markets for assets	easy to convert or sell	no markets available, substantial costs to retire
4 Shared facilities	few free-standing plants	substantial and interconnected with important businesses
5 Vertical integration	little	substantial

Source: Adapted from Harrigan (1980)

it is earning sub-normal returns on its investment or even making losses. Table 7.3 lists some potential exit barriers, and these are looked at more closely below:

1   Whether the firm needs to make any additional investment in order to remain competitive can be important in affecting its decision to remain in a market. High investment expenditure to keep production costs competitive, or to meet pollution control requirements, may prompt the firm to leave the market because they increase the capital employed in the business without necessarily increasing the firm's profitability.

2   The age of the firm's assets used to serve the particular market and the extent to which they have depreciated have to be taken into account. Where depreciation charges on old assets are low then operating costs will be lower and this may encourage the firm to remain in the market despite low prices. On the other hand, with fully depreciated assets, the firm would suffer little capital loss in writing off these assets and exiting the market.

3   The nature of the firm's assets is significant. Specifically, if the assets are special-purpose, as with chemical plant, and so difficult to redeploy to other uses, or the firm's plant and equipment is not easily resaleable in second-hand markets (other than for scrap), then the firm may be encouraged to remain in the market. In cases where the

firm leases rather than owns many of its assets then it may be in a position to exit the market as the lease periods on these assets expire or if it is able to cancel leases without undue penalties.

4 The extent of shared production and distribution facilities is also important. For example, where a multi-product firm's plant produces a number of different products rather than just one, then a decision to drop one product could affect the cost and availability of the other products.

5 The extent of vertical integration is another significant point. For example, a vertically integrated petrochemical firm may find it difficult to drop one product without affecting downstream operations which use that product as a raw material, or upstream operations which rely upon the product as a use for their intermediate material. Where firms enter into long-term contracts with independent suppliers or customers they may be less locked into a market than vertically integrated businesses, although where such long-term contracts involve severe cancellation penalties they may encounter similar exit problems.

In addition to the above, a number of other factors may act as exit barriers. The costs of dismantling facilities, the cost of meeting redundancy payments and contractual arrangements to supply spare parts to past customers may all discourage the firm from leaving the market. Managerial resistance to closures and sell-outs may also be important, and managers' emotional commitment to the business may act as an exit barrier. This may be particularly pertinent for a single-product firm since if it ceases to make the product, then the firm will stop trading altogether and managers and workers will lose their jobs. By contrast, a diversified firm would find it easier to exit from one particular market since it has many others available, and could minimize redundancies by redeploying managers and workers to other areas of the business. (See box 7.4.)

In sum, barriers to exit determine the ease with which firms can leave declining markets, and thus affect both the profitability of firms and the smooth functioning of markets.

Rivalry

The combination of falling industry demand and the persistence of excess supply capacity due to exit barriers will serve to increase rivalry between suppliers, tending to depress prices and profit levels. The extent to which prices and profits are squeezed depend upon a number of factors:

1 The *extent of inter-firm rivalry* within the industry will depend upon the extent to which they all compete *directly* in the same target market

---

Box 7.4   Market exit and barriers to exit in the UK steel casting market

In its 1990 report on the acquisition of three smaller steel casting companies by William Cook, the market leader (market share 30–35 per cent), the Monopolies and Mergers Commission welcomed this development as a further contribution to the rationalization of an industry in long-term decline. Between 1975 and 1981, 13 plants were closed; in 1981 and 1982 a rationalization scheme organized by the Department of Industry (which involved cash payments to firms prepared to leave the industry) led to a scrapping of 14 plants. Taking these two phases together, about one-quarter of the industry's capacity was closed down, primarily by diversified firms with other engineering interests rather than single-plant operators. Despite these moves, overcapacity has continued to be a problem. The tendency for firms to 'linger on' despite low profitability and losses has been attributed to a number of factors:

'Some of the barriers to exit from the steel castings industry are considerable. The cost of lay-offs and plant closures include both substantial cash payments (which may exceed the cash available to an unprofitable foundry) and management time. Closed plant has to be dismantled (at a cost) and sites cleared up and made safe. For single-plant firms closure also means the loss of all management jobs too, and in some cases only bankruptcy can force managers to consider closure.' (Paragraph 2.58.)

---

or belong to a number of dissimilar strategic groups serving different market segments.

2   The intensity of rivalry and pressures to cut prices will depend upon the *size of cost penalties* encountered by firms as contracting sales force them to produce at output levels below minimum efficient scale. In industries where firms compete primarily on costs and prices the pressure to maintain sales volumes in order to cover fixed overhead costs can easily lead to the outbreak of price wars. By contrast in industries where product differentiation forms the basis of competitive activity, rivalry may intensify through increased advertising and promotional expenditures designed to maintain individual brand loyalty amongst the declining industry customer base.

3   The *bargaining power of customers and distributors* in forcing down industry prices may be significant if there are few of them and if customer-switching costs are low.

4   The *bargaining power of suppliers* in forcing up industry input prices will tend to be high where the industry is a relatively unimportant customer of the supplier's, and where suppliers are few in number.

These pressures from customers and suppliers serve to increase inter-firm rivalry as customers and suppliers seek to exploit their improved bargaining power by playing off firms against each other.

The ability of a particular firm to compete effectively in the face of increased rivalry depends upon its strengths relative to its rivals. Where a firm has superior product design and engineering skills, production advantages, marketing and selling skills or financial advantages, then it may be able to exploit these strengths to outperform its rivals.

Other motives for market exit

Whilst market or 'external' adversity factors may cause firms to exit a market, more strategic, firm-specific considerations may also determine whether a firm remains in a market or decides to leave it. The firm may close or sell one or more of its operating units (e.g. a production plant) or a whole business division. In the former case, divestment usually occurs in order to rationalize production and/or to concentrate the firm's output in a more modern plant. In contrast, the divestment of a whole business division represents a more fundamental strategic decision on the part of the firm. Divestment in this case may reflect a number of considerations, including a desire to pull out of an unprofitable, loss-making activity deemed to be incapable of turnround; the wish to shed peripheral businesses in order to release cash and managerial resources which, in opportunity cost terms, could be more effectively redeployed in the firm's other activities; or a major re-think of a firm's strategic position involving a retrenchment back to 'core' businesses. This final motive may be particularly important for large, highly diversified companies where the process of continuing diversification can often lead to a lack of focus in the company. In such situations, the firm may seek to create an identity through its 'mission statement' which, amongst other things, defines its core business interests and its main growth paths.

Endgame Strategies

Although an industry which has moved into the decline phase of the industry life cycle is characterized by a general fall in demand and problems of excess capacity, it nonetheless may still offer attractive returns to firms possessing competitive advantages over rival suppliers. For others, immediate exit from the industry rather than 'hanging on' may be appropriate to the situation. Each industry differs in its make-up so that an appraisal needs to be made of: the particular reasons for decline, the rate at which demand is declining, whether there are growth segments in the market; the structure of the market in terms of levels of market concentration, buyer characteristics or factors influencing the volatility of competition; and the firm's own perceived strengths and weaknesses *vis-à-vis* other competitors in the industry.

Four main strategic possibilities for operating in declining markets are suggested by Harrigan (1980):

1 *Hold or increase investment.* This involves maintaining or increasing the firm's investment in the market to expand its market share and, simultaneously, removing excess capacity from the market in order to achieve market leadership. This is a high-risk strategy but acceptable if the firm possesses competitive advantages (low costs, superior products) and the industry itself exhibits certain favourable endgame characteristics, e.g. a slow rate of decline in overall demand coupled with the existence of profitable market segments. If the increased investment is in new equipment the risk is that the firm will be increasing the capacity of an industry which already has excess capacity. Acquisition of other businesses reduces this risk. Less ambitiously, the company could invest sufficient to maintain its position by replacing worn-out and obsolete machinery and maintaining existing plant and machinery. This is also a high-risk strategy as it is dependent on maintaining sales in a declining market by increasing market share. This is only likely to be profitable if other firms exit. To facilitate the removal of other firms from the market, a firm seeking to achieve market leadership can adopt several tactical manoeuvres. First, it can engage in short-run aggressive pricing and marketing to build market share and dispel rivals' hopes of battling it out. Second, the firm can reduce rivals' exit barriers by buying up their product lines; buying and retiring their production capacity or taking over their long-term contracts. Third, the firm can increase incentives to rivals to leave the industry by reinvesting in new products or process improvements which competitors would have to match in order to stay in the business.

2 *Shrink selectively.* Shrinking selectively involves refocusing the firm by exiting from unprofitable sectors of the market and remaining in profitable segments. This requires the firm to identify at an early stage segments or niches of the declining industry capable of maintaining demand or declining slowly and that have structural characteristics allowing high returns. The firm must then move pre-emptively to gain a strong position in this segment whilst disinvesting from other segments.

3 *Harvest the investment.* This strategy involves the firm maximizing the cash flow from its declining business by maintaining its operation

	Competitive strengths	Competitive weaknesses
Hospitable market for decline	Hold/increase investment	Shrink selectively or harvest the investment
Inhospitable market for decline	Shrink selectively or harvest the investment	Quick divestment

Figure 7.7 Endgame strategies

with a minimum of expenditure and making no effort to maintain its market position. A harvest strategy often involves curtailing new investment, cutting maintenance of facilities and reducing advertising and R & D; and may also involve reducing the product range and number of distribution channels, lengthening delivery times to reduce finished good stocks and cutting back on repair and sales staff. Thus, a harvesting strategy involves deliberately running down the business for a period of time before it is then divested.

4   *Quick divestment.* Divestment involves the firm in selling its declining business to competitors as a going concern or liquidating it and selling off its individual assets. Quick divestment is generally undertaken during the early phases of market decline where the firm feels that it can find buyers more easily at this stage and thus recover more of its investment.

The selection of an appropriate endgame strategy involves matching the remaining opportunities in the market with the company's competitive position. Figure 7.7 shows the strategic options open to a company in a declining market. A strong firm operating in a slowing declining market may choose to hold/increase its investment; whilst at the other extreme a weak company operating in a rapidly declining market would tend to exit quickly. Where the market is declining slowly and is relatively hospitable, even competitively weak firms may have the option of shrinking selectively or harvesting the investment; by contrast where the market is declining quickly and is relatively inhospitable, then only those companies with particular competitive strengths would be able to shrink selectively or harvest the investment with any success.

Summary

Firms are normally attracted into a market by the prospects of profitable long-term growth and similarly may be encouraged to leave a market by poor profit and growth potential. In addition to general market conditions, various firm-specific considerations such as potential synergy or 'strategic fit' may cause firms to enter or leave markets. Market entry and exit can be constrained by the operation of various 'barriers to entry/exit' which, depending upon individual firm and market circumstances, may represent minor or severe obstacles. In order to successfully overcome market entry impediments and establish a long-term sustainable market position a greenfield entrant might have to have some competitive advantage over incumbent firms, either in the market as a whole, or in particular segments of the market in the form of lower supply costs or product differentiation advantages. Alternatively, a firm may enter a market by acquiring an established supplier thereby reducing the overall costs and risk of entry. The take-over mode of entry is often adopted by diversifying 'cross-entrants' seeking to enter a market but lacking in-house experience of the target market.

Questions

1   Discuss the nature and significance of barriers to entry.
2   What tactics may be adopted by established firms to reduce the likelihood of new entry?
3   'Successful market entry is usually based on exploiting the weaknesses of established firms.' Discuss.
4   Examine some of the main factors encouraging/facilitating successful new entry.
5   Discuss the nature and significance of 'strategic groups' in a market.
6   Discuss the factors likely to encourage firms to leave a market and indicate some of the obstacles hindering market exit.

References

Baumol, W. J., Panzar, J. and Willig, R. D., 1982. *Contestable Markets and the Theory of Industry Structure*, Harcourt, Brace and Jovanovich.

Bloor, I. and Cockerill, A., 1989. 'Competition and the UK Brewing Industry', *Economic Review*, vol. 6.

Harrigan, K. R., 1980. *Strategies for Declining Industries*, D.C. Heath & Co.

George, K. D., Joll, C. and Lynk, E. L., 1992. See especially chapter 10 of *Industrial Organization*, Routledge, 2nd edn.

Hay, D. A. and Morris, D. J., 1991. See particularly chapter 3 (section 3.6), chapter 5 (section 5.4), chapter 8 (section 8.6) and chapter 15 (section 15.6) of *Industrial Economics and Organization*, Oxford University Press, 2nd edn.

James, B. G., 1984. *Business War Games*, Penguin.

Porter, M. E., 1985. *Competitive Advantage*, Free Press.

Further Reading

Grant, R. M., chapters 2 and 3, *Contemporary Strategy Analysis*, Blackwell, 1991.

Luffman, G., Sanderson, S., Lea, E. and Kenny, B., chapter 13, *Business Policy*, Blackwell, 2nd edn, 1991.

Thomson, J. L., chapters 7 and 19, *Strategic Management*, Chapman and Hall, 1990.

8

Frameworks for Analysing Markets and Competitiveness

Introduction

A firm's choice of broad growth strategy – horizontal, vertical, conglomerate and international – has to be made in the context of its success in competitively supplying particular products. No matter how few or many product markets the firm chooses to be in, its corporate prosperity depends fundamentally on how well it succeeds in the *individual* product markets making up its business. This requires the firm to formulate plans aimed at ensuring that it is able to meet and beat its competitors in supplying particular products. As Porter emphasizes: 'Competition occurs at the business unit level. Diversified companies do not compete; only their business units do. Unless a corporate strategy places primary attention on nurturing the success of each unit, the strategy will fail, no matter how elegantly constructed' (Porter (1980)).

Market attractiveness

As chapter 6 demonstrated, industrial economics provides a framework for analysing the characteristics of markets, focusing upon the effectiveness of a market in ensuring the efficient supply of a product at reasonable prices, and how this depends to a large extent upon (1) the structure of that market, which will tend to influence (2) the conduct of firms in that market, and (3) their market performance. Market structure embraces such characteristics as seller and buyer concentration and ease of market entry. Market conduct includes the growth and profit objectives pursued by firms, their pricing and product differentiation strategies and the extent to which firms coordinate their behaviour. Market performance depends upon the efficiency with which goods are produced and distributed, the relation between prices and production and distribution costs, and the extent of process and product innovation.

Whilst this framework identifies many of the key parameters influencing the resource allocation efficiency of markets its emphasis is essentially upon the competitive processes at work in markets and not upon the strategic choices available to firms in markets. This latter perspective stresses the pro-active role of firms in developing 'competitive advantages' over rival suppliers against the backdrop of the general structural and behaviourial characteristics of the market.

The attractiveness or otherwise of a particular market must be judged in terms of its present level of profitability, its current size, growth potential, the degree of seller concentration, the nature of the product and the ease of market entry when viewed in relation to a firm's own skills and resource capabilities. This will determine whether the firm remains in this market or exits from it. Likewise, the attractiveness of a particular market will determine whether new firms choose to enter this market.

Competitiveness

'Competitiveness' may be defined as the ability of a firm to meet and beat its rivals in supplying a product on a sustainable (i.e. long-term) and viable (i.e. profitable) basis. This definition rules out, for example, situations where a firm attempts to 'buy' market share by selling the product at unprofitable prices. Competition between firms to win and retain buyer demand can take a number of forms including product design, price cuts, advertising and sales promotion, quality improvements and packaging. Fundamentally, competitive success in deploying these weapons is underpinned by the possession of firm-specific competitive advantages over rival suppliers and the particular marketing mix chosen by a firm will be determined in large measure by the company's firm-specific competitive advantages over rival suppliers. The text under the heading 'The Nature of Barriers to Entry' in chapter 7 elaborates upon these issues and chapters 9 and 10 discuss them in detail. Initially, however, it is important to establish a framework for analysing the market opportunities and threats which form the background to competitive behaviour. Porter's 'competitive strategy' model provides a useful starting point in this respect.

The Porter framework

Porter's analysis breaks the strategic decision-making process into two stages: (1) industry analysis and (2) the choice of a strategy to adopt to secure a favourable competitive position in a particular industry. Industry analysis is orientated towards an assessment of industry attractiveness, and is intended at the company level to answer the question 'Do we want to be in this market?' Specifically, Porter emphasizes that: 'The first and fundamental determinant of a firm's profitability is industry attractiveness. Competitive strategy must grow out of a sophisticated understanding of the rules of competition that determine an industry's attractiveness' (Porter (1985)).

The choice of an 'in-market' strategy assumes that the answer to the question of industry choice was yes, and that the firm is now interested in maximizing profitability and return from the opportunities it has or can develop in the market. This requires the firm to select appropriate cost, price and differentiation strategies paying due attention to not only the characteristics of the market itself (i.e. the external environment) but also its own (i.e. internal) resources and skills (see chapter 1, 'Strategic Analysis').

Analysis of Industry Structure

Competitive strategy aims to establish a profitable and sustainable position against the 'forces' which determine industry competition. Competition in an industry continuously works to drive down the rate of return on capital towards the competitive floor rate of return ('normal profit'). Inevitably this will vary between industries and within a single industry over time, as the level of demand and competitive activity, for example, are not constant. Firms will choose to operate in markets which they feel will offer above-normal profit opportunities, although they may then find the attractions of their chosen markets will tend to change over time. Thus, for example, a market which appears highly attractive because it is currently expanding rapidly and exhibits low levels of seller concentration may, in the course of time, become unattractive as it moves into the maturity phase of its industry life cycle (see chapter 7, 'Endgame Strategy').

Porter (1980) identifies five factors which affect the nature and degree of competition in an industry: the presence and strength of existing competitors (both domestic and international), the threat of new entrants to the market, the threat of substitute products, the bargaining power of input suppliers and the bargaining power of customers. These five forces are depicted in figure 8.1, along with a sixth element which often has an important influence on market processes, namely government regulatory policies.

Rivalry amongst direct competitors

Rivalry for customers involves competitors continuously seeking to improve and defend their market positions and returns. In most industries, firms are mutually interdependent in that moves by one firm have

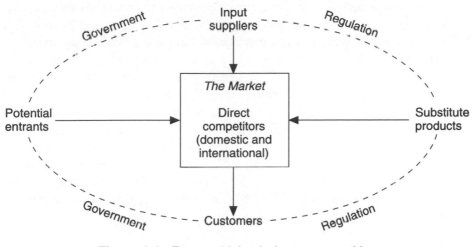

Figure 8.1 Forces driving industry competition
Source: Adapted from Porter (1980)

noticeable effects on its competitors. Competitive moves may incite retaliation and the move/counter-move cycle may or may not leave the firm and the industry any better off. Firms compete against each other in a variety of ways, including pricing, product innovation, advertising and sales promotion campaigns and increased service or warranties. Some of these, notably price rivalry, are highly unstable and quite likely to erode the industry's underlying profitability. Advertising rivalry, on the other hand, may well expand demand and benefit all firms. In markets characterized by a high degree of mutual interdependency suppliers might well seek to 'control' competition so as to promote 'orderly and profitable' trading conditions by, for example, establishing price-fixing cartels.

The degree of rivalry will depend upon such factors as the following:

1 *The number and size distribution of sellers.* Where competitors are numerous and are roughly balanced in size and power then rivalry is likely to be intense as each firm seeks to advance its position. On the other hand, when a market is dominated by one or a few large firms these leaders can impose 'discipline' on smaller competitors and may play a coordinating role in price-setting. Finally, where a small group of equally sized sellers account for the bulk of industry sales then they may either engage in intense rivalry or seek to collude formally through cartels, or informally through such mechanisms as price leadership (see chapter 9).
2 *The diversity of sellers.* Firms display considerable diversity in terms of the origins of the firm, the personalities of their top managers and

the relationship with, in some cases, parent companies. Consequently rivals may have different goals, time frames and approaches to competition all of which will affect their strategies. This may make it difficult for sellers to discern each other's motives and so establish a *modus operandi* for competing in the industry. Foreign competitors in particular often add a great deal of diversity.

3   *The nature of the product.* Where sellers offer standardized or homogeneous products competition is usually focused on price, whereas in markets characterized by buyers' demand for a wide variety of product and quality mixes, product differentiation, competition such as advertising and new product development will be emphasized. In markets with high levels of seller concentration, firms tend to prefer product differentiation competition to price competition because of the mutually ruinous consequences of price wars.

4   *Product perishability.* Another important product characteristic which can affect rivalry is perishability of the product. Where products such as fresh fruit and vegetables have a very short shelf life, sellers may be under considerable pressure to reduce prices in order to clear their stocks of the product before it becomes worthless.

5   *Switching costs.* Where the cost to the buyer of 'switching' to an alternative seller's product is high this would tend to reduce the intensity of competition. Switching costs are mainly encountered by buyers of industrial products and include such elements as retraining workers to use alternative machinery, additional stocks of spare parts and changes in product design to incorporate new materials or components.

6   *Cost structures.* In industries characterized by a high ratio of fixed costs to variable costs, sellers are under pressure to sustain sales volume in order to 'cover' their fixed costs and, with low variable costs, may be tempted to practise marginal cost pricing, cutting prices to levels just in excess of variable costs. Such pressures to cut prices are particularly acute during depressed market conditions.

7   *Industry growth.* Rapid industry growth permits firms to expand as new customers come into the market. However, as the industry matures and its growth rate slows, firms can only maintain their own growth by winning market share from rivals which is likely to intensify competition.

8   *Supply capacity.* A slowing down in industry growth rate may lead to the emergence of long-term overcapacity with sellers finding their existing capacity becoming increasingly under-utilized. Under such circumstances firms may well compete intensively to maintain their sales volumes and keep their plants working at full capacity. The problem of maintaining a balance between industry supply and demand is often exacerbated in capital-intensive industries by the fact

that additional capacity can often only be added in large increments as new plant is brought on-stream.

9 *Exit barriers*. Ideally, industries suffering from overcapacity need to curtail supply by plant rationalization and closure and, possibly, through the departure of some firms from the market. However, there are usually barriers which prevent easy exit from a market such as possession of specialist assets with no resale value or high redundancy costs. High exit barriers may encourage even loss-making firms to stay in the industry.

Bargaining power of input suppliers

Suppliers of raw materials, components or services can exercise bargaining power over the firms in an industry by threatening to withhold essential supplies, raising prices of inputs, by reducing the quality of inputs supplied or delaying delivery of supplies. As emphasized in chapter 3 on vertical market relationships where a number of independent firms operate at different stages in the 'value-added chain', then the share of total value added (and hence profitability) of the firms at each stage will depend upon their power relative to that of firms at other stages. The proportion of the total profit generated through the value chain accruing to firms at any one stage will depend largely on the transfer prices which those firms must pay for their inputs and are able to charge for their outputs. Where the firms in an industry are confronted by powerful input suppliers then their own profitability could be 'squeezed' by having to pay high prices for their inputs. Even where these firms enter into collaborative arrangements with their suppliers through, for example, just-in-time supply contracts the prices and other supply terms they are able to negotiate with powerful suppliers are likely to pressurize their profits.

The power of input suppliers depends upon a number of factors including the following:

1 *The number and size distribution of input suppliers*. Where input industries are dominated by one or a few large suppliers and are more concentrated than the industry stage they sell to, these monopoly or oligopoly suppliers may have considerable power. On the other hand, where input industries are atomistic in structure and the industry stage they sell to is dominated by one or a few large buyers then these monopsony or oligopsony buyers will have the upper hand. Finally, where an upstream monopolist faces a downstream monopsonist (a situation referred to as bilateral monopoly), the resulting transfer prices between the two will depend upon their relative financial resources and withholding power.

2   *Dependency of input suppliers on buyers' industry.* If the industry being supplied is not an important customer of the input suppliers, buyers in that industry will be unable to exert any degree of influence over input suppliers because their custom represents only a small fraction of the input suppliers' total sales.

3   *Importance of input suppliers' product to buyers' industry.* Where a particular input constitutes an essential or critical component or service in the production of the buyer's product, suppliers of that input can often influence the supply terms of the item for the buying industry.

4   *Availability of substitute inputs.* Even where suppliers of particular inputs are dominant suppliers of those inputs, their power to influence supply terms to the buying industry may be circumscribed where buyers have access to alternative inputs. For example, a coffee producer would be in a strong bargaining position in dealing with its metal can suppliers where it is able to turn to alternatives such as glass jars or plastic containers.

5   *Switching costs.* Where a supplier's inputs are differentiated or where there are high switching costs to buyers in moving from one supplier to another, buyers' bargaining power will be limited. For example, if the coffee manufacturer has geared its product, promotional activity and physical distribution systems to the use of glass packaging, it would be reluctant to switch to alternative packaging materials unless the supply terms for glass become particularly onerous.

6   *Threat of forward integration.* If input suppliers have the resources to undertake forward integration into the buyers' industry by either greenfield development or take-over, then the very threat that they might undertake such integration itself increases their bargaining power in dealing with buyers.

The conditions determining suppliers' power are subject to dynamic change, e.g. the entry of new suppliers which serves to expand output and choice. Moreover, a firm can sometimes improve its situation relative to suppliers through, for example, finding and cultivating alternative suppliers, perhaps overseas suppliers, and by redesigning its products or changing its marketing approach in order to reduce switching costs.

Bargaining power of buyers

Buyer groups will be powerful *vis-à-vis* firms in the industry in circumstances which are broadly the corollary of those making for powerful input suppliers. Buyers can intensify rivalry in an industry by playing competing suppliers off against each other in order to force down selling prices, improve product quality or services, or secure better credit terms.

The power of buyers to influence the supply terms of inputs and final products in the value-added chain, and thus to secure a large share of the total profit potential of the supply chain, is governed by a number of factors, including the following:

1 *The number and size distribution of buyers.* If buyer industries are dominated by one or a few large buyers and are more concentrated than the industry stage they buy from, then these monopsony or oligopsony buyers may wield substantial buying power. Under these circumstances buyers can dictate terms of supply and obtain favourable bulk-buying discounts.

2 *Dependency of buyers on the industry.* Where the products or services produced by the industry represent a significant proportion of the buyer's total purchasing costs then it would be worthwhile for the buyer to 'shop around' in an attempt to obtain the best deal.

3 *Importance of the industry's product to buyers.* In situations where the industry's product is not an important component or service for buyers and where the quality of that product has little effect upon the quality of the buyer's own product, the industry has little influence on buyers.

4 *Availability of substitute products.* Even where an industry is dominated by one or a few large firms, their power to influence supply terms to buyers may be limited where buyers have access to alternative products 'outside' the industry (see below).

5 *Switching costs.* Where the firms' products are undifferentiated or where there are low switching costs to buyers in moving from one firm to another, buyers will have significant bargaining power since they can play off one competing firm against another, depressing these firms' prices and profit margins.

6 *Threat of backward integration.* If buyers have the resources to undertake backward integration into the industry, the threat that they might do so increases their bargaining power in dealing with suppliers. This threat is particularly credible from a buyer who already produces part of his own requirements and buys the remainder on the open market, since such a firm will have more precise information about supplier costs.

Over time the conditions affecting buyer power may well change, e.g. mergers and take-overs amongst buyers may increase their market power in relation to sellers. More pro-actively, firms can reduce their vulnerability to buyer power by differentiating their products and increasing switching costs to enhance customer loyalty, or by concentrating on particular buyer groups.

Threat of substitute products

Potential substitute products limit the potential return of an industry by placing a ceiling on the prices it can charge. The strength of the threat of substitutes depends upon the degree of substitutability of these alternatives for the industry's product and this is reflected in the cross-elasticity of demand between them. Commodity-type products like many agricultural goods have close potential substitutes and the high cross-elasticity of demand for substitutes constrains price in such markets. Again, fuels, such as gas, and electricity serve as fairly close substitutes for one another as sources of heating, although here the switching costs involved in replacing/adapting existing equipment to use the alternative fuels may constrain the switching decision. In industries with highly differentiated products, there may be no close substitutes to challenge consumers' allegiance to the industry's product. The more attractive the price/performance alternatives offered by substitutes, the greater is the threat from substitutes and the lower the ceiling on industry profits.

The identification of substitutes is often not immediately obvious and substitutes can emerge over time from areas seemingly far removed from the industry. For example, the mechanical wrist-watch industry persevered with the further refinement of this technology whilst developments in the seemingly unrelated area of electronic microchips spawned the development of electronic watches which rapidly superseded mechanical ones.

Firms need to consider such threats, and identify what minimizing steps can be taken, perhaps through cost reductions or product differentiation, and, more positively, what potential exists for the industry's products to substitute for some other product. Thus, for example, producers of feature films for showing at cinemas initially felt threatened by the advent of television as an alternative form of entertainment as they feared it would result in the reduction of cinema audiences, but eventually they found that television provided opportunities to make films and serials for showing on television.

Threat of new entrants

Where the established firms in an industry are securing attractive (i.e. 'above-normal') profit returns then this can serve as an inducement for new suppliers to enter the market and, in the process, lower industry profitability. Alternatively, entry may be motivated by the failure of established firms to fully perceive or exploit the growth and profit potential of the market. Greenfield entry brings new capacity and new resources to compete for market share and prices can be bid down or established firms' costs driven up as they take defensive action to preserve their market share against entrants. Alternatively, where entry is effected through merger or take-over of an established firm the threat to industry prices and profitability may be less severe.

As discussed in chapter 7, the seriousness of the threat of a new entrant depends upon the barriers to entry present and the reaction from existing competitors that the entrant can expect.

Government regulation

In addition to the threats and opportunities presented by the firms' immediate market environments the efforts by governments to regulate trade and industry also play a broader part in affecting competitive processes. First, government competition policy can constrain firms' conduct by prohibiting various anti-competitive practices and agreements such as exclusive dealing or the formation of cartels, and it may prohibit firms from merging with, or taking over, other firms in the interests of maintaining competitive market structures. Second, government industry policies covering such matters as investment incentives, subsidies and industrial location can provide firms with financial inducements to expand or remove capacity, enter new markets and innovate new products. Third, government trade policy in respect of tariffs, quotas and export incentives will influence competitive processes by making both domestic and international markets more 'open' or 'closed'. Finally, government's general macroeconomic policies in the area of inflation control, unemployment, balance of payments and economic growth affect firms' investment, output and international competitiveness.

In conclusion, the strength of the forces outlined above will determine an industry's attractiveness both to established firms and potential entrants. These competitive forces tend to change over time and can be influenced by the firms themselves and by government. When competing in a given industry it is essential to recognize and understand the composition and relative importance of the underlying forces driving competition. The dominant forces will have a significant impact on the selection of competitive strategy and on the strategic choices available.

The Formulation of Competitive Strategy

Porter (1980) advocates that the aim of a competitive strategy should be to create a profitable and sustainable position in an industry against competitive forces by either defensive or offensive action. A firm should identify its strengths and weaknesses in the light of the various competitive forces facing it, e.g. Are there any imminent new entrants? or Has a major competitor integrated forwards or backwards? Then the firm can devise a plan which may include (1) positioning the company so that its capabilities provide the best defence against the competitive force; and/ or (2) influencing the balance of competitive forces through strategic moves; and/or (3) anticipating shifts in the factors underlying the competitive forces and responding to them.

Sustainable above-average performance can only be achieved through competitive advantage as Porter emphasizes: 'Competitive advantage grows fundamentally out of value a firm is able to create for its buyers that exceeds the firm's cost of creating it. Value is what buyers are willing to pay, and superior value stems from offering lower prices than competitors for equivalent benefits or providing unique benefits that more than offset a higher price' (Porter 1985).

The key to a successful competitive strategy is to establish a position which is less vulnerable to attack from competitors (whether established or new) and less vulnerable to erosion from buyers, suppliers and substitute goods. There are many means of establishing such a position – solidifying relationships with important customers, differentiating the product either substantively or psychologically through marketing, integrating forward or backward, or establishing technological leadership.

The choice of competitive strategy for any firm in an industry is invariably unique. Nevertheless, there are two central questions which underlie the choice of competitive strategy for any firm: (1) Is the industry an attractive one as regards long-term profitability? and (2) What are the determinants of relative competitive position within the industry?

The aim for any firm should be to develop a distinctive competence greater than its competitors. Distinctive competence is concerned with identifying those particular strengths which give the company an edge over its competitors and those areas of particular weakness which are to be avoided. Porter (1985) identifies *three generic strategies* for achieving above-average performance in an industry:

- cost leadership;
- differentiation;
- focus.

The Generic Strategies

Figure 8.2 describes the generic strategies of cost leadership, differentiation and focus. Each is a fundamentally different approach to creating and sustaining competitive advantage, and to be an above-average performer a firm must generally make a choice amongst them rather than attempt to address all at once.

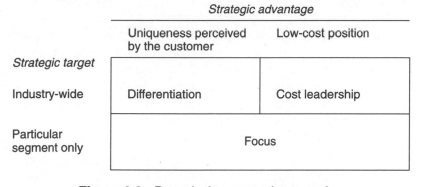

Figure 8.2   Porter's three generic strategies
Source: Porter (1980)

The cost leadership and differentiation strategies are aimed at securing competitive advantage in a broad range of industry segments, whereas focus strategies are targeted more narrowly.

Cost leadership

If average or near-average prices can be obtained for its products, cost leadership will enable a firm to enjoy above-average profit performance. There are many potential sources of cost leadership, the principal ones being cost-effectiveness in production and cost-effectiveness in physical distribution.

Production cost advantages over competitors are of two major types: absolute cost advantages over competitors (i.e. cost advantages over competitors at all levels of output) and relative cost advantages (i.e. cost advantages related to the scale of output). Absolute cost advantages can arise from, for example, the integration of input and assembly operations and the use of superior (latest vintage) production technology. In addition, the use of 'offshore' production facilities in low-cost countries can provide cost advantages over domestic producers (see chapter 5). Relative cost advantages accrue through the exploitation of large-scale production involving the concentration of output in plants of minimum efficient scale and through cumulative 'learning curve' effects. Over time, investment in plant renewal, modernization and process innovation either through in-house R & D initiatives or the early adoption of new technology developed elsewhere may be essential to maintain low-cost market leadership.

Physical distribution cost advantages over competitors are also of two broad types: locational (transportation) cost advantages and distribution channel cost advantages. In the former case, a firm's 'sphere of operations' and the nature of its product (bulky or light) influence the size of distribution costs; in general terms, distribution to local and regional markets is less expensive, on a unit cost basis, than servicing national and international markets. An important consideration in this respect is often the requirement to 'balance' the lower production costs achieved by single-plant operations (but with higher distribution costs), against the lower distribution costs achieved by decentralized, multi-plant operations (but with higher production costs).

Functionally, most products find their way into the hands of final consumers via a manufacturing – wholesaling (holding stocks and breaking bulk) – and retailing (point of sale) chain. Depending upon the 'traditions' of the trade, the nature of the product and the characteristics of the market served, a number of distributive channel configurations may be identified. Channel transactions can be conducted on an arm's-length basis or they can be internalized as noted in chapter 3. In either case there is scope for the establishment of competitive advantage by controlling outlets directly through ownership or through contractual arrangements. This enables the firm not only to reduce transaction costs but also to use transfer-pricing policies to competitive advantage and to limit or even deprive market access to competitors.

Cost leadership usually requires a single leader. Where there is more than one aspiring leader, rivalry may be high as each may consider market share to be crucial to continue to expand scale economies. A cost leader can continue to earn above-average returns since leadership provides some protection from competitive forces. Their effects on profit erosion will eliminate the profits of the next most efficient competitor before those of the low-cost firm.

Porter points to various potential vulnerabilities in the cost leadership strategy which could limit its effectiveness. These risks include the following:

1 If the firm's management concentrates on cost they may fail to perceive product or marketing changes and thus may fail to adapt their products and marketing strategies to meet shifting market requirements. Such marketing myopia may cause the firm to concentrate excessively upon what Drucker (1989) terms 'efficiency' ('doing things right') rather than 'effectiveness' ('doing the right things').
2 The situation may arise where rising costs narrow the firm's ability to maintain enough of a price differential to offset competitors' product differentiation advantages. This pressure could arise where the firm experiences difficulty in containing its own costs or where rising prices of factor inputs which are outside the firm's control threaten its cost and price margins.
3 There may be a time when industry newcomers or current competitors are in a position to match easily and cheaply the low production

and distribution costs of the industry cost leader through investing in state-of-the-art facilities or by imitating the industry leader to take advantage of its learning curve. If the industry cost leader is heavily protected by patents on its production technology and has produced much of its own specialist production machinery then its production technology will be difficult to copy.

4   Where technology changes rapidly this can render obsolete past investments and accumulated experience of the industry cost leader.

Differentiation

In a differentiation strategy, a firm seeks to be unique in its industry along one or more dimensions valued by its customers. A differentiator aims at the ability to demand a price premium based on the perceived value added by differentiation. Brand loyalty and the resulting reduced sensitivity to price help insulate against rivalry. Entry barriers are provided through loyalties and the need for a competitor to overcome uniqueness. Differentiation yields higher margins as a cushion against supplier power and mitigates both buyer power and substitution by its uniqueness and perceived value.

The means for differentiation are peculiar to each industry and might be based on the product itself or perhaps the means of delivery or associations generated by advertising and so on. This covers a number of interrelated marketing-mix facets, but two are especially important: the ability to 'capture' and maintain a primary demand (i.e. customer base) for the firm's product, and the servicing of that demand by ensuring that the product is readily available.

Creating and sustaining a primary demand requires the firm to have first and foremost a marketing-orientated (i.e. consumer-based) as opposed to a production-orientated (i.e. firm-based) competitive strategy. Competitive advantage can then be built on the selection of appropriate consumer-driven product ranges, and consumers' demand for quality, sophistication, variety and other product differentiation attributes. Sensitivity to consumer perceptions of product attributes and value-for-money considerations in turn enables competitive advantage to be secured by the selection of appropriate marketing-mix variables.

Product availability can be secured by forward integration into retail outlets, but for many types of product this is not a financially viable proposition. As retailers' power has grown with the emergence of multiple-store groups, explicit recognition must be paid to the pro-active role retailers play in the channel structure. It is important that the manufacturer is able to offer the retailer a distinctive branded product, with appropriate marketing back-up, which commands a sizeable share of demand, if the retailer is to give the product adequate shelf space.

Finally, over the long run a critical factor in maintaining competitive advantage is *product innovation*. In a dynamic market setting, a firm's existing products may become obsolete through advances in technology, the innovatory nature of competitors' products or through changes in consumer tastes. A firm is thus obliged, to a greater or lesser degree, to introduce new brands or modify existing ones to retain its product differentiation advantages.

Again, Porter warns of certain risks associated with the pursuit of a differentiation strategy, including the following:

1   The price differential between low-cost competitors and the differentiated firm's product may become too great for differentiation to succeed in defending market share. Here buyers sacrifice some of the features, services or image possessed by the differentiated firm in return for large price savings.

2   The situation may arise where customer requirements for the differentiating factor(s) lessen or disappear. This can occur as buyers become more sophisticated or knowledgeable, or where product technology becomes commonplace so that the product takes on the characteristics of a commodity.

3   The situation may arise where imitation of a firm's product erodes perceived differentiation so that customers are less prepared to pay a price premium for it. This is a common occurrence as industries mature and imitators' products begin to closely match the performance and image of the innovator's brands.

Focus

The cost leadership and differentiation strategies generally seek competitive advantage across the whole industry whilst focus strategies aim at either a cost or a differentiation advantage, but within particular segments of the market. This strategy involves purposely selecting a narrow scope, with the focuser selecting one or a group of industry segments and tailoring its business to serving them to the exclusion of others. The intention is to achieve competitive advantage within target segments, despite having no overall competitive advantage.

Focused cost advantages may arise either in respect of production or distribution costs. For example, mini steel mills producing a limited range of steel products, using primarily recycled scrap, may be able to achieve lower costs than a large steel mill which produces a wide range of steel products for all market segments. Again, for example, a small soft drinks manufacturer servicing a compact local market may be able to achieve physical distribution cost advantages over larger competitors whose distribution systems serve the national market. Products such as soft drinks, beer, bricks etc. which are bulky, heavy and low-value-added offer particular opportunities for cost-focused strategies.

Focused differentiation advantages depend upon the identification of particular market niches and the servicing of these segments through specialized products and distribution systems; e.g. a hosiery firm might specialize in marketing thermal and hiking socks, whilst another such as Sock Shop might seek to sell socks through specialist outlets.

Both variants, cost focus and differentiation focus, rely on the differences between the target segments and the other segments in the industry. The target segments must have buyers with special needs or else the production and distribution systems that best suit the target segments must differ from those of other industry segments. The focus strategy implies that the target segments are poorly served by broadly targeted competitors. The focus strategy also requires that the target segments be structurally attractive. The competitive forces discussed above act on different parts of the same industry in different ways and some industry segments are much more profitable than others. If a firm can achieve sustainable cost focus or differentiation focus in its segment (and the segment is structurally attractive), then the focuser will be an above-average performer in its industry. However, there are risks associated with a focus strategy:

1 The cost differential between broad-range competitors and the focused firm may narrow to eliminate the cost advantages of serving a narrow target or offset the differentiation achieved by focus.
2 Where the differences between the customer requirements of the market segment and those of the overall market diminish there will be less scope for pursuing a focused strategy.
3 Where competitors focus on even narrower market segments within the focused-firms target segments they may be able to 'outfocus' the focuser and undermine its particular advantages in servicing its market niches. This is a particular danger where firms focus upon comparatively broad industry segments.

Box 8.1 shows the application of the generic strategies to UK food retailing.

Choice of Competitive Strategy

A competitive strategy based on cost leadership, differentiation or focus involves positioning a business to maximize the value of the capabilities which distinguish it from its competitors. Which of these strategies a firm chooses depends on the nature of the industry, the strengths and

Box 8.1   Generic strategies in UK food retailing

The Porter framework provides a basis for identifying the strategic 'positioning' of firms in an industry. The figure below shows the trading strategies adopted by various UK food retailers. Each attempts to maintain its individual store image in the eyes of the shopper. In some cases these images are based upon high-quality, high-priced products sold in stores projecting an up-market ambience (e.g. Marks and Spencer); whilst others are based upon reasonable quality products at moderate 'value-for-money' prices (e.g. Tesco). Cost focusers offer customers a limited line of basic products at heavily discounted prices through warehousing-style stores (e.g. Aldi and Netto). Differentiation focusers typically offer a limited range of speciality lines at relatively high prices, e.g. delicatessens and health food stores. It should be borne in mind that the scales of the boxes are continuous and thus Marks and Spencer and Sainsbury do not occupy exactly the same position although they have the same generic strategy.

	Strategic advantage	
	Uniqueness perceived by customer	Low-cost position
Strategic target Industry-wide	*Differentiation* Marks and Spencer Sainsbury	*Cost leadership* Tesco Asda Argyll (Safeway)
Particular segment only	*Focus*	
	Delicatessens Health food stores	Morrisons (limited area) Kwik Save (limited line) Aldi (limited line) Netto (limited line)

weaknesses of the firm and its competitors, and also the stage of evolution of the industry (see above under 'The Generic Strategies'). The generic strategy chosen by a firm must be sustainable and its competitive advantage should be strong enough to resist competitor retaliation or industry evolution.

Porter (1980) argues that, in general, firms should aim for *exclusive* concentration on either cost leadership or differentiation, although he argues that a firm should always aggressively pursue all cost-reduction opportunities that do not sacrifice differentiation and also pursue all differentiation opportunities that are not costly. Furthermore, he suggests three conditions under which a firm can simultaneously achieve both cost leadership and differentiation:

- where the firm has no competitors which have significantly lower costs or better products so that no competitor is well enough positioned to force the firm to opt for either cost leadership or differentiation to the exclusion of the other;
- where a firm pioneers a major product or process innovation which enables it to achieve significant product and/or cost superiority over competitors;
- where cost is strongly affected by market share and a firm's established brands give it a sufficiently large market share to operate at or above minimum efficient scale, whilst competitors or potential entrants are unable to achieve comparable sales volumes to operate at equivalent cost levels.

Outside these three particular circumstances, Porter argues that firms should generally pursue one or other strategy and avoid being 'stuck in the middle' between the two strategies of providing a low-cost, high-volume product or a differentiated quality product: 'The worst strategic error is to be stuck in the middle, or to try simultaneously to pursue all the strategies. This is a recipe for strategic mediocrity and below average performance' (Porter (1980)).

However, there is some confusion regarding exactly what 'stuck in the middle' actually means. As Kay et al. (1990) suggest, this could refer to positioning of *particular* products, i.e. where a good or service is to be found relative to its competitors in the market-place. In this sense, a Mini Metro is positioned differently from a Rolls Royce in the car market. If 'don't be stuck in the middle' is a statement about such product positioning, then it is obviously false, as revealed by the long list of companies which have succeeded with products placed firmly in the middle of their markets, e.g. the Ford Mondeo. Alternatively, for some this notion relates more broadly to the strategic thrust of the *whole* firm and suggests that attempts to achieve both differentiation and cost leadership are likely to lead to failure in both. However, again, there are many instances of companies which have succeeded in pursuing high-quality and low-cost strategies, e.g. Sainsbury's in the UK grocery retailing sector.

Thus, whilst in some industries it may be necessary for firms to choose either low cost or differentiation as alternative strategies, in other industries differentiation and cost leadership/low price may be used as complementary competitive strategies. In the latter case, differentiation competition may be seen as a means of commanding 'premium prices' which boost profitability whilst attention to cost-cutting strategies can further increase price–cost margins and profits.

Structure within Industries

Industries are not homogenous but frequently consist of a series of sub-markets or market sectors, often served by different groups of firms referred to by Porter (1985) as 'strategic groups'. Strategic groups are separated from other strategic groups serving other market segments by 'mobility barriers' (see chapter 7). These concepts provide a useful basis for examining intra-firm rivalry within an industry.

A strategic group is made up of a number of firms within an industry, each of which pursues broadly similar policies in respect of product and market coverage, channel selection, product innovation, product quality, price, advertising and promotion policy, service policy and vertical integration. The firms within an industry can be broadly classified into groups according to this list of dimensions.

The profit potential may well vary *between* different strategic groups since some groups will have adopted a more successful orientation in dealing with the competitive 'forces' discussed earlier is this chapter. The profitability of particular firms *within* a group will differ primarily because of the individual firm's ability to implement the common group strategy.

Industry Evolution

So far this chapter has employed a structural analysis for understanding the competitive forces that are crucial for developing competitive strategy in an industry. However, since industry structures change as industries evolve, it is also necessary in strategy formulation to recognize what stage the industry is moving through and to be able to predict the kind of changes to expect because of this. The familiar concept of the industry life cycle can be used to illustrate industry evolution through stages equivalent to introduction, growth, maturity, saturation and decline. These are shown in figure 8.3. In order for a firm to sustain its position as an above-average performer in an industry it must respond to changes in the industry life cycle by, for example, continuously reducing its costs, differentiating its products or by focusing on selected market segments. The transition from industry growth where good profits are readily available to market maturity is often a critical period for firms in an industry, and requires a careful review of competitive strategy.

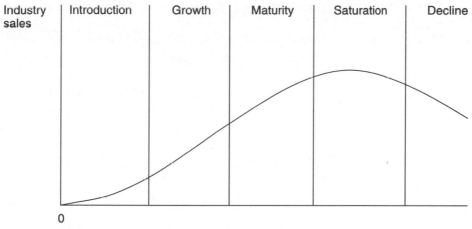

Figure 8.3 Industry life cycle

As an industry matures, a number of important changes are likely to occur in the industry's competitive environment:

Changes in competitive environment

1   Increased competition for market share. This occurs because merely holding its market share no longer provides the firm with any growth. Outbreaks of price, service and promotional rivalry are common events around the transition to maturity. Previous analysis of competitors' characteristics and likely reactions, used to help formulate past strategic moves, may cease to be relevant.

2   Buyers are likely to be experienced and sophisticated. This occurs since firms are increasingly selling to repeat buyers rather than new, relatively ill-informed buyers. Brand and product knowledge will be high.

3   Emphasis on competition shifts to greater cost-effectiveness or service. This shift can require big changes for companies used to competing on other grounds. The added pressure on costs may increase capital needs for the firm to acquire more modern plant.

4   Overshooting of capacity relative to demand is common. The addition of new capacity will require careful timing in some industries as rapid growth will no longer rapidly eliminate industry overcapacity. This effect will add to rivalry between firms, especially in industries with high fixed costs.

5   Methods of manufacturing, marketing, distributing, selling and research are often all undergoing change simultaneously. Changes are

caused by fiercer competition for market share and increased buyer sophistication.

6 New products and applications are harder to come by, since most radical new products and applications have already been conceived and fully exploited.

7 International competition often increases as product and process technology spreads and as firms attempt to sustain their growth by penetrating one another's national markets.

8 Buyer/dealer power may increase as the squeeze on their own profits causes some dealers to leave the industry, so that producers are forced to trade with a smaller number of dealers.

All of the factors listed above are likely to cause a significant deterioration in industry profitability so that even above-average performers in the industry may find themselves experiencing declining profitability.

Implications for strategy

The implications for strategy arising from the move into industry maturity include the following:

1 *Exposure of strategic sloppiness*: Industry growth tends to mask strategic errors and allows most companies to survive. Strategic experimentation is conducted, and mediocre or mixed strategies might be pursued without penalty. The transition to maturity generally exposes strategic sloppiness and firms may be forced, for the first time, to face the need for pursuing one of the three generic strategies in order to survive.

2 *Greater attention to cost*: Cost analysis becomes more important in order to rationalize the product mix by pruning unprofitable items and focusing attention on items which have some distinct advantage in their segments. Ways and means of reducing cost might be expected to play a more prominent part in running the business.

3 *Organizational changes*: Improvements in cost-effectiveness may themselves require organizational changes, in particular the need for centralized control of operations over formerly autonomous divisions or business units. In addition, firms may need to scale down expectations for financial performance in budget-setting, and pay particular attention to maintaining staff morale and loyalty.

4 *Increasing the scope of purchases*: In mature markets, firms may find it more desirable to try to increase the purchases of existing customers rather than seeking new ones which may well involve an expensive battle for market share. An effect of this approach may be some horizontal diversification into the supply of related goods or peripheral equipment and services.

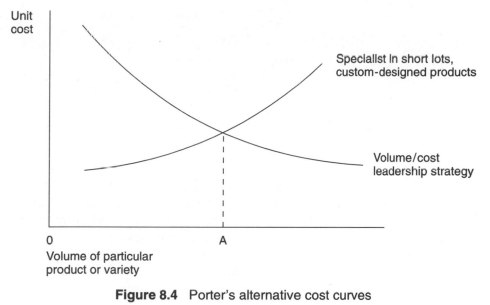

Figure 8.4 Porter's alternative cost curves
Source: Porter (1980)

5 *Acquisition of cheap assets*: Assets or companies may be sold off quite
    cheaply by competitors in a mature industry, which might provide
    the firm with an opportunity to establish or consolidate a low-cost
    position in the industry so long as technology is not changing too
    quickly.
6 *Exploiting different cost curves*: Firms with no prospect of moving to
    overall cost leader position in a mature market may be able to adopt
    a cost focus strategy and become the low-cost producer for certain
    types of buyers, product varieties or batch sizes, by concentrating on
    the volume range 0A illustrated in figure 8.4. Additionally, firms
    which have the foresight to contract their asset commitments into
    niches in their basic industry may be able to use the capital released
    to diversify.
7 *Competing internationally*: A firm may seek to escape from adverse
    home-market conditions by establishing, or extending further, its
    international operations through, for example, exporting, licensing
    or foreign direct investment (see chapter 5).

   Notwithstanding the above considerations, in mature industries some
firms continue to fall into the same traps where their self-perception and
perception of the industry are inaccurate, and they fail to identify and
utilize the optimum competitive strategy. Firms often continue to invest
in increased capacity even though attempting to increase market share

		Size of competitive advantage	
		Small	Large
No. of approaches to achieve advantage	Many	Fragmented	Specialization
	Few	Stalemate	Volume

Figure 8.5 The 'new' BCG matrix
Source: Boston Consulting Group (1989)

in a mature industry is dangerous and the likelihood of gaining an acceptable return on the investment is poor. Firms also tend to give up market share too easily, ignoring potentially lucrative 'harvesting' profits (see chapter 7, 'Endgame Strategy'). Firms suffering in a competitive mature industry very often complain about their competitors' pricing and distribution policies, and also tend to concentrate too much on new product development as opposed to aggressively selling and 'milking' existing ones.

Competitive Environments and Strategy

The concept of strategic advantage has been utilized in order to understand the competitive environment by the Boston Consulting Group (1989). This is shown in figure 8.5.

1 *Fragmented businesses* are often small and regionalized. Economies of scale are difficult to obtain because of the costs of complexity. Profitability is not related to size. Competitive advantage is gained by market focus, innovativeness and by adding value. Examples of this type of industry would include restaurants, precision engineering, handicrafts etc. There is no premium in becoming larger at the expense of the factors which sustain the business.
2 *Specialized businesses,* as their name suggests, specialize in one segment. Their ability to gain a strategic advantage keeps them somewhat immune from competitors who, like them, will be concentrating on another segment. Such businesses are characterized by steep learning curves and scale effects. Thus it pays a company to dominate a segment. Such companies will compete with each other at the edges of segments. Companies which can operate successfully as discriminating monopolists in more than one segment can lower their costs. Examples of specialist businesses would include book publishing, pharmaceuticals and computing.

3   *Volume businesses* such as volume cars are those with significant fixed costs where scale and experience can have a significant impact on lowering costs. Success thus comes from increasing volume to lower costs. This, however, is constrained by market differentiation or segmentation.

4   *Stalemated businesses* where it is difficult to gain any advantage because technology is available for all players. In many cases the only advantage is to lower labour costs by, say, offshore production in lower labour costs economies. In these industries the prizes accrue to those who can remain in business after others have been shaken out.

There is, of course, a dynamic to this analysis as technologies and markets grow and mature with consequent effects on learning and scale effects.

Competitive Advantage and Strategic Choice

In chapter 1 the basic notion of strategic management was introduced, namely the relationship between a firm and its environment. If the concept of the competitive position of the firm is juxtaposed against market attractiveness then a number of consequent strategies can be seen. There are a number of so-called directional policy matrices which demonstrate these relationships, one of which is shown in table 8.1.

As can be seen from table 8.1, wherever a company locates itself or its strategic business units then consequent strategies regarding investment and strategic direction can be identified. Market attractiveness or potential is a composite of growth rate, the state of technology, market structure, stage of the product life cycle etc. Competitive position is a composite of market share, financial strength, strength of the product mix etc.

A refinement to the Directional Matrix Approach is the SPACE (Strategic Position and Action Evaluation) technique of Rowe et al. (1986) (see figure 8.6). The authors state that SPACE is a diagrammatic representation of the PIMS study (see chapter 2).

As can be seen in figure 8.6, SPACE involves the definition and positioning of four factors:

–   financial strength;
–   competitive advantage;
–   industry strength;
–   environmental stability.

Table 8.1 Directional policy matrix

Industry attractiveness	Competitive position		
	Strong	Average	Weak

High	grow
	seek dominance
	maximize
	  investment
		evaluate
		  potential for
		  leadership via
		  segmentation
		identify weaknesses
		build strengths
			specialize
			seek niches
			consider
			  acquisitions

Medium	identify growth
	  segments
	invest strongly
	maintain position
	  elsewhere
		identify growth
		  segments
		specialize
		invest selectively
			specialize
			seek niches
			consider exit

Low	maintain overall
	  position
	seek cash flow
	invest at
	  maintenance
	  levels
		prune lines
		minimize cost
		position to divest
			trust leader's
			  statesmanship
			time exit and
			  divest

Source: Hofer and Davoust (1977)

Like other such models, these variables are composites as shown below:

Financial strength factors (FS)
- Return on investment
- Leverage
- Liquidity
- Capital required/capital available
- Cash flow
- Ease of exit from the market
- Risk involved in business

Competitive advantage factors (CA)
- Market share
- Product quality
- Product life cycle
- Product replacement cycle
- Customer loyalty
- Competitors' capacity utilization
- Technological know-how
- Vertical integration

Industry strength factors (IS)
- Growth potential
- Profit potential
- Financial stability
- Technological know-how
- Resource utilization

Environment stability factors (ES)
- Technological change
- Rate of inflation
- Demand variability
- Price range of competing products

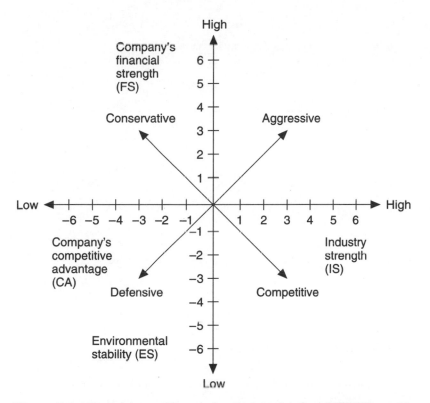

Figure 8.6   Strategic position and action evaluation (SPACE) matrix
Source: Rowe et al. (1986)

- Capital intensity
- Ease of entry into market
- Productivity, capacity utilization

- Barriers to entry into market
- Price elasticity of demand

The task of the managers is to assign values for each of the factors and then to plot the scores on the appropriate axis. The results of this process is a four-sided polygon describing the current situation. The four *generic strategies* available are:

- *Aggressive* – available when the market is attractive and the business has strong finances with definite competitive advantages.
- *Competitive* – unstable but attractive industry. Competitive advantage important but not as important as financial strength which the company needs in order to grow.
- *Conservative* – stable, slow growth market. Emphasis on cost-cutting to improve cash flows for reinvestment in new products and markets.

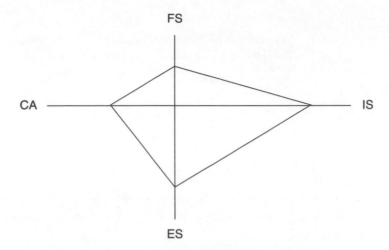

Figure 8.7   An illustration of SPACE

- *Defensive* – relatively unattractive industry where the company has little competitive advantage or financial strength. Heavy emphasis on harvesting strategies (cost-cutting, variety reduction) prior to exit.

By way of illustration, a particular configuration is shown in figure 8.7. The company has a weak financial position with a low competitive position in a turbulent environment. The weight of the evidence points to a competitive strategic posture but the company is financially un-stable. Thus the company will have to acquire external funding if it is to take advantage of the market. Much will depend upon the make-up of the figure, for example, can the company attract new funds? Should the funds be used for marketing or reducing costs? The diagram is a corporate-wide picture and the chosen strategy needs to be based on the wider analysis afforded by the factors in the lists above.

Choosing a Generic Strategy

As can be seen from the Porter framework, the directional policy matri-ces and the SPACE approach, strategy is based upon the strengths and weaknesses of a business in relation to its competitors together with available strategies of differentiation, focus and cost reduction. In reality differing businesses within one organization will be following differing strategies. Figure 8.8 and table 8.2 attempt to combine the differing approaches into a coherent framework.

The four generic strategies identified in figure 8.8, which in many respects are similar to Porter's, can be used to identify which best fits

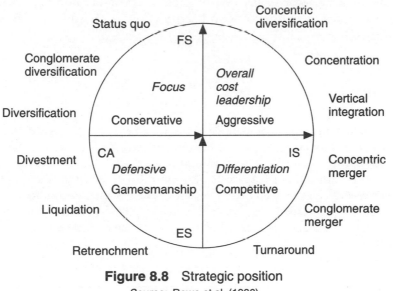

Figure 8.8   Strategic position
Source: Rowe et al. (1986)

Table 8.2   Strategic options

Strategic posture as determined by SPACE	*Appropriate generic strategy*
Aggressive posture	Cost leadership through concentration, concentric diversification, or vertical integration
Competitive posture	Differentiation, e.g. through strong R & D effort funded by merger with cash-rich company
Conservative posture	Focus and selective diversification through acquisition of companies in other market segments
Gamesmanship posture	Defensive, particularly survival tactics, such as retrenchment, divestment, or liquidation

Source: Rowe et al. (1986)

different parts of the organization as in table 8.2. The task of management is to prioritize and choose between the alternative means of achieving the generic strategy.

The literature of strategic management abounds in devices, matrices, models and systems for translating market analysis into strategic action. This chapter has discussed a number of the most important approaches. Of themselves they do not make the decision. Their most important use is in exposing managerial thinking and the inherent assumptions in decision-making. Nor is any one of them a complete and sufficient tool. Differing methods ought to be utilized as they each add a differing view of the problem.

Summary

To formulate appropriate competitive strategies a firm must recognize the various forces driving competition in its chosen markets and the various strategic groups operating in these markets. This appraisal of its markets must take into account the dynamic nature of such markets and the need to constantly re-appraise its competitive strategies to keep them relevant to current market conditions. Whichever of the generic strategies it pursues in a market, the firm must have appropriate and effective management processes to convert these strategies into superior performance.

Questions

1 Show how a market of your choice might be analysed in terms of the Porter 'forces driving competition' framework.
2 Indicate the nature of Porter's 'three generic strategies' for competitive success, analysing the possible advantages and disadvantages of each.
3 Examine the implications of the 'industry life cycle' for the formulation of competitive strategy.
4 Examine the implications of 'strategic groups' for the formulation of competitive strategy.
5 Discuss some of the factors relevant to a firm's 'strategic positioning' in a market.

References

Boston Consulting Group Inc., 1989. *The BCG's Advantage Matrix.*
Drucker, P., 1989. *Managing For Results,* Heinemann.
Hofer, C. W. and Davoust, M. J., 1977. *Successful Strategic Management,* A. T. Kearney Inc.
Kay, J., Davis, I. and Cronshaw, M., 1990. 'On Being Stuck in the Middle', working paper, Centre for Business Strategy, London Business School.
Porter, M. E., 1980. *Competitive Strategy,* Free Press.
Porter, M. E., 1985. *Competitive Advantage,* Free Press.
Rowe, A. J., Mason, R. O., Dickel, K. E. and Snyder, N. H., 1986. *Strategic Management,* Addison-Wesley.

Further Reading

Grant, R. M., chapters 2, 5, 8, 9 and 10, *Contemporary Strategy Analysis*, Blackwell, 1991.

Luffman, G., Sanderson, S., Lea, E. and Kenny, B., Part II, *Business Policy*, Blackwell, 2nd edn, 1991.

Thompson, J. L., chapters 7 and 15, *Strategic Management*, Chapman and Hall, 1990.

9
The Nature and Significance of Cost-Effectiveness

Cost leadership in an industry was identified in chapter 7 as one possible generic strategy for competing successfully in a market. Where a firm possesses superior raw material supplies, low-cost plants, more efficient distribution systems etc., this gives it a competitive edge over rival suppliers. Such cost-effectiveness enables the firm to meet and beat competitors on price. Cost advantages are a crucial factor in markets for 'standardized' products, exhibiting little product differentiation and where competition is primarily price-driven. More specifically, low-cost producers are in a better position to survive adverse trading conditions such as cyclical downturns in market demand and market entry by new suppliers which tend to exacerbate price competition and in the extreme lead to cut-throat 'price wars'. More pro-actively, cost advantages may enable a firm to exercise considerable influence over its rivals in setting prices, informally by means of price leadership or more formally by setting prices for a cartel. Finally, even in markets where product differentiation is the primary form of competition and firms can command premium prices for their product, lower costs provide the firm with better profit margins than competitors or additional resources to finance the promotion of its brands.

Cost advantages over competitors are of two major types: (1) absolute cost advantages, i.e. lower cost than competitors at all levels of output deriving from, for example, the use of superior production technology; (2) relative cost advantages, i.e. cost advantages related to the scale of output accruing through the exploitation of economies of scale in production and marketing and through cumulative 'experience curve' effects. Over time, investment in plant renewal, modernization and process innovation (either through in-house R & D or the early adoption

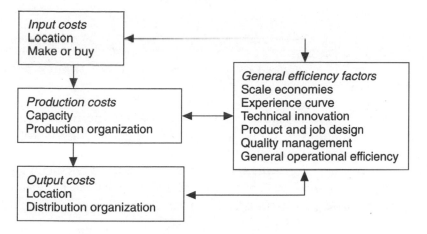

Figure 9.1   Sources of efficiency improvements
Source: Adapted from Grant (1991)

of new technology developed elsewhere) is essential to maintain cost advantages.

All firms operate as transformation units, converting inputs into higher value outputs, whether these outputs be goods or services. A firm's efficiency in undertaking this transformation process is a key factor in giving it competitive advantage. Figure 9.1 follows this broad input–output sequence in grouping potential sources of efficiency improvements. However, it is important to recognize that cost savings are not necessarily made just at one stage of the total value-creating chain but may be achieved through careful analysis of the interrelationships between conversion stages and through a broad view of the total operations of the firm. *Productivity*, which measures the relationship between physical output of products and the factor inputs used to produce that output, provides a key measure of a firm's efficiency.

Productivity improvements enable a firm to produce a *given* output at a lower resource cost thus enabling the firm to supply this output at a lower price, or alternatively produce more output from the *same amount* of inputs, enabling the firm to increase its profits through increased sales. Productivity is usually measured in terms of output per employee hour, and a firm can improve its productivity in a variety of ways including the adoption of better working practices and pay incentive schemes; the adoption of methods for economizing on stockholding; and the use of superior production methods.

In exploring the potential savings to be made in input costs two broad considerations, location and make or buy, are important:

Location

The choice of a geographical site or sites by a firm to perform its economic functions is influenced by a range of factors, but two are particularly important:

1 the nature of the industrial activity that the firm performs (e.g. raw material extraction or crop cultivation, the manufacture of intermediate or final products, the provision of a service), and
2 the relative costs of production at different locations balanced against the cost of physical distribution to target markets, and the importance of closeness to customers as a basis for establishing competitive advantages over rival suppliers.

Some activities are highly *location-specific*. For example, the extraction of iron ore can only occur where there are deposits of the metal. Likewise, many service activities, e.g. retailing, have to be located in and around customer catchment areas, whilst some suppliers of components may find it advantageous to operate alongside their key customers in order to synchronize better with the latter's input–production requirements. The manufacture of final products tends to be more *'footloose'*. Certain locations may be preferred for their production advantages, because of, for example, lower labour costs, or the availability of investment subsidies through government's regional policy or the supply of skilled workers and access to technology and related facilities. Furthermore, where a number of firms in the same industry locate in close proximity, specialist secondary services such as training facilities, machine tool suppliers etc., may develop to service these firms, and the effectiveness of these secondary services can provide 'external economies of scale' which lower supply costs. On the other hand, high distribution costs, especially in the case of bulky, low-value-added products such as coal, or, in the international context, the imposition of tariffs and quotas on imports, tend to favour a market-orientated location.

For firms operating on a *multi-plant* basis, particularly multinational companies (MNCs) with plants and distribution facilities sited in several countries, location decisions can have a critical effect upon their competitiveness. Thus, for example, cost considerations might induce an MNC to establish part of its production operations in overseas plants in order to take advantage of the lower cost structures of 'offshore' production centres.

Alternatively, MNCs might establish overseas operations in order to improve their access to superior technology; e.g. Japanese pharmaceutical companies have sought to overcome the lack of a strong home-based research tradition in drugs by setting up R & D facilities and forging joint venture links with established drug companies in the US and UK. Location decisions may be influenced by the need to *protect 'core' technologies*. Many UK pharmaceutical companies, for example, produce the key patented 'active ingredients' of their drugs in the UK and export these to overseas plants where they are made up and packaged for sale. Thus, the pursuit of cost-minimization in making location decisions needs to be tempered by consideration of other aspects affecting the firm's competitive position. Furthermore, location needs to be subject to continuous review in the light of changing market circumstances and comparative cost levels between regions and countries, and firms may need to overcome inertia and loyalty to existing localities and relocate facilities in order to maintain their cost-competitiveness.

Make or Buy

A second major factor which is relevant to the consideration of input costs is whether the firm purchases its raw materials, components and services requirements from outside suppliers or produces them for itself as part of a vertically integrated operation (see chapter 3). The main advantage of using outside suppliers who specialize in the production of an input and produce for a large number of customers (not just one as in the case of self-supply), is that they are able to benefit from the lower costs associated with economies of large-scale operations. Thus, it may be cheaper for the firm to buy in the input rather than to produce it internally – the more so if the firm has access to a number of supply sources (both domestic and international) and can take full advantage of price competition between them. Where the firm concerned is a large customer for a particular raw material, component or service, it may be able to use its bargaining power to secure advantageous bulk-buying discounts.

Rather than dealing at arm's length with a number of alternative suppliers, often on an *ad hoc* and opportunistic basis, it may pay a firm to enter into *long-term cooperative arrangements* with a limited number of input suppliers. This facilitates better coordination between the firm and its suppliers over order sizes, the timing of deliveries, input quality and possibly even product development. Where suppliers undertake to supply the firm on demand with small consignments at frequent intervals through, for example, a 'just-in-time' arrangement this reduces the stock-holding costs to the firm, reduces its storage and space requirements and may enable it to achieve faster manufacturing rates. Where suppliers undertake to meet the firm's input specifications then this serves to reduce the firm's goods inward inspection, sampling and testing costs. Additionally, the firm may involve its suppliers in the design of new products and production planning for new products, capitalizing on the expertise of suppliers to improve product quality and reliability.

Reliance upon independent suppliers for inputs carries the risks in certain cases of over-dependency on particular suppliers, leading to possible problems of overcharging and disruptions to the firm's production schedules arising from supply shortages, failure to meet delivery times, and inputs lacking the desired degree of quality or precision. For these reasons a firm may decide to make an input for itself rather than buy it. *Backward vertical integration* may be a viable proposition for a firm if its requirements for an input are sufficiently large that it can take full advantage of economies of scale of producing that input to minimize its costs (i.e. it can achieve the minimum efficient scale of operation). (See box 9.1.) Furthermore, backward vertical integration may enable the firm to achieve economies of scope by linking together technologically related processes, and reduce various transaction costs in using the market (e.g. finding suppliers and negotiating contracts with them). Backward vertical integration may also provide an opportunity for the firm to acquire low-cost input sources.

Even when the firm's own user requirement is less than the minimum efficient scale of operation it may still decide to produce its own inputs, producing at the minimum efficient scale or above and selling surplus raw materials and components on the open market. (Box 9.1.) Alternatively, the firm may still choose to make its own inputs even though this involves some cost penalty in order to secure reliable supplies of inputs and avoid the potential overcharging and disruption problems indicated above.

However, when contemplating backward integration a firm must bear in mind that this will change its cost structure, substituting high fixed costs of owned assets for the variable costs of buying. Furthermore, the firm also reduces its flexibility in dealing with demand fluctuations since it is geared to produce a given volume of its input requirements. Finally, the firm, in making rather than buying, forgoes any benefits it might obtain from innovations by independent suppliers which reduce input costs or improve input quality.

Production Costs

Production costs are influenced by a number of factors including capacity planning and utilization and production organization, together with scale economies, experience/learning curves, product and job design etc. Capacity and production organization are discussed in the two sections that follow. Scale economies, experience/learning curves etc. in so far as they affect all stages of the value chain, not just production, are discussed later in the chapter.

Box 9.1   Costs and the make or buy decision

Firms can either buy an input on the open market or undertake self-production.

The figure below shows the costs to a firm of producing an input internally. LATC is the unit cost of producing various quantities of the input; the minimum efficient scale of operation is $0X_3$. $0P$ is the market price for the input. Self-production is clearly economical if the firm's typical requirement for the input is greater than $0X_2$. In the output range $0X_2$–$0X_4$ the firm is able to produce the input for itself at a cost which is below the supply price. On the other hand, if the firm's typical requirement for the input is, say, $0X_1$, production for self-consumption only is uneconomical. However, even in this case the possibility exists that a firm could undertake self-production, producing at the minimum efficient scale of output, $0X_3$, consuming $0X_1$ units itself, and selling the remainder X_1X_3 to other businesses at any price between $0P$ and the minimum unit cost of production.

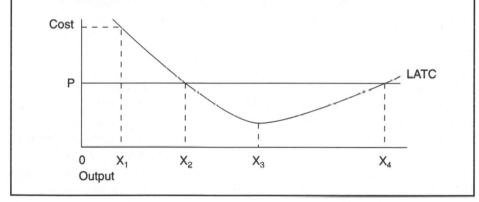

Capacity

Production capacity refers to the amount of output that a firm is physically capable of producing given full and efficient use of its existing plant or plants. This capacity is dependent upon the planned number of days and hours per week of production operations, making allowances for machine downtime, maintenance, cleaning etc. Some automated plants with high capital costs are planned for three-shift, 24 hour, 6- or 7-day working, paying premium labour shift rates; whilst less automated plants which involve larger labour inputs might plan for single-shift, 5-day working.

In order to minimize its costs a firm must plan over the long term to create production capacity which matches long-term demand for its products. This requires reliable forecasts of total future market demand

and the firm's likely market share. The number of plants which a firm chooses to operate in order to satisfy likely demand for its products depends upon the minimum efficient scale of each plant, given existing production technology. However, the decision as to how many plants to operate is governed by the need to balance minimizing production costs in each plant and subsequent distribution costs. Where a firm produces products which are bulky and expensive to distribute it may deliberately choose a large number of sub-optimal-sized plants in order to reduce distribution costs.

Over time, a firm may adjust its capacity to meet changes in demand and the competitive situation facing it, investing in new plant or extending existing plant to meet an increase in demand, or closing down plant, permanently or temporarily (mothballing), to meet a situation of overcapacity. In addition to rationalizing its scale of operations to reduce overcapacity, a firm may also rationalize the number of plants it operates in order to improve efficiency, closing high-cost plants and concentrating production in larger, more modern, plants. Whereas rationalization to reduce overcapacity only needs to be considered infrequently when a long-term decline in market demand or falling market share necessitates adjustments, the firm should *continuously* seek to explore rationalization opportunities which improve efficiency.

In situations where demand is volatile, firms need to decide whether to establish sufficient productive capacity to meet peak demand or whether to restrict capacity to some 'notional' base level of demand, meeting peak demand from buffer stocks held for such contingencies. Service industries, such as electricity and banking which cannot store their products, are unable to use buffer stocks to meet fluctuating demand and face a stark choice of creating excess capacity or having disaffected queueing customers, in establishing appropriate service levels.

Although over the long term a firm can vary the number and size of its plants to match changes in demand, in the short term plant capacity is more or less fixed and changes in demand can only be accommodated by changing plant utilization rates. Operating a plant below capacity output will involve cost penalties, in particular fixed costs will be spread over a smaller volume of output. In capital-intensive industries where fixed costs form a large proportion of total costs and where, as a consequence, the break-even output volume is high, excess capacity can raise unit costs substantially and may even force the plant to operate below break-even volume (see box 9.2 in the section entitled 'Scale Economies'). On the other hand, attempting to push output of a plant beyond its normal capacity working in order to meet high demand would also entail extra costs through overtime working and additional shifts paid at premium wage rates, and through faster machine operations and reduced maintenance which increase scrap rates.

Production organization

The efficiency with which a firm manages the value creation process depends upon a careful consideration of the factor inputs which the firm uses and how these might be combined in the most cost-effective manner to produce the firm's products. In seeking to achieve its planned levels of output of goods and services the firm will need to control the physical quantities of inputs such as materials, labour and capital which it uses to produce that output (a relationship often referred to as a firm's 'production function'). The firm's demand for inputs is derived from its need to satisfy demand for products and all of these inputs must be purchased or hired by the firm; and their prices will determine the firm's production costs (a relationship often referred to as a firm's 'cost function'). The proportions in which a firm mixes factor inputs to produce output may be constrained by the nature of its production processes and the existing state of technology so that the firm, in effect, uses factor inputs in fixed proportions to produce output. However, where a firm has some discretion in mixing factor inputs its choice of factor proportions will be influenced by their relative prices so that, for example, as wage rates rise relative to the price of capital equipment firms will seek to automate production processes, substituting comparatively cheap capital for expensive labour inputs. Again, where wage differentials between skilled and semi-skilled workers widen the firm will have an incentive to reorganize, mechanize and simplify production operations to facilitate the substitution of semi-skilled for skilled labour.

Achieving production efficiency A firm's efforts to control and minimize the costs of producing goods or services will be guided by the need to economize on the use of resource inputs, although more specifically a number of considerations need to be borne in mind:

1 *Minimizing the number of transformation operations* undertaken in making products. Careful value analysis of products may suggest opportunities for redesigning products to simplify their processing, without impairing the value in use or function of the product. For example, reducing the number of working parts in a product may offer opportunities for eliminating some production operations altogether. Alternatively it may be possible to combine production processes, undertaking several processes simultaneously to effect cost-savings.
2 *Speeding up production throughput* at each operational stage and between operations. This shortening of production cycle times should enable the firm to meet customer order requirements more quickly thereby saving on the need to carry large finished goods stocks. In addition, speeding up production may serve to reduce or eliminate

interprocess stocks as each production operation is fed by its immediate predecessor on a just-in-time basis. Standardization of products or components can contribute to speeding up production by
minimizing machine set-up times. Long production runs of a limited
number of products reduces the amount of idle time when machines
are being reprogrammed for different products, whilst a totally
dedicated production line should eliminate idle time due to machine
change-overs. Plant maintenance programmes can also contribute to
reducing machine downtime due to breakdowns.

3 *Minimizing materials handling.* The careful design of plant layouts
can serve to reduce materials handling both during and between
production operations, avoiding excessive double handling of materials or components. The use of conveyor belts and other materials-
handling devices can effect savings in labour costs.

4 *Production line balancing* by the assignment of equal amounts of work
to sequential production operations on the production line in order
to avoid idle time at any production operation. Good balancing should
serve to cut costs by reducing the amount of surplus capacity carried
at particular stages of the production process.

5 *Quality control* of production inputs and production processes to
minimize the amount of scrap product generated and reworking costs
of rectifying defects.

All of these cost-savings require prompt and regular data about costs
and output in order to properly monitor and control production costs.

Production methods Most goods and services can be produced using
a number of alternative production methods, and a firm will seek to use
a production method which is appropriate to its underlying production
technology and which is cost-effective. Production methods for goods
are of several major types:

1 *Process* production involves the continuous production of a good in
bulk often by chemical means, e.g. petrochemicals. Process production is used whenever raw materials in liquid or gaseous form need
to be blended, heated or distilled, and the flow of these materials is
facilitated by using pipelines which connect the various production
stages.

2 *Mass* production involves the production-line or assembly-line
production in very large numbers of goods such as motor cars or
domestic appliances. Mass production is used wherever demand for
a product is sufficiently large and the product sufficiently standardized
to justify laying out a specialized production-line or assembly-line for
it in order to achieve the cost-savings associated with economies of
scale, reduced machine set-up times, lower interprocess stocks etc.

3   *Batch* production involves the manufacture of similar goods together in batches and is used where demand is insufficient for mass production or the product cannot be standardized. In batch production, batches of product are subjected to a series of processes such as machining, drilling and grinding in work stations specializing in these processes, with machines generally being reset after each batch, ready to process the next batch. Batch production offers the advantage of greater flexibility but generally involves higher cost of machine set-ups, larger interprocess stocks etc.

4   *Hybrid* production systems such as group technology and flexible manufacturing systems (FMS) combine various features of mass production and batch production methods, using automation and computers to facilitate the low-cost production of a variety of low-volume components or products. *Group technology* involves grouping together several products or components which are sufficiently similar in terms of their processing requirements for them to be produced using the same machines, with a minimal amount of machine resetting from product to product. In *FMS systems* computer-controlled machines can be quickly switched from the production of one component or product to another by reprogramming the machines. Such reprogramming also facilitates the smooth running of the production system by allowing a component or product to be processed on several different machines, thus avoiding production bottlenecks or delays caused by machine breakdowns.

The advent of *computer technology* has enabled firms to integrate all facets of production planning and control, including product design, factory layout planning, production scheduling and stock control through the use of *computer-integrated manufacturing* systems (CIM). CIM systems embrace *computer-aided design* (CAD) to design new components or products and redesign existing products. Components or products can be subjected to various tests of strength, performance etc. using *computer-aided engineering* (CAE) software without having to build prototypes; thus changes in product design can be made quickly and cheaply. CAD can also be linked to *computer-aided process planning* (CAPP) to determine the best methods by which to manufacture a product. Finally, the firm may employ *computer-aided manufacturing* systems (CAM) to impart operating instructions to numerically controlled machines and robots employed in production systems. CAM enables production scheduling to be completed more efficiently and quickly, particularly in rescheduling production to accommodate new or redesigned components or products. For example, CAD/CAM computer software packages can provide design specifications and parts lists for components or products directly to the machines that will produce these items.

Developing in-house process technology   The development or adoption of superior production techniques can be an important source of cost advantage to a firm. However, where these process innovations are undertaken largely by the firms' suppliers of capital equipment or components, this innovation can be rapidly diffused and taken up by competitors, thus providing no lasting advantage to any one firm. Many of the computer-based design and manufacturing systems developed by computer manufacturers and software suppliers fall into this category. Firms which are growing rapidly and so have a high rate of investment will find it easier to maintain some transitory technological leadership of this kind over slower growing firms. More substantial and lasting cost advantages are likely from the firm's own in-house process innovations since they are based upon the firm's own specific in-house expertise and know-how, employ specially commissioned capital equipment and may be protected by patents. Thus they are not readily transferable to competitors except on terms dictated by the process innovator through, for example, licensing arrangements.

Although process innovations of this kind may take the form of large, dramatic innovations such as Pilkington's revolutionary 'float glass' process, firms can also maintain a technological lead over competitors by smaller, incremental process innovations. Many schemes for plant modernization take the latter form, gradually updating production processes on a piecemeal basis as changes in technology create opportunities for improvement. Exploiting the productivity benefits of incremental process innovations requires an alertness to the possibilities offered by changing technology and the willingness and ability of the firm to change its organization, management and working practices to accommodate it. The problems of overcoming inertia and introducing new production processes are more acute when developing new methods on a piecemeal basis and fitting them into an existing production process alongside established processes compared with a 'greenfield' plant where all production processes can be planned from scratch.

Distribution organization

In addition to seeking cost-savings in production, a firm may also secure cost-savings by examining its physical distribution arrangements in respect of stockholding, warehousing and transport, and in promoting products and generating customers amongst wholesalers, retailers and consumers through the distribution channel.

Earlier it was emphasized that a firm's choice of production location might be influenced by the need to minimize its input costs by siting production near to raw material or component sources. Equally, however, 'closeness to the customer' considerations may prompt the firm to locate its plant(s) in or near its main markets in order to improve its market servicing effectiveness. Plants near to customers not only minimize physical distribution costs to customers, which may be important when products are heavy or bulky to transport, but also facilitate the provision of high customer service levels and may enable the firm to identify changing market needs more quickly. The final choice of plant location(s) will depend upon the balancing of 'input' costs considerations which favour location near to input sources and 'output' costs considerations which favour location near to customers. However, this balance must also allow for production cost factors so that, for example, a firm may tolerate higher input or output costs in the interests of siting its production in a few large plants rather than several small ones in order to achieve production cost-savings from economies of scale.

Distributing products

Typically, the distribution of products involves a distribution channel consisting of the wholesaling and retailing functions, and various associated channel functions: customer generation, promotion and transport.

Wholesaling The wholesaling function involves the stockholding/warehousing of products in relatively large quantities which are then sold in smaller quantities to retailers or final customers. The optimum location of inventory is dependent on a number of factors including (1) the ratio of stock to sales required to maintain a given quality of service to trade and final buyers; holding large stocks enables firms to turn round customer orders quickly, but holding large stocks increases inventory costs; (2) economies of scale. The technology of warehouse design favours the larger warehouse, since the ratio of cubic capacity to surface area increases with size and larger warehouses facilitate mechanization of order processing, loading etc. These factors encourage the centralization of stockholding; but against these factors must be set the additional costs of long-distance transportation, which may favour a decentralized network of warehouses and local depots.

Retailing The retailing function involves the provision of a 'point of sale' such as a shop or store. In consumer markets the location of retailing operations is generally determined by the geographic spread of consumers and population densities in particular areas. In some cases, however, it is possible to dispense with a 'physical' retail outlet by selling through mail order, or as with many industrial products direct selling through sales representatives.

Agents   In most marketing channel systems there is a need, at some stage in the channel, for agents, whose primary function is to generate new business contacts. Typically, agents and other similar intermediaries do not take title to the goods, they simply generate contacts. They may be used at the stage of the wholesaler/distributor to generate new retail customers or end-users or at the level of the manufacturer contacting end-users direct or finding new wholesalers to handle its products.

Trade promotion   An important facet of a firm's distribution policy is to secure adequate availability of its products in the distribution channel, i.e. unless wholesalers are prepared to handle a product and retailers are prepared to give it shelf space then contact with final customers is lost. Trade promotion to wholesalers and retailers is required alongside product promotion and advertising aimed at the final consumer to encourage wholesalers and retailers to stock the product.

Transport   The movement of products from the factory to warehouses, depots and retail outlets and final customers can be undertaken in a variety of ways – by road, train, ship and air. A firm is required to select an appropriate mode of transportation for its products bearing in mind the costs of alternative transport systems and their convenience for customers, especially in respect of delivery times and the avoidance of damage to products in transit.

Distribution arrangements

In broad terms, a firm may use independent distributors and agents to perform the distribution functions of stockholding, warehousing, transport and channel promotion on its behalf or, alternatively, the firm may internalize some or all of these functions by forward vertical integration.

Wholesaling   In the case of the wholesaling function, critical factors in the choice of which form to follow are the relative costs of operation and the extent to which the firm is able to control the distribution arrangements for its product. There may be heavy fixed costs in establishing a wholesaling facility but offsetting advantages in having stable internal transfer prices for wholesaling functions. By contrast, using independent wholesalers avoids these fixed costs but involves the additional expense of constant renegotiations on price with independent wholesalers. The major advantage to a producer of operating through an independent wholesaler is that the cost of managing inventories and distribution is passed on to the wholesaler. However, the producer runs the danger of control loss – the producer must rely on the wholesaler stocking enough volume to serve retail demand, maintaining the quality of products in transit and storage and also selling to appropriate retailers (i.e. those who serve the market to whom the products are targeted).

Retailing   In the case of retailing, the large number of outlets and wide geographic spread necessary to serve retail demand generally makes internalization of such operations costly and difficult to manage centrally. In practice, the ownership of retail outlets by producers of consumer goods is limited, particularly in those areas where the development of 'one-stop shopping' has meant that one individual producer cannot provide the breadth of product range necessary to cater for this kind of buying behaviour. In some cases, however, integrated manufacturing, wholesaling and retailing is viable where firms buy in other suppliers' products to augment their own range (as exemplified in the UK by Boots the chemist, Bass the brewer and W. H. Smith the newsagent). In some consumer goods markets and most industrial markets specialist dealers are perhaps more easily integrated by producers, particularly those who manufacture a complementary range of products.

Independent agents   The relative cost advantages/disadvantages of using independent agents as opposed to a company-based sales force has been summed up by Kotler (1984) thus: 'The fixed costs of engaging a sales agency are lower than those of establishing a company sales office. But costs rise faster through a sales agency because sales agents get a larger commission than company sales people.' Moreover, there are various 'agency costs' in using independent market intermediaries and policing contracts.

Trade promotion   Trade promotion costs in obtaining adequate product representation by independent wholesalers and retailers may be substantial but would not in themselves justify forward integration. However, the coordination of promotion (both distributor and final customer based) with the performance of other functions is crucial to competitive success. This process is highly information-intensive, and gathering relevant information on which promotional campaigns may be based is often perceived as facilitated by internalizing functions (i.e. production, wholesaling, retailing and sales/marketing).

Transport   The mode of transport (road, rail etc.) used by producers and distributors will depend mainly upon the availability and relative cost of each mode; the characteristics of the products themselves (bulk, weight, perishability, unit value etc.); and the distances over which goods are to be transported (short-haul, long-haul). The latter in turn depends upon the extent to which production and wholesaling is centralized or decentralized and the geographic scope of the firm's outlets (local, regional, national, international). The high cost and specialist expertise involved in providing transportation services would usually incline firms to favour independent hauliers etc. However, there are various products like petrol, ready-mixed concrete and frozen foods where the producer may find it more cost-effective or safer to move the product himself using customized transport.

Whilst the above discussion has concentrated sequentially upon potential cost-savings in dealing with inputs, production and distribution, a number of other factors bearing upon cost-effectiveness must be considered which, to a greater or lesser degree, affect *all* stages of the value chain. These include economies of scale, learning curve effects, technical innovation and operational efficiency.

Scale Economies

The economies of scale or unit cost reductions secured by a firms as its scale of operations is increased (using a particular technology) are an important means of establishing cost advantages over rivals and potential entrants. Scale economies can be obtained by operating larger *plants* to secure production economies or by operating larger *firms* to secure purchasing, marketing, distribution and financial economies, as indicated in chapter 2. In chapter 2 the concept of the 'minimum efficient scale' (MES) was introduced, this being the minimum output a firm is required to produce to achieve cost-effective production (output 0X in figure 9.2). In some industries the MES is so large in relation to total market size that the market can only support a limited number of cost-effective suppliers.

A number of qualifications, however, must be borne in mind. First, the cost 'penalty' experienced by a firm whose planned scale of operations is smaller than the MES may be severe (NL at output 0Y on cost curve B) or small (ML at output 0Y on cost curve A). Second, a firm may have a planned scale of operations which is equal to or greater than the MES (0X in figure 9.2) and so should, in *principle*, be cost-effective but may be unable to achieve sufficient sales volume and market share to operate at this level because, for example, it is unable to overcome the product differentiation advantages of competitors or because of industry overcapacity. (See box 9.2.) The extent to which operating below planned capacity increases unit production and distribution costs depends largely upon the ratio of fixed to variable costs; the higher the ratio of fixed costs the higher the cost disadvantage. Finally, a firm may avoid the cost penalty associated with operating below MES using a *particular* technology

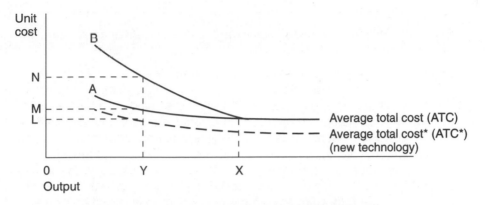

Figure 9.2 Minimum efficient scale and costs

by adopting *alternative* technologies. Where such technologies are available and exhibit different cost–output characteristics it may be possible for a firm operating on a relatively small scale to match the unit cost performance of larger scale competitors. An example of this is provided by the US steel firm Nucor. Nucor was far too small to build a blast furnace to smelt iron ore – the capital-intensive method used by the integrated manufacturers to process basic steel. Instead it took a much cheaper route recycling scrap metal by melting it down in an electric arc furnace. Nucor found it was able to make steel at the commodity end of the market at a price which undercut both the big manufacturers and imports.

In addition to scale economies a firm may be able to reduce its unit costs by taking advantage of economies of *scope*, supplying a greater range and variety of product by using its existing physical and human resources more comprehensively.

The Experience Curve

As the managers and labour force of a firm gain greater experience of a new technology by repetitive contact, they become more efficient at operating it, which enables unit costs of production and distribution to be reduced. Familiarity reduces costs by lowering the time required to complete jobs, improving coordination between jobs and reducing scrap and defects. The economies of learning are particularly important for complex production and distribution activities such as aircraft production. Learning effects tend to be cumulative and are often depicted in the form of an 'experience curve' such as the one presented in figure 9.3 which shows the estimated reduction in total cost per square foot

Box 9.2 Minimum efficient scale and capacity utilization in the UK plasterboard market, 1990

Estimates of the minimum efficient scale in the manufacture of plasterboard vary. (Monopolies and Mergers Commission, plasterboard report, 1990.) According to one company, RPL, it was around 25 million square metres, whilst another company, Knauf, quoted an annual production rate of 20 million square metres. BPB, the market leader (76 per cent market share in 1990), considered that costs per square metre of plasterboard produced would continue to fall as scale increased (as lower running costs offset higher capital costs), but estimated that 'above the capacity range of 20–30m square metres, further falls in unit costs were modest' (paragraph 4.51).

A comparison of these estimates with BPB's, RPL's and Knauf's actual installed capacity is given below and indicates the market is supplied by plants of minimum efficient scale. However, because of an overcapacity problem some of these plants were only barely breaking even ('the minimum economic output lies in the range of 60–70% of plant capacity', paragraph 9.48). The industry's capacity utilization rate was estimated at 63 per cent in 1990 (nominal UK plasterboard capacity = 314 million square metres compared to industry sales in 1990 of 197 million metres).

UK plasterboard capacity, 1990

		million square metres
BPB	East Leake plant	63
	Kirby Thore plant	54
	Robertsbridge plant	36
	Sharpness plant	26
	Sherburn plant	51
		230
RPL	Bristol plant	38
Knauf	Sittingbourne plant	46
		314

accruing from accumulated increases in the production of float glass using the 'float glass' process.

In the early stages of dealing with a new technology a considerable amount of management and worker time is required to closely supervise and operate the new process. However, over time as managers and workers become more accustomed to the technology, they are able to perform their operations more efficiently and coordinate their activities more effectively, reducing the need for detailed management supervision. Whilst some learning benefits might be expected to accrue in any

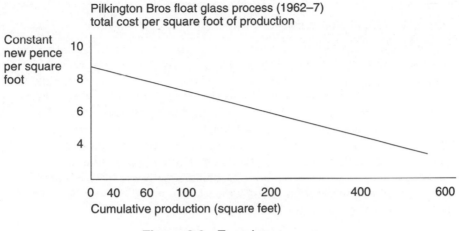

Figure 9.3 Experience curve

Source: Monopolies and Mergers Commission, float glass report, 1968

firm, substantial learning effects will occur only in firms which consciously strive to manage costs down by continuously seeking ways of performing tasks better. Firms which pursue cost-minimization programmes will attempt to develop their own experience and know-how and transfer experience between business units and departments within the firm. Such firms are likely to move down the experience curve more rapidly than more passive competitors and thus acquire cost advantages over them. However, a firm may be able to speed up its learning to some extent by benefiting from the experiences of superior competitors through observing closely how these competitors make and distribute products and by hiring competitors' former employees.

The effective assimilation of existing technologies and a firm's unique embodied experience of those technologies can enable it to establish competitive advantages over rival suppliers. Additionally, familiarity with a technology and the development of associated skills and expertise can provide a platform for further technological advances. (See box 9.3.)

Technical Innovation

In many industries, cost leadership can only be sustained over time by the firm being an *active* innovator of new production and distribution processes or an early adopter of technologies developed by others. From a competitive advantage perspective the former is the more attractive option since it offers the firm a 'head start' over rivals, and there is the possibility that the innovation may be protected against competitive

Box 9.3   Experience curve for microchips

Improvements by semiconductor firms in the way that they produce memory chips by etching circuits into silicon wafers using lithographic equipment have increased the power and reduced the cost and price of dynamic random access memory (DRAM) chips, as shown in the figure below. The prices of 1-megabit chips and 4-megabit chips have fallen sharply; next generation 16-megabit chips began to appear on the market in 1991 (one year ahead of schedule), and 64-megabit chips have been produced on an experimental basis. The smaller space and lower power needed to provide memory as chips have increased in capacity have brought considerable benefits to the main customer for semiconductors – the computer industry.

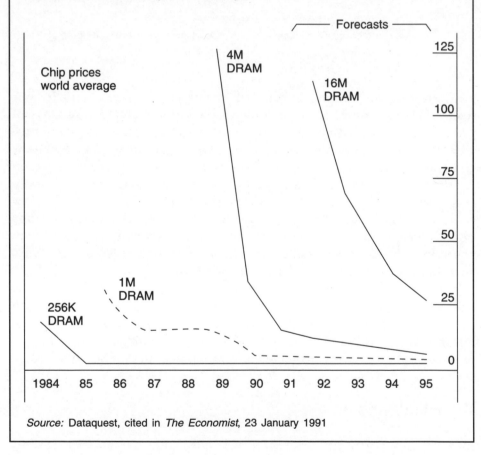

Source: Dataquest, cited in *The Economist*, 23 January 1991

encroachment by taking out patents and keeping know-how secret. Process innovation may enable a firm to lower its unit costs at all levels of output (e.g. allowing it to operate on cost curve ATC* in figure 9.2) and thus give it a cost advantage over rivals operating older technologies (ATC in figure 9.2).

In most cases innovations are incremental, involving small technical improvements to current equipment and processes arising from experience of operating existing technology, e.g. the substitution of optical and laser measurement devices for mechanical ones in engineering firms. In other cases more dramatic innovations in production or distribution methods may be instituted. For example, the US steel firm Nucor significantly changed the process of producing sheet steel products by replacing the conventional process which involves extruding eight-inch-thick slabs of metal which then have to be repeatedly rolled and reheated to 'squeeze' the slab into a thin sheet. To avoid the heavy capital investment and time which this entails, Nucor used a new type of (German-designed) funnel mould which casts steel straight into two-inch-thick slabs which can be immediately compressed into thin sheet steel. In both cases, the active management of technological innovation requires a firm to monitor and forecast technological developments in its own and other industries, to undertake R & D into process technologies, to be receptive to opportunities for technology transfer, to invest in new equipment and to adapt existing operating procedures to accommodate new technology.

Technological advances can have a dramatic impact upon operating efficiency and costs, as box 9.4 demonstrates for the data processing industry.

Product and Job Design

Substantial cost-savings may be effected by careful consideration of the design of a product both in terms of the *'value in use'* of the product and its *'manufacturability'*. The former relates to the way in which a product performs and adequately fulfils its product functions, whilst the latter relates to the ease with which it can be made and assembled. This requires an evaluation and review of a product's design, with the aim of reducing its material or manufacturing cost without impairing its function or performance. By examining all a product's components and their manufacture, and by consulting component suppliers, it may be possible to identify cheaper raw materials to replace expensive ones, or opportunities to reduce the degree of precision with which components are made, or to reduce the number of components. In addition, product design may make provision for the use of modular sub-assemblies to facilitate the interchange of standardized components and to assist in the

Box 9.4   Advances in computer technology

The figure shows the time and cost for a computer to process 1,700 typical operations. Early electric computers based upon vacuum tubes/valves were slow and expensive to operate although the speed and cost of data processing fell with the introduction of transistor circuits. Solid state circuits and silicon microchips have continued to accelerate cost reductions in computing, and continuing improvements in the capacity and cost of microchips (see box 9.3) are likely to offer further scope for cost improvements in computing. However, future developments in computers cannot be expected to rely on electronics alone as the technological base since there are physical limits to the number of components per chip, and because the speed with which electronic signals can be transmitted places limits on computer speed of operation. The next generation of computers are therefore likely to rely on the merging of electronics, optical fibre and laser technologies in order to overcome the speed-restricting resistance of silicon chips.

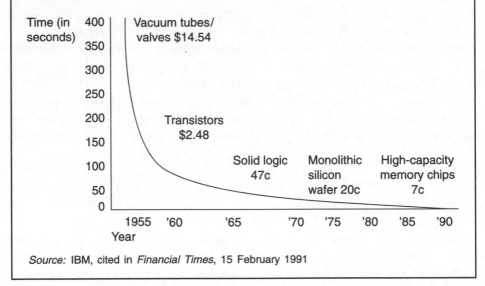

Source: IBM, cited in *Financial Times*, 15 February 1991

automation of production and assembly operations. The efficiency gains from the value analysis of products can be achieved both in relation to new products where manufacturability should be an important facet of product design and established products where changes in materials characteristics and prices, and production techniques may offer opportunities for beneficial product redesign.

Alongside product design firms also need to consider *job design*, i.e. the way in which work tasks are organized and grouped to form individual jobs. The products which a firm makes and the way in which it makes them have important implications for job design which in turn can significantly affect the efficiency with which products are made and distributed. Job design needs to strike an appropriate balance between specialization and worker discretion over the job concerned. Specialization can be an efficient approach to job design insofar as it reduces training requirements and facilitates the use of unskilled labour performing limited numbers of routine tasks. On the other hand, specialization can reduce job satisfaction, particularly amongst better educated workers, giving rise to conflict, industrial disputes, absenteeism and high labour turnover which reduce productivity. To enhance job satisfaction and productivity it may be necessary to redesign jobs by, for example:

- *job enlargement*, where additional tasks are given to the worker so as to provide more variety;
- *job enrichment*, where workers are given greater scope in deciding how the tasks should be performed;
- *job rotation*, where workers rotate around the jobs in their department on a regular basis, on the grounds that greater variety will lead to greater job satisfaction;
- *work groups*, where workers are allowed to decide amongst themselves how to distribute and exercise work tasks.

Underpinning job design and redesign are the *training* processes necessary to extend and improve the skills and knowledge of a firm's managers and operatives so as to improve their job performance. Vocational training concerned with the acquisition of specific vocational skills can assist in improving the performance of current tasks, although it is important to ensure that training programmes improve the flexibility and adaptability of managers and workers to help them successfully cope with new work practices associated with technological innovations. Training needs programmes can be instituted to identify what skills are necessary to achieve the firm's current and future goals and to identify any deficiencies by comparing requirements with current skills available.

Quality Management

As well as improving the efficiency and reducing the costs of manufacturing and distributing products, a firm must also ensure that the quality of its goods or services meets specified performance criteria in terms of product reliability, durability, ease of operation, ease of servicing and repair etc. *Traditional quality control methods* involve:

- Interpretation of product specifications which itemize product components and production operations.

- Inspection of components and products, including sampling procedures, to select items for testing and the use of testing equipment to check the performance of components or products and detect those that are defective. The results of such tests enable production operations to be modified quickly to prevent further defectives being made and thereby save on rectification or scrap costs.
- Cooperation with product design, production, R & D and outside suppliers over improvements in product quality.

Traditional quality control is concerned specifically with detecting and rectifying cases of failure and waste. However, it may be more effective to prevent quality problems arising in the first instance through '*total quality management*' (TQM). Total quality management is a business philosophy which seeks to instil in all employees of a firm an individual as well as a collective responsibility for maintaining high quality standards, in respect of both the products supplied by the firm and the attention paid to customer services and requirements. TQM has both an internal and an external dimension. Fundamentally, the success or failure of the firm will depend on its ability to satisfy the demands of its external customers. Product quality may well be the most important source of a firm's competitive advantage over rival suppliers. TQM emphasizes that the firm's ability to generate and sustain quality advantages stems from the totality of its internal operations. The firm is made up of a network of interrelated departments, each one standing in a customer or supplier relationship with others in terms of the internal flow of raw materials and components, processing and assembly operations, through to final product, stockholding and dispatch. TQM seeks to establish a unity of interests and commitment to the maintenance of the highest possible quality standards at each of these interfaces. Individual commitment to quality can be reinforced by the operation of quality circles which meet periodically to discuss ways in which the quality of the firm's products can be improved.

General Operational Efficiency

In addition to the specific opportunities for cost reduction identified above, firms need to pay attention to broader considerations of operational efficiency and seek to reduce overhead costs. Most firms tend to exhibit inefficiencies in their organizations (variously termed '*organizational slack*' or '*X-inefficiency*') in the form of excess staffing and facilities over and above those strictly needed to perform the firm's productive functions. This results in the firm's cost structure being raised above the minimum attainable level through inefficiencies such as restrictive labour practices, overmanning, demarcation rules, bureaucratic rigidities in the management of resources and excessive perquisites (such as generous travel budgets and expense accounts, lavishly furnished offices, company cars etc.). The understandable tendency for managers and workers to avoid the strains of operating at maximum efficiency means that inefficiency will always tend to occur, although these tendencies are likely to be exacerbated in large bureaucratic organizations which operate in markets where there is a lack of effective competition 'to keep them on their toes'. If demand conditions deteriorate or market competition intensifies putting pressure on the firm's profitability, the firm is likely then to seek ways and means of cutting costs generally. In the extreme, when a firm's future is threatened by financial crisis, the shedding of unnecessary costs will become an important part of corporate turnround.

The dividing line between what is 'necessary' expenditure and what is 'excessive' expenditure is a blurred one since many employee facilities, such as canteens and medical care, have a beneficial effect on workers' health, motivation and productivity. In some cases it may be possible to identify quite clearly where improvements might be made; e.g. the elimination of shop-floor overmanning and restrictive work practices through productivity-bargaining between management and workers. Other savings may be effected by reducing head office staffing and reducing the management levels. For example, the US steel firm Nucor has a very small rented head office building, employing just twenty people to manage an organization employing over 5,000 people by devolving responsibility to operating businesses. Ford UK has recently revamped its corporate structure of seven management layers which it felt was too weighty, time-consuming and bureaucratic to just five layers, and in the process reduced its white-collar work force by around 12 per cent.

Interrelationships between Cost-cutting Programmes

In principle, although it is possible to search for cost-savings in each of the various areas identified above, in practice cost-cutting programmes tend to be multi-faceted and need to take an integrated view of the effects of efficiency programmes upon procurement, production and distribution. The following examples highlight the need for the coordination of cost reduction initiatives:

Havelock Europa, the UK store-fitting company, embarked upon a comprehensive factory reorganization programme in 1991 designed to eliminate various inefficiencies. The firm found that one of its leading products, a shop counter, required 116 steps in the production process, including moving the semi-finished product and collecting components to fit it, yet only 22 steps added value to the product. Furthermore, each counter travelled almost one mile on its way round the factory during processing. In addition, the lead time needed to produce a counter from the time it was scheduled for manufacture to the time it left the plant was seven weeks, yet the actual process time was only approximately four hours. Long lead times meant that the firm had to hold a large buffer stock of finished goods totalling up to £2 million of surplus stock, which incurred high interest charges. Most of these problems arose because the firm's main factory had been expanded in an *ad hoc* way so that processing equipment was in an illogical order, causing dislocations and delays in altering settings of machines and in searching for and obtaining materials and tools.

This led the firm to change the layout of the plant, move equipment and reorganize production flow to avoid unnecessary setting time in the main machines and to break down joinery shop work into 'cells' with each joiner concentrating on one process at a time. In addition, the factory moved to just-in-time manufacturing. The early benefits from this reorganization have been encouraging. The number of steps involved in production have been reduced from 116 to 68 (with eventual scope for reduction to 34), and the distance travelled has been trimmed from 1 mile to 300 metres. Lead times have been reduced from seven weeks to one week (with an eventual target of one day). Stocks have been reduced dramatically through just-in-time ordering.

The experience of *Caterpillar*, the US construction equipment-maker, highlights some of the opportunities and problems associated with plant modernization. In 1987, the firm introduced its 'Plant with a Future' (PWAF) programme to modernize its production facilities at its main plants as the cornerstone of its long-term strategy of maintaining its position as a low-cost producer. Its programme was designed to generate an aggregate 18 per cent drop in product costs and a one-fifth fall in inventory. The programme involves the use of computer-integrated manufacturing systems, the use of manufacturing cells and heavy capital expenditure on new capital equipment. Table 9.1 sets out the goals of the project. The project has achieved some successes, e.g. the dumper-truck production plant at Decatur has reduced production costs by 12 per cent and cut fabrication times from 20 to 5 days. However, the firm is still needing to deal with upgrading the education and training levels of its work force, and changing work habits and work force attitudes with respect to operating computerized interlinked production machinery, and as a consequence has experienced delays and cost over-runs on its plant modernization programme.

Costs: Strategic Implications

Cost, output and profitability

The intrinsic cost structures of firms have an important effect on the sensitivity of their profits in relation to their outputs.

Table 9.1   Caterpillar's 'Plant with a Future' project

	1989 %	1990 %	1991 %	1992 %	1993 %	Goal %
Capital spent	45	69	85	97	100	–
Employment reduction	7	14	21	27	30	33
Inventory reduction	9	10	12	16	20	22
Throughput days reduction	31	53	67	76	79	79
Product cost reduction	4	8	10	13	15	18
Return on investment	–	–	–	–	22	30

Source: Caterpillar, cited in *Financial Times*, 6 June 1990

Figure 9.4 shows the cost structures for two firms, A and B. Firm A in figure 9.4(a) has a lower proportion of fixed costs (FCA) to total costs (TCA) than firm B in figure 9.4(b). The two firms break even at output levels 0X and 0Y respectively, since at these output levels total revenue (TRA and TRB) just covers total costs (TCA and TCB). At any outputs smaller than 0X or 0Y respectively, the firms make a loss, whilst at larger outputs than 0X or 0Y respectively, they make a profit. For firm B the penalties of not achieving break-even volume are greater than for firm A as indicated by the wide angle between TRB and TCB.

By contrast the rewards at outputs beyond break even favour firm B which makes profits at an incrementally faster rate than firm A, as can be seen by an examination of the respective angles between the total revenue (TR) and total cost (TC) curves of firms A and B. Firm B is more volume-sensitive in that it needs a higher volume to get past break even. Alternatively, one could examine the two firms in terms of the '*contribution*' which they make towards fixed costs, where total contribution is defined as the difference between total revenue and variable cost or the difference between selling price and unit variable cost (unit contribution). Firm A with high unit variable costs makes a small unit contribution to its fixed overheads, whilst firm B with lower unit variable costs makes a larger unit contribution to its fixed overheads.

Where market conditions permit a firm to sell high volumes of product then firms like B can readily achieve sales volumes beyond break even and benefit from their low variable costs and high unit contributions to generate large profits. By contrast, where market conditions are more hostile then firms with high fixed costs, like B, are at a cost disadvantage in so far as they find it difficult to achieve sufficient sales volumes to earn enough contribution to cover their fixed costs and thus break even. Under these latter circumstances, firms like B may be forced to cut

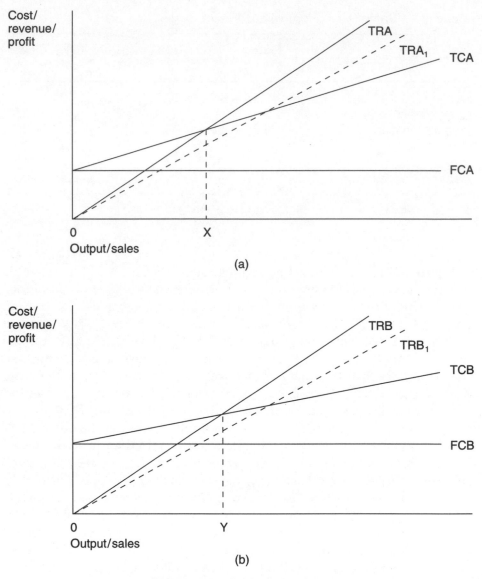

Figure 9.4 Costs and volume

prices below the level which covers their full cost and set prices at levels which cover their variable costs and make some contribution to fixed overheads. Companies with high fixed costs like banks, theatres, building societies, railways and airlines often have to offer such pricing deals at below full cost in order to attract enough business to pay their fixed costs.

The total revenue lines TRA and TRB show the relationship between total revenue and volume at a *given* selling price. If selling price were to fall then this would have the effect of moving the total revenue line downward to a new position such as TRA_1 and TRB_1. Firms like A which have a lower ratio of fixed to total costs but high unit variable cost are more price-sensitive. This is because the rate at which they make or lose profit as a result of price changes is greater (as indicated by the narrow angle between total revenue and total cost). Thus any change in the total revenue line (TRA) caused by a drop in price will have a large effect on company profits. By contrast firm B's profits are less sensitive to price changes since its total costs (TCB) rise less steeply than those of firm A (TCA).

Strategically an important question is whether or not any firm can alter its cost structure to gain a competitive advantage. This may be difficult, but certainly as market conditions change then there may well be some advantage in being the fastest to change. For example, banks are currently slimming down their branch network in order to reduce fixed costs and at the same time trying to sell more products through this network. Similarly, a firm through vertical integration or disintegration can change the balance of its fixed and variable costs, vertical integration increasing the firm's fixed costs whilst reducing variable costs and vice versa (see chapter 3).

Organization and cost

Reference has been made earlier in the chapter to the adverse impact on costs of poor coordination of activities within a company's production/distribution system. A further aspect of the impact of organizational behaviour on cost occurs where there are many subsidiaries or strategic business units (SBUs). As variety and complexity increase in a company as a consequence of widening the product/market mix there is a greater need for coordination. Indeed, many diversified companies have to create departments whose functional role is to coordinate the activities of others. This cost of coordination or complexity can outweigh the gains of diversity. Good inter-SBU relationships can limit rises in cost by avoiding duplication, sharing expertise and facilities as well as generally knowing what each other's strategy and role are. This can be accomplished in many ways (see chapter 4), but chief amongst them are the senior management decisions surrounding the generic strategies of the firm's various subsidiaries or SBUs. Thus, when subsidiaries know what is expected of them in terms of performance and how their strategy fits into the whole corporate strategy there may be a better chance of managing costs.

Decision-making and cost

As emphasized in earlier sections of this chapter, management, through its decisions, can have a big effect on costs. Whilst there are always

pressures to reduce costs and increase efficiency, the task of management is to make balanced choices. Thus, care has to be taken to ensure
that 'efficiency drivers' in one part of the firm do not increase the costs
or lower the efficiency in other parts of the firm. A further aspect of
decision-making is timing. Getting decisions out of sequence, particularly at the implementation stage of a strategy, can result in cost penalties. Examples include launching new products, bringing new plant
on-stream, purchasing new assets, mergers and divestments. Indeed, one
of the major problems involved with large structural changes such as
merging or divesting is the impact on the firm's cost structure.

Dangers of strategies based on cost

As has been pointed out in several places in this book, there would
appear to be overwhelming potential strategic advantage in pursuing
strategies that result in lower costs which can then either increase profit
and/or lower prices. The purpose of this section is to look at some of the
problems associated with cost-based strategies.

Perhaps rather obviously in a low-cost game there is only one winner.
Thus for those close to the winner there will be strong pressure to
reduce costs and for the winner there is equal pressure to reduce costs
further to stay ahead of the competition. Whilst there may be a finite
limit on cost reduction such unremitting pressure to reduce costs can
have serious strategic implications for firms. For example, firms may
become obsessed with saving money rather than earning it. Thus ideas
for product improvement or market extension will fail on cost grounds.
Low-cost obsession often results in strategies based on a fixed product/
market scope with little emphasis on corporate spending on R & D.

Finally, strategies based on cost, in order to have lower prices, assume
that low price is a key determinant of demand and that low price is a
strong buying motive. Whilst this may be true, there is abundant evidence that for many buyers price is an indicator of quality and that buyers
are more interested in quality than price. Moreover, quality may not just
be confined to the product but could include service.

Cost-effectiveness and pricing

Where firms are able to establish cost leadership over rivals they may
choose to exercise this advantage by cutting prices in order to secure
market share at the expense of rivals, or they may choose to match the
prices of competitors and take the benefits of their lower costs in the
form of enhanced profit margins. However, although being a low-cost
supplier gives a firm potentially more latitude over pricing the firm must
be mindful of the wider competitive implications of its pricing behaviour

as regards the sustainability of its own profitability and that of the industry. Thus, a low-cost supplier might practise forbearance in its attitude towards competitors, not capitalizing on its lower costs to attempt to drive competitors out of the market, but instead exercising its low-cost advantages in more subtle ways as part of collaborative arrangements such as price leadership systems and cartels. Whether a firm chooses aggressive or collaborative strategies depends upon its assessment of the short-term losses it would have to bear in the form of reduced profits in order to undercut rivals' prices; how long it would need to do so before it eventually destroyed its competitors; and what longer term profit enhancement would result if it were able to achieve a more dominant position in the market. This trade-off between shorter term and longer term profits will be very much influenced by the firm's *perception* of the extent of its cost advantage.

In practice, aggressive price competition tends to be avoided by firms operating under oligopolistic market conditions where firms recognize that their fortunes are interdependent and thus perceive price wars to be mutually ruinous. Where there is a possibility of expanding the total market by their actions, or a danger of ruinous price war, oligopolists have strong incentives to engage in some form of collusion, for this can increase their joint profits. By seeking to raise the growth rate of total market demand or countering a decline in prices and profits through their pricing strategies, oligopolists may all gain. Such motives may cause oligopolists to establish formal arrangements like cartels with pricing and product promotion rules for members; or engage in less formal collusion through price leadership arrangements. (See Technical Appendix – 'Oligopoly'.)

Summary

The present chapter has identified the various ways in which a firm may seek to establish itself as a low-cost supplier through the choice of an appropriate location for its production and distribution activities and appropriate external purchasing and self-supply policies. Establishment of an appropriate scale of operations which balances production and distribution costs is an important aspect of securing low costs. Over time the firm needs to 'manage down' its costs by taking advantage of experience curve effects, technical innovation and product and job design. Such cost management inevitably involves an examination of all the interrelationships between a firm's production and distribution activities with the aim of securing across-the-board cost-savings. Whenever cost-savings are achieved, they can be devoted either to cutting product prices to achieve price advantages over rivals or to boosting profit margins. The type of market in which the firm operates will play an important part in determining which of these strategies the firm pursues. In particular, in a situation where firms operate in concentrated markets they are likely to avoid aggressive price competition and use their cost advantages to secure higher profits.

Questions

1 What are the possible advantages and disadvantages of a competitive strategy based on cost leadership?
2 Under what circumstances might it be more attractive for a firm to produce an input for itself rather than procure it on the open market?
3 Examine the implications of the 'minimum efficient scale' of production and the 'experience curve' for a firm's cost-effectiveness.
4 Consider the view that process innovation by a firm is fundamental if it is to remain a cost-effective supplier in a dynamic market.
5 What is 'X-inefficiency' and how can it be kept in check?
6 Discuss the attractions of adopting a 'total quality management' philosophy in order to achieve competitive success.

References

Grant, R. M., 1991. *Contemporary Strategy Analysis*, Blackwell, chapter 6.
Kotler, P., 1984. *Marketing Management: Analysis Planning and Control*, Prentice-Hall, 5th edn.

Further Reading

George, K. D., Joll, C. and Lynk, E. L., chapter 7, *Industrial Organization*, Routledge, 4th edn, 1992.
Hay, D. A. and Morris, D. J., chapters 2 and 8, *Industrial Economics and Organization*, Oxford University Press, 2nd edn, 1991.
Luffman, G., Sanderson S., Lea, E. and Kenny, B., chapter 7, *Business Policy*, Blackwell, 2nd edn, 1991.
Porter, M. E., *Competitive Advantage*, Free Press, 1985.
Thomson, J. L., chapter 11, *Strategic Management*, Chapman and Hall, 1990.

10

The Nature and Significance of Product Differentiation

Differentiation was identified in chapter 7 as one possible generic strategy for competing successfully in a market. The purpose of product differentiation is to create and sustain a demand for the firm's services or products by nurturing consumer brand loyalty. Product differentiation is an important means of establishing competitive advantage over rival suppliers, and in some market structures, most notably oligopoly, it is regarded as constituting a more effective competitive strategy than price competition. The attraction of product differentiation competition over price competition lies in the fact that whereas price cuts, for example, can be quickly and completely matched by competitors, a successful advertising campaign or the introduction of an innovatory product is less easily imitated. Moreover, whereas price competition lowers firms' profitability, product differentiation tends to preserve and even enhance profit returns. In particular, the establishment of product uniqueness may allow firms to command premium prices over competitors' offerings. Finally, product differentiation may serve as a barrier to entry, thereby protecting existing market shares against new competition.

Product differentiation needs to be based upon a careful consideration of the 'product' offered, which Thomas (1988) suggests consists of three elements as shown in figure 10.1: the *core product* which reflects the consumer's basic reason for buying it, e.g. a motor car as a means of personal transport; the *physical product* which is the particular model of car; and the *total product* which is the sum of all benefits received if the product is purchased.

Suppliers attempt to distinguish or differentiate their own products from those offered by competitors in two basic ways:

1   They can vary the physical appearance and attributes of the product by differences in design, styling, colouring and packaging, and

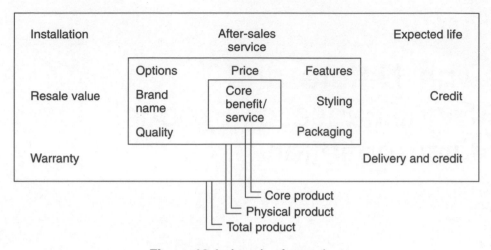

Figure 10.1 Levels of a product
Source: Thomas (1988)

differences in quality, composition, innovatory features and performance results.
2 Broadly similar products may be differentiated in the minds of buyers by the use of advertising and sales promotion techniques which
emphasize imputed or subjective aspects of the product: e.g. 'better
than', 'cleaner and whiter than'.

Identifying Customers and Their Needs

A differentiation strategy involves the firm in identifying customer requirements and satisfying them by providing customers with appropriate
products in order to achieve the organization's objectives. This goes
beyond merely selling what the firm produces, but starts by identifying
underlying consumer needs through marketing research; generating
products which satisfy these needs through new product development;
promoting these products to consumers through various marketing-mix
policies (pricing, advertising, sales promotion etc.); and physically distributing products to customers through distribution channels. This
requires a firm to take a broad view of its markets rather than taking a
narrow, myopic view of the markets it currently serves and thus ignoring
wider market opportunities. For example, a producer who viewed his
market solely as that for 'potato crisps' would be ignoring the potential
for selling related products into the much larger 'snack products' market. Such a 'marketing orientation' stresses the superiority of a customer-
based marketing approach over a production orientation which is largely

concerned with persuading customers to buy what the firm has chosen to produce.

Industrial and consumer markets

Where a firm aims to generate profits by the recognition and satisfaction of customer needs, its starting point must be a careful consideration of the purchasing decisions of buyers as shaped by their functional and psychological motivations and needs. A broad distinction can be made between industrial buyers and consumers in general. Industrial buyers purchase products largely on the basis of functional or technical requirements: the producer of a motor car, for instance, may seek to buy suitable components such as tyres, batteries, etc. for incorporation into a particular car model. Consumers too buy many products on the basis of some functional or physical requirements, e.g. a consumer may decide to purchase a motor car as a means of personal transport. However, a consumer's decision to buy a product such as a car is also influenced by his or her personality and the image he or she wishes to project to others ('extrovert', 'sporty', 'affluent' etc.).

It is thus important for producers of consumer goods to understand the psychological impulses of prospective buyers of their products as well as their practical needs. This requires careful market research into the motivation and perception of buyers aimed at matching products with identified customer needs, and the deployment of appropriate marketing-mix strategies (product quality, pricing, advertising etc.) designed to maximize sales potential.

Market segmentation

Successful differentiation requires a firm to identify sub-markets or segments each of which has its own particular customer profile and buyer characteristics. A market can often be divided up broadly into major customer segments as well as more narrowly into various sub-markets within each of these segments. In marketing terms, markets can be segmented in a number of ways as box 10.1 indicates, pyramiding down from the identification of major sub-groups of customers, and their particular product-type requirements and preferences with reference to such things as a range of quality gradations, colouring and packaging. Further elements in market segmentation include the distribution outlets used by buyers to make purchases and the geographical boundaries of the market which could be regional, national or international in scope.

Depending upon the complexity of a market as revealed by market segment analysis, a firm may choose to operate 'across the board' or decide to focus on a limited number of segments. Since most markets

Box 10.1 Market segmentation matrix for paint

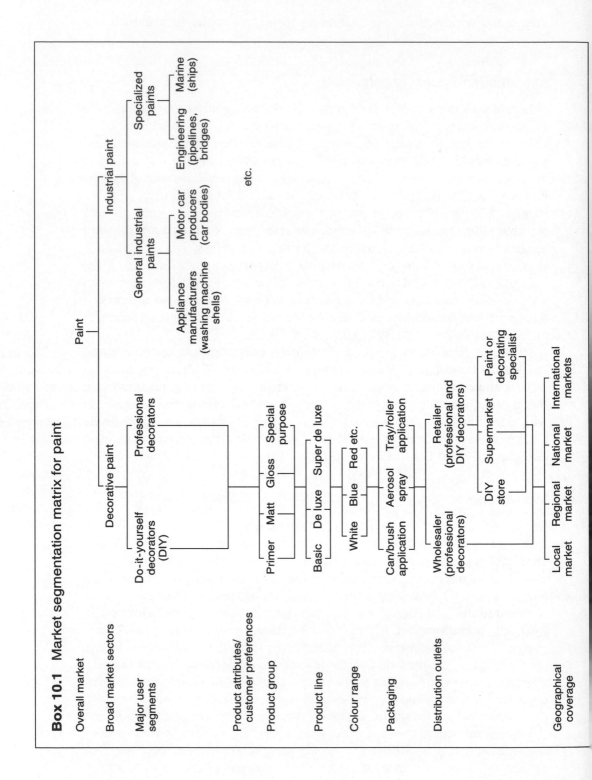

in practice possess segmentation characteristics to a greater or lesser degree, a uniform marketing strategy involving the same marketing-mix approach across all segments is likely to be of only limited effectiveness. A more attractive approach in these circumstances is a marketing strategy which involves various 'customized' marketing-mix formulations, each tailored to match the buyer characteristics of the segments targeted. A third, more concentrated, marketing strategy may be applied where the firm decides to target the whole of its marketing effort on one particular segment.

Differentiation is based on the identification of consumer needs which may differ both between market segments and within segments. As the earlier example made clear, a first important distinction may be made between industrial buyers and consumers in general insofar as they may require different products, different back-up services and the use of different distribution channels. In the case of industrial buyers it is often possible to identify the precise nature of buyer requirements from product specifications, tender details or by direct contact with buyers. By contrast, general consumers tend to be more amorphous and, for practical purposes, it may be necessary to group together these potential buyers in terms of certain common personal and economic characteristics. Such groups are likely to differ in the level and pattern of their spending and thus can be used as the basis for identifying strategic market segments which can then be exploited by targeting 'customized' products to meet the particular customer requirements of those segments.

Socio-economic groups

A commonly used general method of classifying potential customers is the 'A to E' social-class grading system:

Grade A   –   'upper middle class': higher managerial, administrative or professional occupations;

Grade B   –   'middle class': middle to senior managers and administrators;

Grade C1   –   'lower middle class': junior managers, supervisory and clerical grades;

Grade C2   –   'skilled working class': qualified tradespersons;

Grade D   –   'working class': semi-skilled and unskilled workers such as labourers;

Grade E   –   pensioners.

For most consumer product marketing, a much finer, more detailed customer profile is required based on such data as sex (male, female),

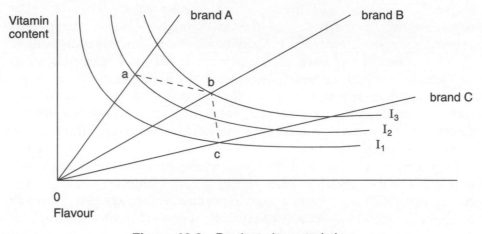

Figure 10.2   Product characteristics

age (1–4, 5–10, 11–18, 19–34, 35–49 etc.), income level (£50,000+, under £5,000), housing status (owner-occupier, council-house tenant), etc.

Using such information it is possible, for example, to establish the approximate number of professional, high-income-earning women, in the age bracket 35–49, who might provide a potential market for a new premium price exotic perfume.

Consumers and product characteristics

The socio-economic characteristics of consumers identified above are important insofar as they influence their purchase requirements and their perceptions of products available. A typical consumer will tend to choose a particular brand of a product rather than some other brand on the basis of their perceptions of the respective attributes of these brands. For example, consumers buying blackcurrant juice may be looking for two principal product characteristics – flavour and vitamin content. Three brands of blackcurrant juice are available – brand A, brand B and brand C – each of which is differentiated insofar as it places a different emphasis on the two product characteristics. The three brands are represented by the rays in figure 10.2 which show the fixed proportions of product characteristics in each brand. Brand A, for example, has a high vitamin content but has little flavour whilst brand C, by contrast, has a lot of flavour but a low vitamin content.

Points a, b and c on these rays show how much of each brand of juice can be bought for a given unit of expenditure at the prevailing prices of the three brands. To find the consumer's satisfaction-maximizing brand purchases it is necessary to introduce a set of indifference curves, I_1, I_2 and I_3, showing the consumer's preferences between the two product

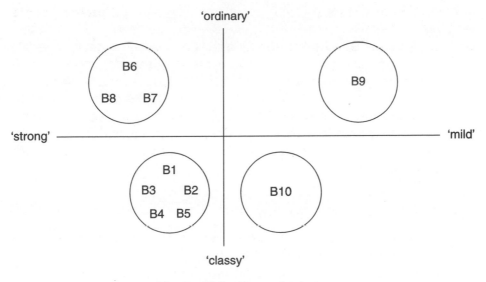

Figure 10.3 Perceptual map

characteristics, each curve showing combinations of product characteristics which yield equal satisfaction to the consumer. The consumer's
final choice will be brand B, as they settle at point b on the highest
indifference curve (I_3) consistent with their limited expenditure on juice.

Perceptual mapping

The technique of 'perceptual mapping' is often used to chart all consumer's perceptions of brands currently on offer and to identify opportunities for launching new brands or to re-position an existing brand.
This technique involves identifying perceived product characteristics which
may be used to classify consumer opinions about brands of a product.
Thus, in figure 10.3 the axes of the 'map' show the perceived product
attributes, 'strong'/'mild' and 'ordinary'/'classy' for cigarettes whilst B1
to B9 on the map indicate consumers' perceptions of existing brands of
cigarettes on offer in terms of these characteristics. Brands show market
segments which are currently being served by existing brands and 'clus-
ters' of brands suggest larger volume segments. Perceptual maps are
generated through market research which requires potential buyers to
assign ordinal rankings to attributes possessed by varieties of a particular
product. In essence a brand's position is the customers' view of the
company's marketing strategy.

A positioning strategy seeks to differentiate the firm's brand from
competitors' brands in terms of product characteristics and 'image' so as
to maximize sales potential. In positioning brands a firm may choose,

in a well-served market segment, to offer a 'copy-cat' or 'me-too' brand which is very similar to competing brands, with minimal product differentiation (brands B1 to B5 in the figure). This stratagem may be viable where this segment represents a high proportion of total market sales so that even a small brand share would result in large sales. Alternatively, a firm's marketing research may reveal untapped demand potential in different market segments, so that it may choose to distance its brand from competing brands with a high degree of product differentiation, introducing a new brand (B10). Clearly, to be of value, the correct axes need to be identified.

Types of differentiation strategy

The Porter (1980) analysis discussed earlier in chapter 8 emphasized that a differentiation strategy could involve promoting the same brand to the whole market or a substantial proportion thereof (a generalized differentiation strategy); or, alternatively, could involve promoting *different* brands to particular market segments (a focused differentiation strategy).

A *generalized differentiation strategy* for a product is based on the use of the same marketing mix format right across the market (uniform pricing, advertising messages, retail outlets etc.). This approach attempts to reach all classes of buyer. It is best suited to a market where the product being sold is relatively standardized and buyers require little in the way of product variety. Mass marketing the product on a uniform basis is simpler to organize and manage than a fragmented approach, and may yield lower unit selling and production costs by enabling the firm to take advantage of economies of scale in advertising and production. On the other hand, generalized marketing may fail to realize fully a product's sales potential because of its inability to appeal to key customer segments.

By contrast, a *focused differentiation strategy* for a product is based on the use of a variety of marketing-mix formats (different prices, advertising messages, retail outlets etc.), each aimed at a particular group of customers in the market. This approach attempts to customize the marketing mix for each particular segment in order to maximize its appeal to the buyers constituting those segments. It is best suited to a market in which the product being sold is capable of being differentiated either by physical variations of the product itself or by its psychological appeal, and where buyers demand a substantial amount of product variety. In these cases, focused marketing is usually much more successful than an across-the-board approach in boosting sales. Moreover, a firm which caters for a variety of market segments is likely to develop organization structures and communication patterns which can rapidly detect changes in the market environment and ensure a prompt response to these changes. However, the targeted approach may prove to be costly in terms of both higher production costs (e.g. with smaller production runs a firm may be unable to lower costs through exploiting economies of scale) and marketing costs (e.g. the need to finance a number of separate advertising and sales promotion budgets). To some extent it is possible to offset some of the higher costs associated with product diversity through the use of flexible manufacturing systems which retain some scale economies; through the use of common standardized components in making a variety of products; and through the use of joint marketing and distribution networks.

In some cases firms may pursue an extremely focused differentiation strategy targeting *one* particular group of customers. Such a concentrated marketing approach is particularly suited to a smaller firm with limited financial and marketing resources or a specialist producer, and could be used by a new entrant to the market as a means of establishing a toe-hold in the market before undertaking further expansion. By concentrating its resources narrowly, a firm may well be in a better position to boost its sales but, on the other hand, may fail to capitalize on the sales potential of other segments. Worse still, dependency on the one market segment leaves the firm unduly exposed to a fall in demand in that segment.

The Marketing Mix

Firms can use a range of 'marketing-mix' measures to establish product differentiation advantages over competitors. Important facets of the marketing mix are outlined in figure 10.4.

The relative importance of these elements will vary according to the particular buyer characteristics of the market or market segments being served by a product. Thus, to take a broad example, in marketing industrial goods technical features of the product, price and personal selling might be stressed, whilst in marketing consumer goods such factors as advertising, sales promotion and packaging might be emphasized. In general, industrial buyers, mainly purchasing/procurement officers, are involved in the purchase of 'functional' inputs to the production process, usually in large quantities and often involving the outlay of thousands of pounds. Their particular concern is to obtain input supplies which are of an appropriate quality and possess the technical attributes necessary to ensure that the production process goes ahead smoothly and efficiently. Consequently, in selling to industrial buyers, personal contacts, the provision of technical advice and back-up services are important. Buyers of consumer goods, by contrast, typically buy a much wider

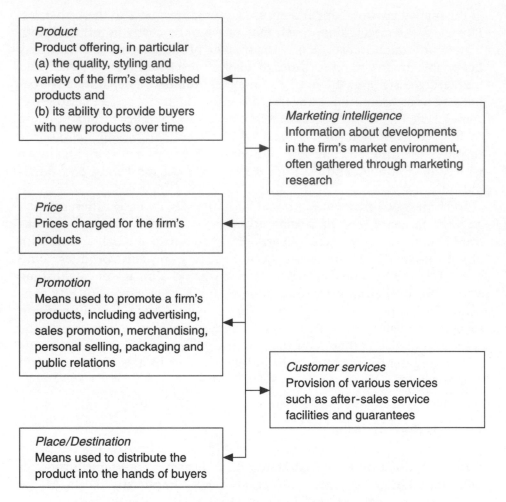

Figure 10.4 Sources of potential differentiation advantage
Source: Adapted from Grant (1991)

range of products, mainly in small quantities. Purchases are made to satisfy some physical or psychological need of the consumer. Thus, it is important for marketers to understand the basis of these needs and to produce and promote brands which satisfy identifiable consumer demands. In this context, advertising and sales promotion are important tools for shaping consumers' perceptions of a brand and establishing brand loyalty. In addition, the marketing mix needs to be modified over time to reflect changes in a product's circumstances as it goes through its life cycle. Thus, for example, in the introductory phase of a product's life cycle product novelty, quality, guarantees etc. would be emphasized, whilst in the later maturity phase price, styling and advertising may become more prominent.

Product Strategy

Product strategy involves the firm deciding on the range of products to be included in its product portfolio. Product strategy requires the periodic updating and modification of the firm's existing products or brands; the introduction of new products; and the phasing out of old products whose sales are declining in order to release production and marketing resources which can be devoted to newer, more active products.

Technological innovations result in new products, new cost-reducing production technologies and new materials. Some innovations can serve to improve existing products or reduce their production costs and so prolong their lives. However, many such technological changes serve to limit the lives of products, shortening the product life cycle and speeding the onset of decline as new products supersede existing products. Furthermore, rapid changes in consumer tastes may render a particular product obsolete after only a short time, as with, for example, fashion products. Consequently, a company's product development policy needs to maintain a constant stream of new products over time if it is to succeed in meeting its growth and profitability goals. Product range strategy should provide for launching new products and deleting old ones so as to avoid having a disproportionate number of products at any one stage of their lives. Indeed, firms may deliberately follow a strategy of 'planned obsolescence', bringing out a continuous stream of new products as a means of increasing their total sales by inducing customers to replace products more frequently.

Product range

A basic decision facing the firm is the number of products and individual brands it intends to sell. Depending upon the firm's degree of specialization or diversification its product range may be classified as follows:

1 *Product line* or product class: a number of closely related products. The products in a line may serve a particular consumer segment or price range, or may be used together by the consumer, or may employ common distribution outlets. For example, a motor car supplier such as Ford offers a number of different versions of a particular model/'brand' of car, say, the Fiesta (differentiated by engine size, trim accessories etc.), within a limited price band designated in box 10.2 as 'basic', 'de luxe' and 'super de luxe'. Alternatively, a kitchenware supplier may market together as a product line such items as food mixers, toasters and kettles.

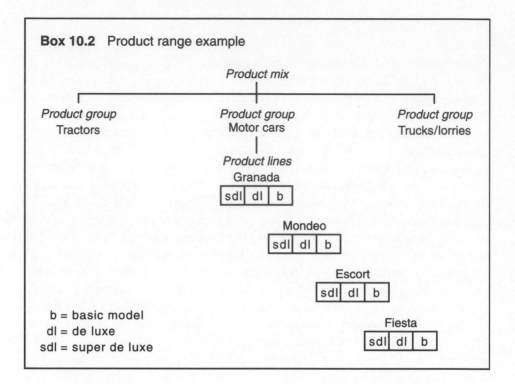

Box 10.2 Product range example

2 *Product group* or product family: a combination of individual product lines which together constitute a firm's product offering to a particular market. A motor car supplier such as Ford, for instance, offers a number of different car models (Granada, Mondeo, Escort and Fiesta) to serve different segments of the motor car market (see box 10.2).

3 *Product mix:* all the product groups and product lines which together constitute a firm's total product offering. The firm's product range might be closely related or very diverse depending upon the spread of the firm's business interests. Ford's product mix for instance, consists primarily of motor cars, trucks and tractors, whilst a more diversified company such as Hanson markets bricks, food products, dry batteries and many other different products (see chapter 4, box 4.1).

Product strategy requires the firm to consider its *product width,* the number of different product lines it offers, and its *product depth,* the number of variants of a product offered by the firm in each of its product lines. How many variants of a product a supplier markets will depend on the degree to which the market is segmented and the number of product variants offered by competitors. In making product variety decisions the firm must consider how to position its brands so as to serve its target market segments without excessive duplication of brands in any segment, and the additional costs of producing and marketing small volumes of many varieties with consequent loss of standardization economies. By offering a number of brands, suppliers may be able to expand their sales and offer a comprehensive range of brands to compete against rivals. However, extensive brand proliferation poses a danger that the firm may 'cannibalize' its own sales, increases in the sales of one particular brand being largely at the expense of its other brands rather than taking sales from rivals' brands.

A firm's product range can be affected by its own production technology where, for example, producing its main products generates a by-product from the common production process which it may choose to market alongside its main products. Thus, for example, oil refiners producing petrol from crude oil also produce by-products such as tar and creosote. Additionally, a firm may choose to buy in products which it does not manufacture itself to augment its product range to obtain the marketing benefits of being able to offer a 'full' product line. In some cases it may be possible to capitalize on consumer awareness of, and loyalty towards, a firm's established brands in order to gain rapid consumer approval and acceptance of new or modified products ('brand transference').

Over time, a firm will need to modify its product range to reflect changing demand conditions. This could involve the alteration of an existing product to update it and improve its competitiveness in existing market segments or to modify it to serve new market segments. Where technological change is rapid or where consumer tastes are changing rapidly, appropriate product modifications may be necessary to extend its life. More radically, instead of updating products the firm may withdraw a product from the market as part of a 'product rationalization' programme. It may withdraw a product because demand for it has fallen to the extent that it is no longer profitable to sell, or the firm may decide to withdraw a number of products from its product range in order to cut costs or focus its marketing efforts more narrowly.

New product development

The imperative to develop new products involves both pro-active and reactive motives. Development of a new product which embodies unique features serves to undermine the position of competing products, creating differentiation advantages which the innovator can exploit in the form of premium prices. Although it may be possible for a firm to 'buy in' the latest technology and products from other firms through licensing deals, this may represent a poor substitute in competitive terms for the establishment of the firm's 'internalized' pool of skills and experience; i.e. it is the difference between the firm being able to assume the position of product leader in the industry as opposed to that of 'me-too' follower. More defensively, firms are forced to develop new brands as changing tastes or technology undermine their existing products if they are to continue to survive (see box 10.3).

Product life cycle   Products typically follow a characteristic pattern of product development of introduction, growth, maturity, saturation and decline described as the *'product life cycle'* (see figure 10.5). Given the dynamic nature of product competition in conditions of rapid techno-logical change, a company's product development policy needs to main-tain a constant stream of new products over time if it is to succeed in meeting its growth and profitability goals. Product range strategy should provide for launching new products and deleting old ones from the range to maintain a balanced portfolio of products, thus avoiding having a disproportionate number of products at any one stage of their lives. If the company has too many products in the maturity phase then its sales growth will suffer, whilst too many products at the launch phase involves cash flow difficulties in financing a number of product launches simul-taneously. Rather, the company's marketing plan must provide for a regulated process of new product launches with new products, such as B and C in figure 10.5 growing as other products like A begin to decline. In addition it may be possible to modify an existing product such as A in figure 10.5 in order to extend its life cycle as depicted in the figure. The marketing plan should also regulate product deaths, phasing out declining products to release resources which can be devoted to newer, more active products.

Generation of new products   The generation of new products typically requires the commitment of resources by firms to scientific research (both 'pure' and 'applied') and the refinement and modification of re-search ideas and prototypes aimed at the ultimate development of com-mercially viable processes and products. Thus R & D is concerned both with invention (the act of discovering new methods and techniques of manufacture and new products) and innovation (the task of bringing these inventions to the market-place).

Invention is often an inspirational act, and studies have shown that the large firm with its well-equipped laboratories and research teams has been no more successful than the individual inventor working alone with minimal facilities (see box 10.4). Innovation, however, is usually very resource-intensive and the substantial capital outlays required to pur-sue development work, coupled with a high risk of failure to come up

Box 10.3   Product development in the UK coffee market

	Nestlé	General Foods	Brooke Bond
1939	L Nescafé		
1947		GF acquires Alfred Bird & Sons	
1954		L Maxwell House	
1955	L Blend 37		
1960			
1962			
1965	L Gold Blend		L Crown Cup
1970	R Granulated Nescafé	R Maxwell House Granulated	
1971			
1972		L Mellow Birds	L Brazilian Blend
1973	L Fine Blend		
1974			
1975	L Nescoré		
1976			L Coffee Time
1977	L Elevenses		
1978	L Gold Blend Decaff.	L Brlm	
1979		GF acquires HAG AG	
1980			
1981	R Nescafé	L Café Hag for general distribution	
1982	L Good Day		L Red Mountain R Brazilian Choice (Brazilian Blend)
1983			
1984	L Gold Blend R&G	L Master Blend R&G	
1985	W Good Day L Alta Rica/Cap Colombie		
1986	L Nescafé decaff. R Blend 37/Gold Blend	L Master Blend (Light & Rich)	
1987	L Blend 37 R&G	GF acquires Kenco Coffee	R Red Mountain
1988		L Kenco Reg. & Decaff. W Master Blend Light Roast	L Red Mountain decaff.
1989	Nescoré becomes granular decaffeinated	L Maxwell House decaff.	W Coffee Time
1990		L Maxwell House Classic	L Café Mountain

L = Launch   R = Relaunch   W = Withdrawal
Source: Soluble Coffee Report, Monopolies and Mergers Commission, 1991

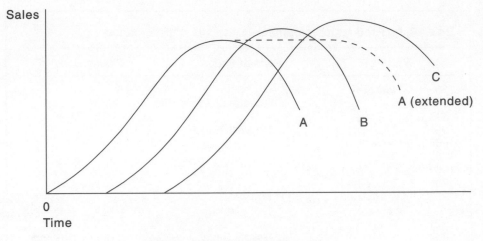

Figure 10.5   Product life cycles

with a marketable product, tend to favour the larger business which is able to cross-subsidize R & D out of profits from existing products and also pool risks. Nonetheless, in many industries small innovative firms continue to coexist alongside large firms as in, for example, computer software and electronics.

From an organizational point of view, R & D activities may be performed within a separate department but with links to the main operating divisions of the firm. Alternatively, a more 'customized' approach may be preferred involving the decentralization of R & D and a close integration of R & D work with the firm's on-going production and marketing operations.

New product development involves a number of steps as indicated in figure 10.6. New product ideas can arise from two broad sources:

1   product concepts based on ideas for new products generated by the firm's own marketing or production staff, or ideas from customers or suppliers;
2   product technology generated by the firm's R & D department or licensed from outside the firm.

Product ideas arising from either of the above sources are then subjected to an initial product screening which explores their viability in terms of possible consumer acceptance, technological feasibility and likely cost. Product ideas which seem viable in terms of this initial screening justify further development expenditures and proceed to the next phase. This phase involves:

Box 10.4   Major inventions in the period 1880–1965, classified by source

* Acrylic fibres: Orlon, etc.
* Air conditioning
* Automatic transmissions
* Bakelite
* Ball-point pen
* Catalytic cracking of petroleum
* Cellophane
  Cellophane tape
* Chromium plating
* Cinerama
  Continuous casting of steel
  Continuous hot-strip rolling
* Cotton picker
  Crease-resisting fabric
* Cyclotron
  DDT
  Diesel electric railway traction
* Domestic gas refrigeration
  Duco lacquers
* Electric precipitation
* Electron microscope
  Fluorescent lighting
  Freon refrigerants
* Gyrocompass
* Hardening of liquid fats
* Helicopter
* Insulin
* Jet engine
* Kodachrome
  Krilium
  Long-playing record

* Magnetic recording
  Methyl methacrylate polymers:
    Perspex, etc.
  Modern artificial lighting
  Neoprene
  Nylon and Perlon
* Penicillin
* 'Polaroid' Land Camera
  Polyethylene
* Power steering
* Quick freezing
  Radar
* Radio
  Rockets
* Safety razor
* Self-winding wrist-watch
  Shell moulding
  Silicones
  Stainless steels
* Streptomycin
* Sultzer loom
  Synthetic detergents
* Synthetic light polarizer
  Television
  'Terylene' polyester fibre
  Tetraethyl lead
* Titanium
  Transistor
  Tungsten carbide
* Xerography
* Zip fastener

* By individuals
Source: Jewkes et al. (1969)

1   further testing of the product concept to gauge its consumer accept-
    ability, perhaps using consumer discussion groups and questionnaire
    field research;
2   product design to make product prototypes and test them in a lab-
    oratory situation.

The results of these two processes will then be subjected to further
screening on marketing, technology and cost grounds, and a product

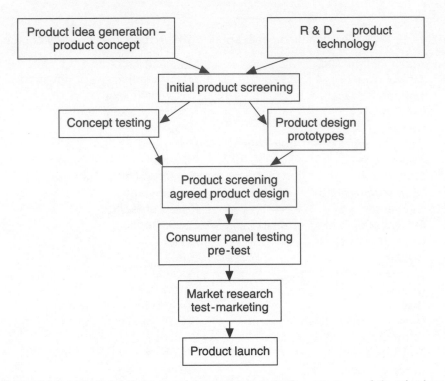

Figure 10.6 New product development: steps in the process of developing a new product

design will be agreed for product ideas which survive the second screening. In order to test further both consumer acceptability and the operating efficiency of the product design, prototypes may be distributed to a consumer test panel for their views of the product. Feedback from this pre-test can then be used to make final modifications to the product design if the basic design proves to be broadly acceptable.

Finally, the firm may undertake marketing research into the potential market for the designed product, establish pilot production facilities for it and 'test-market' it in a limited geographical area in order to gauge consumer reaction. If test-marketing proves successful then full-scale production facilities will be created and a full product launch undertaken, backed up by appropriate advertising and sales promotion.

A very high proportion of new product ideas are eliminated by the firm through its screening processes. Despite this screening only a small proportion of those surviving new products which are launched succeed in establishing themselves in the market.

Patent protection The high-risk nature of new product development and the considerable expenditures involved in generating a limited number of successful new products makes it imperative for the firm to protect the 'uniqueness' of its new products against imitation. In many cases this is done by the innovator securing a patent or copyright in respect of their invention. In the UK, for example, under the Copyright, Designs and Patents Act 1988, the Patent Office can grant a patentee a monopoly to make, use or sell the invention for a maximum of twenty years from the date on which the patent was first filed. In order to obtain a patent approval, inventors are required to supply full details of the invention to the Patent Office and satisfy it that the invention contains original features and that it has a demonstrable industrial application.

Patents registered in one country may be valid in other countries if filed in a country which is party to a reciprocal treaty. The UK, for example, is a member of the thirteen-country European Patent Convention (EPC) which allows inventors to obtain patent rights in the EPC countries by filing a single European patent application. In addition, a company can apply simultaneously for patent protection in many other countries under their particular patent rules.

The protection given by a patent is not usually enforced by the patent-granting authorities. Thus it is the responsibility of patentees to look after their rights by detecting whether someone else is infringing them and then seeking redress for infringement through the courts. A benefit of patent protection is that firms may be able to charge high prices and have low costs, i.e. be in both of Porter's generic strategic 'boxes'.

Accelerating product development Increasing globalization of markets and products, and rapidly advancing technology, have shortened product life cycles in many industries and emphasized the importance of *rapid* new product development as a key factor in achieving competitive advantage. In order to sustain technological advantage in the face of accelerated global diffusion of technology a firm needs to structure its product development programmes appropriately.

First, it may need to run in parallel the phases of the design and development process, not only of new products but also of the machines which will make them and the components and systems which input into them. Coordination of this kind serves to get new products onto the market more quickly than traditional, sequential R & D efforts, where much time is wasted in designing and redesigning new products to achieve the performance, manufacturability and cost criteria as they proceed from research to production planning etc.

Second, the firm may need to organize interdisciplinary project teams involving functional specialists from design, engineering, production, costing and marketing in order to improve collaboration in developing a new product rapidly. Third, it may need to adopt an incremental approach to innovation, limiting the degree of product change from one generation to the next so as to make product development and production start-up easier and speedier to manage compared with the processes involved in starting up a radically different product.

Finally, firms need to tailor their product development strategies to the particular competitive and technological situations of their company and industry, but should generally avoid following a single product development formula. In adopting appropriate product development formulae firms need to avoid, on the one hand, hasty development programmes which compromise the performance of the new product and, on the other hand, painstakingly slow development which is likely to miss out on opportunities in fast-moving markets. These various organizational changes collectively serve to compress the time needed for new product development, making 'time management' a key competitive performance variable. (Stalk and Hout (1990).)

Pricing Strategy

Product price is often considered to be one of the most important of the marketing-mix variables since it alone generates revenues and profits, other variables such as advertising being, by contrast, elements of cost.

Pricing objectives and methods

The firm's pricing strategy will depend upon its pricing objectives and firms may adopt a number of pricing goals, including:

1   pricing to achieve a target return on investment;
2   pricing to achieve stabilization of prices and margins;
3   pricing to reflect product differentiation;
4   pricing to match competition;
5   pricing to maintain and expand market share.

These objectives will determine the prices which the firm sets and the target profit margins it aims for. In setting prices a firm may use a number of pricing methods. Three basic pricing methods may be distinguished:

1   *Cost-based pricing* which relates the price of a product to the costs of producing and distributing it.
2   *Demand-based pricing* which relates the price of a product to the intensity of total demand for it and acknowledges differences in demand intensities between sub-groups of buyers.
3   *Competition-based pricing* which relates the price of a product to the prices charged by rivals.

In practice, firms use a combination of these methods in setting their prices.

In considering the pricing strategy and methods which it might adopt in relation to its various products, a firm needs to consider a number of elements, in particular changing demand patterns and opportunities for price discrimination.

The product life cycle and pricing

A firm may vary its prices over time as demand for its products changes as a result of business cycles, charging higher prices when demand is strong and shading down prices in conditions of weak demand. More specifically, particular products will be subject to variations in demand over their product life cycle with implications for pricing. High *'skimming'* *prices* may be charged for a new product in the early launch phase of its life cycle where high-income, pioneering customers are attracted primarily by the novel features of the product and where premium prices often reinforce the quality image of the untried product so that demand is price-inelastic. By contrast, in the later growth and maturity phases of a product's life cycle, as the product becomes more familiar and available, buying patterns for the product tend to become more price-sensitive so that firms often charge a low market *'penetration' price* to secure growing sales and a higher market share.

Price discrimination

Firms may also practise price discrimination, varying prices between types of customers, the location of customers, the time of purchase and versions of a product. Customer-based pricing recognizes the different price-sensitivity or bargaining power of potential buyers and seeks to capitalize on this by charging whatever price particular customers are prepared to pay. Such price discrimination is worth while when the price-sensitivity or price-elasticity of demand in each market is different.

There are two key conditions which make price discrimination possible:

First, it must not be possible to move products easily from the high-price market to the low-price market – otherwise customers or traders could buy up products in the low-price market and resell them in the higher price market. This makes goods with high transport costs particularly susceptible to discrimination.

Second, it must not be possible for consumers to move easily from one market to another, otherwise they will simply shop in the cheaper market. Branding and styling differences between products can serve to discourage customers from such cross-shopping.

Price discrimination between market segments may be practised in the following circumstances:

1   By *type of customer*. For example, in pricing theatre tickets, special low prices may be charged to low-income consumer segments such as students and pensioners. In the supply of personal services such as taxation or legal advice, the supplier can set a separate price for each client on the basis of his detailed knowledge of that client's financial status. The power of particular consumer groups as sources of demand may also influence supplier's prices through the granting of favourable discounts, rebates etc. on large bulk-buying orders.

2   By *location of customer*. For example, a firm may distinguish between the prices charged to domestic customers and those charged to foreign customers, sometimes charging a higher price to foreign customers to reflect the higher distribution costs incurred or uncertainties about domestic currency receipts caused by exchange rate movements, or to exploit the higher incomes and lower price-sensitivity of foreign buyers. Alternatively, foreign customers may be charged less where competitive conditions are more intense. In other cases firms may simplify their pricing arrangements by means of a 'uniform delivered price system' which involves charging the same price to all customers irrespective of their location (e.g. post office letters). Alternatively, customers may be grouped into a number of delivery zones and a common price charged to all customers in each zone. Such 'basing point price systems' involve some cross-subsidization of delivery costs between customers in the interests of maximizing the firm's total sales.

3   By *time of demand*. Different prices may be charged for a product on different days of the week or at different times of the day. The timing of demand is particularly important for firms providing services which cannot be 'stored', since here the firm must decide the maximum production capacity to offer in order to cater for peak demand and may thus have considerable excess capacity at off-peak times. In the case of railway services, for example, full fare prices may be charged to commuters during 'rush hour' times with lower off-peak prices being charged for travel at other times. Charges for electricity, theatre tickets etc. may be varied similarly.

4   By the *type of product*. A firm producing a number of groups of similar products (e.g. a car producer supplying luxury saloon cars like the Ford Granada, medium saloons like the Ford Mondeo, light saloons like the Ford Escort and small cars like the Ford Fiesta) needs to pay careful attention to relativities *between* these product lines. In addition *within* a particular product line like, for example, the Ford Fiesta, the firm must establish price relativities between

various versions of the product – the basic, de luxe and super de luxe versions.

Appropriate price relativities between and within product lines are complicated by possible overlaps between product lines like that, for example, between the super de luxe version of the Ford Fiesta and the basic model of the Ford Escort. The firm may create additional flexibility in matching its product range with customer requirements by offering appropriately priced 'optional extras' for each model. The final set of prices charged will seek to exploit the relative sophistication, quality and cost of each version and model *vis-à-vis* equivalent competitors' offerings and the prices they are charging.

Other examples of price differentials related to the type of product offered include: whether the product is sold as part of original equipment or as a replacement part; differential packaging of hard- and soft-backed books; and differential theatre ticket prices for seats in different parts of the theatre.

Consumer perceptions and price

Finally, in considering its pricing a firm must pay particular attention to the effect which a product's price has upon consumers' perceptions of the product. This has a number of dimensions including:

1   the charging of very high prices for certain (generally high-quality) consumer products to convey an impression of product exclusiveness. High prices may appeal to particular high-income customers who wish to possess the product as a status symbol ('conspicuous consumption');
2   the charging of high prices for technologically sophisticated consumer products in order to convey an impression of superior product quality and performance. This may play an important part in the buying decision when consumers are ignorant about the comparative properties of the brands of the product facing them, and thus use price as an indicator of quality;
3   the charging of relatively low prices for frequently purchased and familiar products so as to create or reinforce an impression of value for money.

Firms cannot make their pricing decisions in isolation but must consider the prices being charged by their competitors, and whether they want to adopt an aggressive pricing stance towards competitors or set prices broadly in line with those of competitors. In addition, the firm needs to consider its pricing in relation to the nature of its products and those other elements of the marketing mix which are outlined below.

Promotional Strategy

Promotional strategy involves the firm selecting the means of marketing its products. A firm can deploy various methods to inform prospective customers of the nature and attributes of its products and to persuade them to buy and repeat-purchase those products. The promotional mix is made up of advertising, sales promotion, merchandising, packaging, personal selling and public relations.

Advertising involves the placement of advertisements in the media (commercial television, newspapers etc.); sales promotion embraces such things as money-off-packs and free trial samples; merchandising is concerned with in-store promotions and displays; packaging assists in emphasizing the attractiveness of products; personal selling involves visits by a firm's sales representatives to prospective customers. Finally, public relations is aimed at promoting the company's image in general to establish a favourable public attitude towards the firm and its products.

In practice, most firms will use a combination of these methods to sell their products, varying the mix according to the product and buyer characteristics of a particular market or market segment. For example, low-price, frequently bought consumer goods like tea are mostly promoted by mass-media advertising and sales promotions, whilst high-price industrial or consumer goods such as cars are promoted largely by personal selling.

Once a firm's product development strategy has created a product which is consistent in terms of quality and performance then it will seek to help customers to identify this particular product in order to ensure a strong demand for it. This will generally be achieved by securing an effective 'brand' identity for the product which distinguishes it from similar products offered by competitors. Brand identities are usually based on a name, term, sign, symbol or design and once established they may be given legal protection against unauthorized use through trade marks and copyrights. When new product brands have been established, consumer goodwill towards the brand can be reinforced by using appropriate promotion to generate 'brand loyalty'.

Product differentiation based upon product 'uniqueness', and underpinned by brand promotion, can often be preferable to attempts to win customers by price competition. The attraction of product differentiation competition over price competition lies in the fact that whereas price cuts, for example, can be quickly and completely matched by competitors, a successful advertising campaign or the introduction of an innovatory product is less easily imitated. Moreover, whereas price competition lowers firms' profitability, product differentiation tends to preserve and even enhance profit returns. In particular, the establishment of product uniqueness may allow firms to command premium prices over competitors' offerings. Finally, product differentiation may serve to act as a barrier to entry thereby protecting existing market shares against new competition (see below).

Opportunities for successful differentiation will depend largely upon the intrinsic qualities and attributes of the firm's brand but may also be swayed by promotional efforts.

Methods of promotion

Advertising Advertising provides a means by which a firm attempts to increase sales of its brand of good or service by communicating with buyers, informing them of the nature and attributes of its brand and persuading them to buy it in preference to competitors' brands.

Advertising is undertaken in a variety of ways, including the use of mass-media channels such as television, national newspapers and magazines, posters etc., and more targeted approaches through 'special interest' magazines and trade journals, and regional and local newspapers.

Although some advertising is largely concerned with providing buyers with information about the product, the majority of advertising is 'persuasive' in orientation. Persuasive advertising aims to encourage consumers to purchase products, and the skill of advertising copywriters lies in designing advertisements which are visually attractive and which appeal to deep-seated consumer motivations, both physical and psychological. If advertisements appeal sufficiently to consumer motives they will encourage repeat-buying of the product, thereby establishing brand loyalty and increasing or maintaining the firm's market share. Individual brand spend on advertising and sales promotion can vary enormously with brand leaders accounting for the majority of these expenditures (see box 10.5).

The selection of the advertising medium will depend upon the market or market segment which is being targeted and the relative costs and effectiveness of using different media. For example, in respect of specialized industrial buyers advertisements may be placed in appropriate trade/professional journals. On the other hand, if large numbers of final consumers are being targeted it may be more cost-effective to use the mass media which, although more expensive in absolute terms, actually costs less per potential customer reached.

Sales promotion Sales promotion is often used alongside advertising and personal selling to increase sales of the firm's products.

In the case of consumer goods, whilst advertising seeks to develop and sustain sales by creating brand loyalty over the long run, sales

Box 10.5   Advertising and promotion expenditure by major coffee suppliers, 1985–1989

		£ million					
	Date launched	1985	1986	1987	1988	1989 television advertising	1989 total advertising and promotion	Cumulative 1985–9
Nestlé		14.7	19.3	25.0	30.3	15.3	30.8	120.1
Nescafé	1939	9.3	12.3	15.7	18.4	6.9	18.5	74.2
Blend 37	1955	0.7	1.0	1.3	1.3	1.4	1.8	6.2
Gold Blend	1965	4.2	5.1	6.4	8.3	6.6	8.4	32.4
Fine Blend	1973	0.3	0.5	0.6	0.6	–	0.4	2.5
Nescoré	1975	0.1	0.1	0.1	–	–	–	0.3
Elevenses	1977	0.1	0.1	0.1	0.1	–	–	0.4
Alta Rica/Cap Colombie	1985	–	0.2	0.3	0.6	0.4	0.8	1.9
Non-brand		–	–	0.4	0.9	–	0.9	2.2
General Foods		10.8	19.2	21.1	28.3	17.5	29.9	109.3
Maxwell House	1954	8.1	11.4	14.2	16.8	8.2	14.5	67.3
Café Hag	1979	1.5	1.9	2.2	4.7	4.1	5.9	16.2
Mellow Bird's	1972	1.0	1.8	1.8	1.8	0.5	1.3	7.8
Kenco	1988	0.0	0.0	0.0	2.7	4.7	5.6	8.3
Master Blend	1986	0.0	4.0	2.9	2.2	0.0	0.3	9.5
Brooke Bond		2.2	3.2	4.4	6.3	2.7	5.8	21.9
Red Mountain	1982	1.4	2.7	4.4	6.1	2.7	5.6	20.2
Other		0.7	0.5	0.1	0.2	–	0.2	1.7

All figures may not total exactly due to rounding.
Source: Soluble Coffee Report, Monopolies and Mergers Commission, 1991

promotions are largely used in short, sharp bursts to support, for example, the introduction of a new brand, to renew interest in a product whose sales have fallen and, periodically, to stimulate extra demand for a well-established brand. A variety of techniques are used for these purposes, including: free trial samples, money-off packs, 'two-for-the-price-of-one' offers, extra quantities for the same price, product competitions offering prizes, coupons offering gifts, trading stamps, in-store demonstrations, point-of-sale displays etc.

These methods can succeed only if the product being promoted is widely available for consumers to buy, so that it is important also to encourage retailers to stock it. This is done using various trade promotions including special cash offers on purchases, free extra quantities, gifts and prizes.

In the case of industrial products, trade fairs, exhibitions and demonstrations are used to back up the most commonly used mode, personal selling.

Merchandising   Merchandising involves in-store promotional activity by manufacturers or retailers at the point of sale, designed to stimulate sales. Such merchandising makes considerable use of point-of-sale display materials and special buying incentives such as free trial samples, money-off packs and gifts.

Packaging   Packaging can be used as a means of selling a product as well as a means of physically protecting the product. Functionally, packaging protects products whilst they are in transit and being stored, enables products to be sold in convenient retail packs in standard weights and measures, and identifies the contents of the package by means of labelling.

In addition, packaging may play an important part in marketing a product, particularly when products are being sold on a self-service basis. The attractiveness of the colour and design of the package is important in attracting the attention of the buyer. In addition, the use of brand names on packaging reinforces the perceptions of the brand at the point of sale.

Personal selling   Personal selling is a means of increasing the sales of a firm's product which involves direct contact between the firm's sales representatives and prospective customers. Unlike passive means of communicating with buyers such as advertising, face-to-face meetings with customers facilitate a more pro-active approach, with sales representatives being able to explain fully the details of a product, advise and answer customer queries about it and, where appropriate, demonstrate the workings of the product.

Public relations   Public relations is a more general means of promoting a business's company image with a view to encouraging customers to buy its products. Public relations management of news about the company's activities and sponsorship of sport and the arts etc. represent an indirect way of building up customer goodwill towards the company's products.

Branding and competitive advantage

Once a firm has cultivated a strongly entrenched brand image for a product through cumulative investments in advertising and sales promotion, this brand can become an important source of competitive advantage to the firm. Indeed, it may be possible in some cases to create a situation where the brand name becomes synonymous with the product offering, as was the case, for example, with Hoover vacuum cleaners. The cost to competitors of establishing an equally prominent brand to challenge a well-established brand through conventional advertising and promotion gives established brands a considerable value to their owners. In such cases, competitors may seek to buy a business largely to acquire its brands rather than its physical assets; e.g. Nestlé's take-over of Rowntree Mackintosh. An additional advantage of having a strong brand name is the potential it offers to capitalize on consumer awareness of, and loyalty towards, the firm's established brands in order to gain rapid consumer approval and acceptance of some other product offered by the firm. *'Brand extension'* or *'brand transference'* may be deployed to move the firm into other market segments or new markets. For instance, Hoover as a well-known manufacturer of vacuum cleaners was able to use its brand name to facilitate its entry into the washing machine market. Such strategies must be used with caution as too much brand-stretching may undermine the original product's brand image if the new products to which it is attached prove to be unsuccessful.

Place/Distribution Strategy

The organization and efficiency of a firm's distribution can be an important source of competitive advantage insofar as it serves to ensure widespread distribution of its products to consumers and distributes them quickly, securely and with minimum cost.

The distribution channels or routes used in the physical distribution of a product from the producer to final buyers typically involve three interrelated operations, manufacturing, wholesaling and retailing (see chapter 3). These operations may be undertaken separately by firms which specialize in a particular stage of the distribution chain or they may be combined and undertaken by one firm as an integrated operation. Small firms generally have insufficient volume and resources to undertake national or international distribution of their products and thus may need to use independent wholesalers and retailers or sales agents to perform distribution tasks. Where firms are large enough to internalize all the distribution functions then they may be able to achieve better control and coordination of the marketing and movement of their products. For example, where a firm uses sales agents to obtain new customers then it may be difficult to get agents to follow strictly the firm's marketing strategies. Specifically, agents may be tempted to go for volume sales and sell a firm's products at a discount to boost their sales commission even though this cheap-price policy may undermine the firm's brand image.

Customer Services

Whilst all elements of the marketing mix are concerned with customers and their needs, a firm's marketing and technical staff who deal with customer service provide the most direct interface with customers. Customer services can involve offering pre-sales services, such as providing advice to customers on their product needs; and after-sales services, such as repair and maintenance back-up and the replacement of faulty products or parts. Customer services are an important means of attracting new customers and reinforcing brand loyalty among existing customers.

Specifically, guarantees and warranties covering replacement, refund or repair of defective products help to assure buyers about the product's expected quality and reliability.

Additionally, customer services can provide valuable feedback about customers' reactions to, and satisfaction with, the firm's products.

Marketing Intelligence

The effective integration of the marketing-mix elements discussed above needs to be underpinned by an appropriate marketing intelligence system. In formulating marketing plans it is important that firms gather information about developments in their market environments. Marketing research involves monitoring the firm's market environment on a regular basis. Such research provides intelligence about competitors and their pricing and marketing policies, effects of proposed legislation on company brands, the potential impact of economic changes such as total consumer spending and social trends such as environmental awareness. In addition, marketing research can be used to obtain specific information about consumer attitudes and perceptions about an existing product. This information could then be used to modify the product or change the marketing mix used to promote it.

Various techniques may be employed to gather market intelligence. *Field studies* may be undertaken amongst samples of the population employing personally conducted or postal questionnaires, telephone and personal interviews, and group surveys. *Focus groups* may be used which involve detailed discussion amongst small groups of invited respondents. *Desk research* can be employed using secondary published information and reports from government or other sources. Finally, information about existing products or prototypes can be gained by recruiting *panels of consumers* who report regularly on their experience of using products; by setting up controlled *experiments* to test consumers' reactions to products and advertising messages; and by *direct observation* of customers who are buying or using a product or service.

Marketing research can be used to identify market trends; to find out about market characteristics; to forecast market potential; to analyse market share; to find a market segment; and to test consumer acceptance of new or existing products. Where a firm develops a superior intelligence-gathering system, it will have a comparative advantage in seeking out new market opportunities and identifying possible threats to the sales of its existing products. In this regard marketing intelligence can help to improve the effectiveness of a firm's marketing-mix elements in securing customers.

Product Life Cycles

Life cycles and the marketing mix

The proportions in which the various elements of the marketing mix are combined must be carefully considered in the context of the nature of the firm's products and customers, and the mix will need to be adapted over time to reflect changes in the product and customer perceptions of it. Specifically, since products tend to follow a characteristic life cycle sales pattern of the type described in figure 10.5, they will require different blends of marketing instruments at each phase of their lives.

The kinds of consumers who buy a product can be divided broadly into groups according to the speed with which they adapt to new products. The people who first buy new consumer goods are typically young, well educated, well-off and socially and geographically mobile ('*pioneering customers*'); by contrast, the people who are last to buy new consumer goods ('*laggards*') tend to be older, less educated, poorer and fixed in their job and residence. In appealing to these different kinds of consumers firms will tend to vary the components of the marketing mix which they stress.

Consider the case of a new consumer durable product. In the introductory phase of the cycle where sales are predominantly to first-time pioneering customers it is important to emphasize product quality and performance attributes in order to overcome consumer resistance to trying an unknown product. Where the product is particularly complex the use of guarantees can assist in reassuring customers of product quality. In addition, a high level of personal selling may be required to provide information about the product at the time of purchase, and an after-sales service may be required to deal with any customer queries or problems. In order to create consumer awareness of the product extensive advertising may be necessary, although much of this advertising copy will be concerned with providing information about the new product and its benefits. At this phase of the product's life, firms may adopt a high market-skimming price to exploit the novel features of the product by charging a premium price to high-income, price-insensitive pioneer buyers.

By contrast, for example, in the maturity phase of the life cycle it may be more important to emphasize other aspects of the marketing mix. By this phase usually other competitors have entered the market making similar products and the market has expanded to embrace a wider range of customers with more modest incomes and life styles. By now sales are dominated by repeat purchases of the product by existing customers who see the product as a familiar 'commodity'. At this stage a heavy emphasis may be placed on competitive advertising and sales promotion, aimed at pursuading customers to purchase a particular brand of the product. In some cases price competition may become more acute as competing firms strive to achieve a high market share and where the mass of consumers are likely to be more price-sensitive.

Industry, product and brand life cycles

In practice many products have life cycles which differ markedly from the pattern shown in figure 10.5, some having life cycles which encompass only a few months, others having life cycles which last many decades, whilst yet others do not embody all of the phases. In this context it is important to distinguish between the industry life cycle, the product life cycle and the individual brand's life cycle. This is illustrated in figure 10.7 for the UK household soaps/detergents industry. The industry grew fairly rapidly during the middle decades of the twentieth century as a result of changes in population and the technology of washing clothes, but has grown much more slowly in recent years. Over this period a number of product innovations have occurred, including the switch from soap flakes to synthetic-based powders in the 1950s; the introduction of enzyme-based (biological) detergents and 'low suds' detergents suitable for use with front-loading washing machines in the late 1960s; and the launch of liquid detergents in the late 1980s. Each of these has followed its own product life cycle as shown in the figure. Persil, one of the original branded soap-based powders introduced by Unilever in the earlier part of the twentieth century, was one of the important brands in the soap powder product market, competing with Proctor and Gamble's Fairy Snow. The introduction of synthetic detergents was led by P & G's Tide launched in 1950 and Daz (1953), in competition with Unilever's Surf and Omo detergents (launched, respectively, in 1952 and 1954).

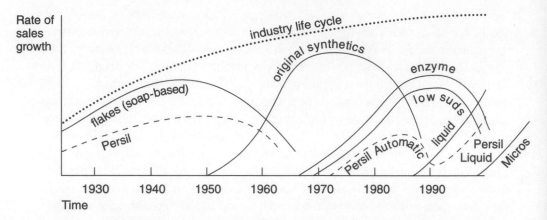

Figure 10.7   Life cycles for UK household soaps/detergents

Persil continued as the leading powder in the now rapidly declining soap powder product market. P & G also led the introduction of enzyme-based detergent products with the launch in 1968 of its Ariel brand in competition with Unilever's Radiant brand, and this led to further falls in sales of soap powders in general and Persil in particular. However, in 1969 Unilever brought out a new product, a low suds detergent launched under the brand of Persil Automatic, followed by P & G's brands Bold and Ariel Automatic. More recently, both companies have introduced a new liquid detergent product and 'concentrated' powders and liquids, again capitalizing on existing brand names by launching such brands as Ariel Liquid, Daz Liquid and Persil Liquid. Thus, it can be seen that in the overall context of a changing industry life cycle a series of new product innovation has undermined the sales of established products, although in some cases the firms have chosen to practise brand trans-ference, attaching their established brand names such as Persil to a series of products to enhance the acceptability of these new products. In this way it is possible to extend the life of a brand name beyond the product to which it was originally attached. Furthermore, it may be possible to manipulate the marketing mix pro-actively in order to extend the lives of products by modifying the product, adding new product features, or modifying its image. For example, Unilever has been able to extend the life of its original Persil soap powder product through continuous adver-tising despite competition from synthetics etc.

Creating Uniqueness

Achieving product differentiation advantages over competitors requires the firm not only to identify what product attributes and values customers

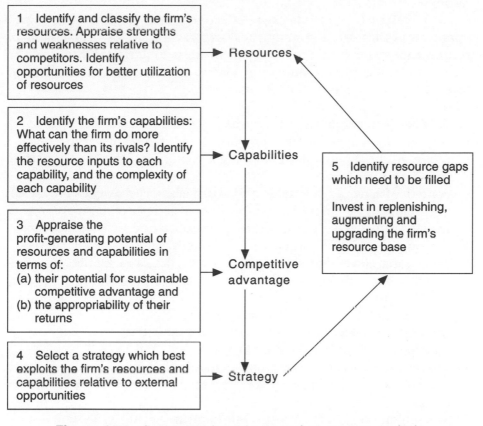

Figure. 10.8   A resource-based approach to strategy analysis
Source: Grant (1991)

demand, but just as crucially to be in a position to *supply* 'uniqueness'. The firm as a 'bundle of internalized resources' must develop a capability to generate and sustain the necessary resources to out-compete rivals in satisfying customer demands. Accessing resources such as basic capital and labour usually is not enough to generate what Porter (1985) calls a 'distinctive competence', i.e. many competitors may have access to funding to build low-cost plants or distribution systems. Thus, 'uniqueness' essentially derives from the skills and capabilities of the firm's personnel as embodied in, for example, proprietary or intellectual property rights, specialized, innovative equipment and products. Grant (1991) has formulated a model, outlined in figure 10.8, which captures the essence of this process.

Identifying and classifying the firm's resources provides a more stable base for defining the firm's identity (i.e. what is the firm's basic business and who are its customers) than an appraisal based solely on market opportunities since these are often volatile. Classification of the firm's resources provides an opportunity to identify the firm's capabilities and assess what the firm can do more effectively than its rivals. The firm's opportunities for creating uniqueness can arise from particular skills or competence in performing any of the business functions. Porter (1985), for example, identifies a number of '*drivers of uniqueness*' over which the firm can exercise control including:

- product features and the performance which the product offers;
- the services which the firm provides (e.g. credit, delivery, repair);
- the intensity of particular marketing activities (e.g. rate of advertising spending);
- content of activities (e.g. type of pre- and after-sales services provided);
- the technology employed in performing an activity (e.g. precision with which products are manufactured, computerized order processing);
- the quality of inputs procured for an activity;
- procedures governing the conduct of particular activities (e.g. frequency of quality control inspections, service procedures, frequency of sales visits to a customer);
- the skill and experience of employees in activities;
- the control procedures used in different activities;
- locations (e.g. with retail stores);
- the degree of vertical integration (which influences a firm's ability to control inputs and intermediate processes).

Differentiation advantage arises from firm-specific skills and know-how, brand reputation and sales and service networks. Such differentiation advantages enable the firm to command premium prices for its products, and as long as the firm can supply uniqueness at a cost which does not exceed the price premium then it should be able to generate 'above-normal' profits from them. The size and persistence of above-normal profits accruing to a firm will depend crucially upon the ability to sustain competitive advantage over time and the extent to which the firm's capabilities can be imitated by rivals. The potential rate at which the firm's competitive advantage is eroded depends upon the particular characteristics of the firm's resources and capabilities. Grant suggests that the *sustainability of competitive advantage* depends upon four major factors:

1   *Durability of resources.* Where rates of technological change are modest, competitive advantage based upon technological leadership may be less vulnerable to encroachment by rivals. In addition, brand reputation may be sustained, with continuous advertising and product upgrading. By contrast, process and brand innovation by rivals may rapidly undermine the value of a firm's resources.

2   *Transparency*. Where it is difficult for competitors to identify and comprehend the precise nature of the firm's competitive advantage, and where it is difficult for other firms to obtain the resources and capabilities to imitate the firm's successful strategy, then the firm's competitive advantage is likely to be long-lived.

3   *Transferability*. Even where rivals are able to identify a firm's sources of competitive advantage they may still find it difficult to acquire the necessary resources to mount a competitive challenge because resources may be geographically immobile, because of imperfect knowledge about the productivity of resources and because firm-specific resources cannot be acquired in the open market.

4   *Replicability*. Where a firm's competitive advantages are based upon complex organizational routines and team-working, it may be difficult for competitors to replicate these advantages.

In the last analysis, the ability of a firm to secure superior profits depends on its ability to protect its competitive advantages through copyrights, patents, brand names, trade secrets etc.

Once a firm has selected a strategy which best exploits its resources and capabilities, it may need to identify any resource 'gaps' which need to be filled by augmenting the firm's resource base.

Strategic Risks of Product Differentiation

From a strategic point of view the benefits of differentiation are that it can attract customers, allow for higher prices and give a competitive edge to a firm's strategy which may be hard for others to emulate. The generic strategy of differentiation is not, however, without dangers:

1   Although differentiation is an important source of advantage, any difference can be imitated to a greater or lesser degree. Firms talk of obtaining a 'position' in the market-place and clearly a product which is patent-protected would be difficult to imitate. However, many firms find their differentiation lead competed away, not through copying but rather by competitors putting a superior product on the market which appeals to the same buying motives of customers.

2   From a marketing point of view customers' preferences change, and where they change appreciably this will undermine the existing differentiation strategy. What was previously valued is now a commonplace. This often gives rise to rapid product innovation in certain industries such as consumer electronics.

3   The basis for differentiation may change as, say, between process and product. In many manufacturing industries it may be difficult to

differentiate the product but the allied production processes may be radically different, giving some companies a marked strategic advantage. This is true in industries such as steel-making, where the differentials arise from production of what is to the market a commodity product.

4   Although it may be attractive to differentiate a product it may also be prohibitively expensive to do so. Firms may be able to offer superior products compared with those offered by competitors but they would not make a sufficient profit to warrant them doing so.

5   The differentiator can be attacked by segmenters or focusers who re-segment the market or find segments with slightly differing needs and thus they can deploy their own strategies of differentiation in smaller market sub-segments. This is often how small firms are able to differentiate their products in order to survive in a market dominated by large companies.

Summary

The present chapter has identified the main ways in which a firm may seek to establish itself as a differentiated supplier offering a 'unique' product. Effective differentiation requires the firm to identify customers and their needs and then to adopt an appropriate mix of marketing instruments which is geared to their needs. The firm can achieve differentiation through its product offerings (range, sophistication etc.); its promotion policies (advertising, sales promotion etc.); its distribution arrangements; its customer services; and its marketing intelligence.

Creating and sustaining competitive advantage through product differentiation requires firms' management both to identify customer demands and to acquire and develop the particular resources and capabilities to satisfy these demands. Successful differentiation strategies enable the firm to become an above-average performer in its chosen markets and insulate it from competitive encroachment by established and potential rivals.

Questions

1   What are the possible advantages and disadvantages of a competitive strategy based on product differentiation?

2   Discuss the view that product differentiation is a superior competitive strategy to cost leadership since the creation of 'product uniqueness' is less easily imitated by competitors.

3   Examine the role of advertising and sales promotion in a differentiation strategy.

4   Examine the implications of the product life cycle for new product development strategy.

5 What factors are likely to be important in determining a firm's product range strategy?

6 Discuss the circumstances in which price discrimination might be an effective policy for a firm.

References

Grant, R. M., 1991. *Contemporary Strategy Analysis*, Blackwell, chapter 7.

Jewkes, J., Sawers, D. and Stillerman, R., 1969. *The Sources of Invention*, Macmillan, 2nd edn.

Porter, M. E., 1980. *Competitive Strategy*, Free Press.

Porter, M. E., 1985. *Competitive Advantage*, Free Press.

Stalk, G. and Hout, T. M., 1990. *Competing Against Time: How Time-Based Strategies Deliver Superior Performance*, Free Press.

Thomas, J. G., 1988. *Strategic Management*, Harp College (US).

Further Reading

George, K. D., Joll, C. and Lynk, E. L., chapters 8 and 9, *Industrial Organization*, Blackwell, 4th edn, 1992.

Grant, R. M. 'The Resource-based Theory of Competitive Advantage: Implications for Strategy Formulation', *California Management Review*, Spring, 1991.

Hay, D. A. and Morris, D. J., chapters 4, 5 and 13, *Industrial Economics and Organization*, Oxford University Press, 2nd edn, 1991.

Luffman, G., Sanderson, S., Lea, E. and Kenny, B., chapter 7, *Business Policy*, Blackwell, 2nd edn, 1991.

Thomson, J. L., chapter 10, *Strategic Management*, Chapman and Hall, 1990.

11
Summary

Core Themes of the Book

The book has addressed two key corporate issues: (1) the strategic direction of the firm and (2) its competitive strategies within the markets it chooses to operate in.

The first of these, *business strategy*, is concerned with the selection of appropriate policies and instruments to achieve a business's objectives. The 'strategic' decision-maker operates in a dynamic business environment, subject to frequent changes in market conditions and where such changes cannot be easily predicted. The decision-maker is faced with a fluid and uncertain economic future and has to formulate appropriate defensive and offensive responses in order to secure and maintain corporate success. The 'strategic' firm consists of a bundle of internalized resources which top management can, at its discretion, deploy between a number of product and geographic markets; over time, it can expand and re-position these resources in accordance with actual and perceived opportunities for profit gain.

Resource deployment can lead the firm in a number of broad directions. It may choose, for example, to pursue *horizontal* expansion in order to secure various cost-savings and to strengthen its market position *vis-à-vis* competitors. Second, the firm could choose to grow *vertically*, integrating backwards to secure sources of supply or forwards to secure outlets for its products in order to improve its efficiency and market security. Third, the firm could choose to *diversify* its activities, changing its product portfolio so as to spread risk, take advantage of growth opportunities and withdraw from unprofitable markets. Each of these three expansion paths could be pursued within the firm's domestic market but increasingly such expansion is likely to be *international* expansion.

The second corporate issue, *competitive strategy*, involves the formulation of plans by a firm aimed at ensuring that the firm is able to meet and beat its competitors in supplying a *particular* market. Competitive strategy constitutes an integral part of overall business strategy formulation (deciding which markets to operate in) since the firm's corporate prosperity depends fundamentally on how well it succeeds in the individual markets making up its business. Thus, the firm must pay specific attention to its immediate market situation. At this level the main concern of competitive strategy is to identify the firm's *own* and its *rivals'* competitive strengths and weaknesses; the possibilities for market *entry* and *exit*; and the nature and strength of the various *forces driving competition* in a market – the bargaining power of suppliers and customers, the threat of new entrants, the threat of substitute products and inter-firm rivalry between established companies.

The key to a successful competitive strategy is then to fully understand what product attributes are demanded by buyers with a view to establishing, operationally, a position of competitive advantage which makes the firm less vulnerable to attack from established competitors and potential new entrants, and less vulnerable to erosion from the direction of buyers, suppliers and substitute products. The two main generic strategies which businesses can adopt are *cost leadership* which emphasizes improving the firm's cost-effectiveness, and *product differentiation* which emphasizes the need to develop product 'uniqueness'.

Critical Success Factors and Businesses' Core Skills

Strategic management is concerned with understanding the environment and the way in which it changes in order to make decisions about the deployment of the businesses resources to produce goods and services for selected markets. Knowledge of the environment and the dynamics of those economic variables which cause change allow a firm to understand those *critical success factors* which it needs in order to be successful. Critical success factors are those elements in a company's strategy which if well identified and managed will lead to success, and if not, will result in failure. Critical success factors represent those elements of strategy which *all* firms in a market need to address in order to gain a competitive advantage and be successful. For example, all football teams know that a major success factor is to attract supporters, all hotels know that success comes from high occupancy levels, and pharmaceutical companies realize that product innovation is a critical element in their success. In a real sense critical success factors are the answer to the question of what a company needs to be good at in order to be successful.

To respond successfully to the critical success factors companies need to develop competencies or core skills. It is the development of these competencies *specific* to the individual firm which results in strategic advantage. Thus a football team may possess a competence in managing its players which is difficult for others to imitate, a hotel chain may be particularly skilled at developing activities which fill beds, e.g. package tours, and a pharmaceutical company may have a strong reputation in a particular therapeutic application such that it attracts better research staff. A list of possible sources of core skills or competencies is shown below. Individual corporate competencies can be deployed by companies in order to gain strategic advantage through the two generic strategies of differentiation and low cost.

Core skills and key resources

Corporate resources
- Corporate image and prestige
- Company size (overcoming entry barriers)
- Government influences
- Flexible and adaptable structure
- Effective R & D
- Effective management information systems

Factors of production and operation
- Benefits of vertical integration
- Materials availability and cost
- Production and process skills
- Experience curve effects
- Flexibility of production equipment
- Processing of by-products
- Buildings and land

Factors of markets and marketing
- Image and prestige
- Benefits of vertical integration
- Efficient distribution and location
- Promotional strength (advertising, public relations, merchandising)
- Sales and after-sales service
- Patent protections
- Marketing research

Factors of finance
- Flexible capital structure
- Total financial strength

Factors of personnel
- Skills and experience of management
- Skills and experience of labour force
- Labour costs
- Trade union relations

Source: Luffman and Reed (1984)

Operationalizing Strategy

Firms need to operationalize the above concepts. They need to discover the appropriate critical success factors. They need to discover their core skills. They need to be aware of the strategic consequences of an environment/skills mismatch.

As indicated in chapter 1 (under the heading 'Strategic Analysis'), a business can conduct a strategic audit by identifying its own strengths and weaknesses and the nature of the environmental threats and opportunities it faces. A framework is given below by way of illustration.

Internal appraisal

The purpose of the internal appraisal is to gain some feeling for the ability of the firm to achieve different strategic alternatives. Such ability stems from the firm's capabilities and resources in its various functional areas. This ability is usually dependent on the firm's activities and resources relative to the strategic alternative pursued (its distinctive competencies) and/or the resources of competitors pursuing the same strategic option (its competitive advantages) rather than on any absolute level of activities or resources.

Such an assessment should be performed for all the firm's activities and resources against both the 'average' of the relevant competitors to determine competitive advantages and the needs of the strategic alternative under consideration to determine distinctive competencies.

Analysis of corporate strengths and weaknesses should be carried out with the key variables of efficiency and effectiveness in mind. Any corporate strength can only be defined in terms of strategic importance – it is no use being good at something unless it contributes to the well-being of the organization.

Where a firm has a strength which is crucially important to its effectiveness, it can be said to have a distinctive competency in that area. The internal appraisal is, of course, essential to ideas for future strategy by matching strengths to future environmental opportunities, whilst avoiding threats and correcting weaknesses.

External appraisal

The purpose of the external appraisal is to assess the firm's various market environments and the opportunities and threats they offer. This requires careful assessment of the boundaries of the markets and market segments which the firm currently services or might enter, and the nature and intensity of competition in these markets and segments. Important elements of this analysis include:

1 How may each market be defined? Segmented?

- What is the size of each market and market segment?
- What is the rate of growth of each market and each market segment?
- At what stage of evolution (life cycle) is the market and each segment of the market?
- What are the characteristics of each market or segment in terms of, for example, buyer concentration, buyer motives, usage rate, brand loyalty, channel loyalty, price-sensitivity, advertising-sensitivity etc.?
- How are these factors changing over time? – method of definition and/or segmentation; stage of evolution (life cycle); characteristics of each segment.
- What market or market segments are not being adequately served now or will not be adequately served in the future?

2 What are the economic characteristics of the business system serving each market or market segment?

- What is the degree of seller concentration?
- What is the number of competitors, the size and market share of each?
- What are the barriers to entry?
- What are the barriers to exit?
- What is the degree of backward integration?
- What is the degree of forward integration?
- What is the relative distribution of economic (market) power amongst the different stages and segments of the markets? – which stages and segments are most concentrated; which stages and segments have the greatest value added; which stages and segments exert the greatest influence over ultimate consumer demand?
- What is the price-elasticity of demand? Are industry profits price-sensitive? Volume-sensitive?
- What economies of scale exist in production? In marketing? In distribution? In purchasing? In R & D?
- What is the present utilization of capacity?
- What are the capacity trends?
- What are the profit centres of the business?

Relative strengths and weaknesses

The assessment of firms' internal resources and capabilities in turn will enable it to judge its strengths and weaknesses in relation to its objectives. Important aspects of this analysis include:

1   *Objectives*

- What are the overall objectives of the firm? (and their time horizon?)
- Are the objectives clear, explicit, measurable, achievable, realistic and capable of communication within the organization?
- Are there operational objectives which are consistent with overall strategic objectives?
- Will the objectives satisfy owners and stakeholders?

2   *Strategy*

- Is the strategy consistent with objectives and the resource capabilities of the organization?
- Does it build directly on strengths?
- Does the strategy realize synergy within the company?
- Is the strategy appropriate for the company's environment?

3   *Structure*

- Is the organizational structure consistent with the declared strategy?

4   *Finance*

- Has the company sufficient financial resources to fund its strategy?
- Is the mix of funding flexible?
- How low is the cost of capital?
- Can the company raise new capital?
- How effective is financial planning and control?

5   *Marketing*

- How efficient and effective are the component parts of the mix?
- How strong (in terms of market share) is the company in the markets served?
- How effective is product development?
- How good is the company at market research and at identifying trends and gaps in the market?
- What is the relationship between turnover and profits?
- What is the relationship between profits and the customer base?

6   *Technology*

- How does the company compare in terms of production cost?
- How does the company compare in terms of production quality?
- How up to date is the production technology?
- How effective are the production systems for maintenance, quality control, production scheduling, stock control?
- How easily can new products be assimilated into production?

- How near to full capacity utilization is the company?
- How flexible is the plant?
- Is production in the right location?
- Is purchasing taking advantage of bulk discounts?
- Is there a major sourcing problem with scarce raw materials?

7 *R & D*

- How technologically competent are the staff?
- How good are the laboratories and equipment?
- How market-orientated is R & D?
- How much is spent on R & D?

8 *Personnel*

- Is the recruitment policy developing the number and quality of people required to implement strategy?
- Is the training policy developing the necessary new skills and improving existing competence?
- Is the management development programme providing the quality of management necessary to implement the corporate strategy?

9 *Systems and procedures*

- Are the systems and procedures providing the means by which strategy can be implemented?

Data sources which can be used to 'flesh out' the above framework are indicated in figure 11.1.

Strategic Choice

This analysis results in a full understanding of a firm's capabilities and the nature of the environment, thus providing the basis for strategic *choice*. The major strategic choices available to firms were discussed in the first part of the book. Which one the firm chooses will be determined by its corporate mission and market opportunities. Additionally, the firm needs to consider the manner in which it chooses to compete in the particular markets it serves, and this will depend upon its core skills and its competitive advantages as discussed in the second part of the book. Managers will make such choices on the basis of their own knowledge and insights of their firm and the opportunities open to it. The present book provides a framework for the systematic analysis of the strategic issues facing the firm.

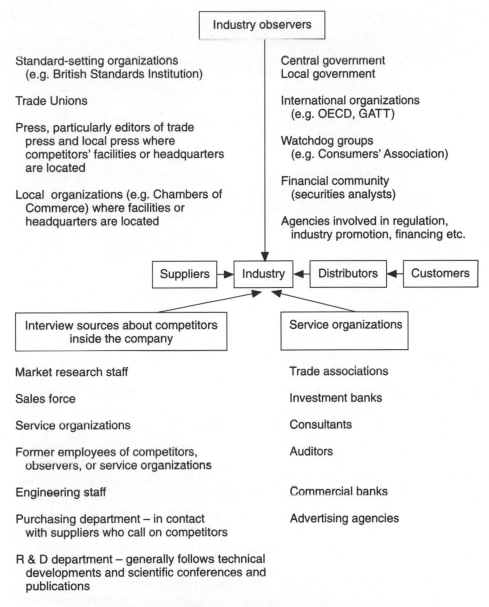

Figure 11.1   Data sources for competitive analysis
Source: Adapted from Porter (1980)

References

Luffman, G. A. and Reed, R., 1984. *The Strategy and Performance of British Industry 1970–80*, Macmillan.
Porter, M. E., 1980. *Competitive Strategy*, Free Press.

Technical Appendix: Theory of Markets

The theory of markets is concerned with how scarce factors of production are allocated between the multitude of product markets in the economy. More specifically, the theory of markets is concerned with the determination of the prices and outputs of goods and services, and the prices and usage of factors of production.

The 'theory of markets' distinguishes between types of markets by reference to differences in their market structure. The main structural distinction is made according to the degree of seller concentration, i.e. the number of suppliers and their relative size distribution. Other structural features emphasized include the character of the product supplied, i.e. whether it is a homogeneous product or differentiated, and the condition of entry/exit to the market. Given these structural distinctions, market theory examines the way in which market structure interacts with market conduct to produce particular patterns of market performance.

The main market 'situations' considered by the theory of markets are the two polar extremes of the market spectrum – perfect competition and monopoly – and two 'intermediate' market structures – monopolistic competition and oligopoly. In order to facilitate a comparison of performance results between these four market types the assumption is made that all firms seek to maximize profits. This body of analysis shows perfect competition to yield performance results superior to those of the other market forms. However, the conventional theory of markets is deficient in a number of respects particularly in regard to its portrayal of firm cost structures and its lack of attention (by definition) to dynamic performance criteria – process and product innovation. Accordingly, it is necessary to take a much broader, more empirically-orientated view of market performance and market structure–conduct–performance interrelationships.

Perfect Competition

Perfect competition is characterized by:

1   many firms and buyers, i.e. a large number of independently acting firms and buyers, each firm and buyer being too small to be able to influence the price of the product transacted;
2   homogeneous products, i.e. the products offered by the competing firms are identical not only in physical attributes but are also regarded as identical by buyers who have no preference between the products of various producers;
3   free market entry and exit, i.e. there are no barriers to entry (hindrances to the entry of new firms) or impediments to the exit of existing sellers;
4   perfect knowledge of the market by buyers and sellers.

In a perfectly competitive market, individual sellers have no control over the price at which they sell, the price being determined by aggregate market demand and supply conditions. Each firm produces such a small fraction of total industry output that an increase or decrease in its own output will have no perceptible influence upon total supply and, hence, price. Further, given that consumers regard the homogeneous outputs of the competing sellers as perfect substitutes, no firm can increase its price above the ruling market price without losing all of its custom. Thus, the demand curve facing the firm will be a horizontal straight line at the ruling market price. In consequence, marginal revenue, MR (the additional revenue obtained from selling one extra unit of output) equals average revenue, AR (total revenue divided by the number of units sold). The competitive firm is a 'price-taker', accepting price as something completely outside its control, and will simply adjust its output independently to the most profitable level at that price. In doing so the firm will need to take into account the cost of producing output, in particular the marginal cost, MC (the additional cost incurred in producing one extra unit of output) and the average cost, AC (total cost divided by the number of units produced): i.e. the firm will continue to produce additional units of output so long as price (= MR = AR) exceeds marginal cost. When the additional revenue obtained from selling one extra unit of output is exactly equal to the additional costs incurred in producing that output then the firm will have achieved a level of output/sales at which it maximizes profits. Figure A.1(a) shows the short-run competitive equilibrium position for a 'representative' firm and the industry. The individual supply schedules (MCs) of 'x' number of identical firms are summed horizontally to obtain the industry supply

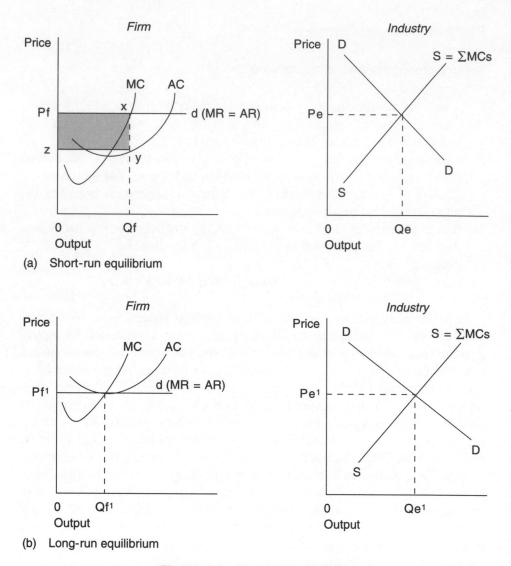

Figure A.1 Perfect competition

curve (SS). Given industry demand (DD), the short-run equilibrium price and output are 0Pe and 0Qe. Taking the equilibrium price as given, the competitive firm establishes its profit-maximizing output at the level 0Qf (P = MC). Since the firm's average costs *include* a 'normal' profit return on capital employed, at price level 0Pf the firm receives an 'above-normal' profit per unit equal to xy and total above-normal profits of Pfxyz.

The long-run equilibrium position can also be ascertained. It is deduced from the assumptions of profit maximization, perfect knowledge and free entry and exit, that unless the returns to the productive resources employed in this market are at a level that could be derived from their use in an alternative market elsewhere in the economy (i.e. they are earning a normal profit), resources will enter or leave this market. In general, outputs will be adjusted to demand until market output is extended (or reduced) and price reduced (or increased) to the point where the average cost of supplying that output is just equal to the price at which that output sells.

If, as in the example given, established sellers are earning above-normal profits then new resources will be attracted into the industry thereby increasing total market supply and reducing market price. This process will continue until the excess profits have been competed away. Figure A.1(b) shows the long-run competitive equilibrium position for the 'representative' firm and the industry. Given an unchanged industry demand (DD) the long-run equilibrium price and output for the industry are $0Pe^1$ and $0Qe^1$. Given the equilibrium price, the firm establishes its profit-maximizing output at the point $0Qf^1$, where $P = MC$ at the point of minimum long-run average cost.

Static market theory shows perfect competition to result in a more efficient market performance than other forms of market organization (see especially the comparison with monopoly). Specifically, market output is optimized at a level equal to minimum supply costs; consumers are charged a price just equal to minimum supply costs, with suppliers receiving a normal profit return.

Monopoly

Monopoly is characterized by:

1   one firm and many buyers, i.e. a market comprised of a single supplier selling to a multitude of small, independently acting buyers;
2   a lack of substitute products, i.e. there are no close substitutes for the monopolist's product;
3   blockaded entry, i.e. barriers to entry are so severe that it is impossible for new firms to enter the market.

In static monopoly the monopolist is in a position to set the market price. However, unlike a perfectly competitive producer the monopolist's marginal and average revenue curves are not identical. The monopolist faces a downward-sloping demand curve (DD in figure A.2) and the sale of additional units of its product forces down the price at which *all* units must be sold. The objective of the monopolist, like that of the competitive firm, is assumed to be profit maximization and it operates with complete knowledge of relevant cost and demand data. Accordingly, the monopolist will aim to produce at that price–output combination which

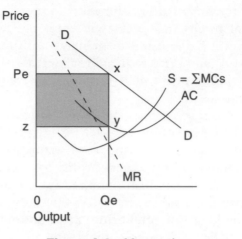

Figure A.2   Monopoly

equates marginal cost and marginal revenue. Figure A.2 indicates the short-run equilibrium position for the monopolist. The monopolist will supply 0Qe output at a price of 0Pe. At the equilibrium price, the monopolist secures above-normal profits (Pexyz). Unlike the competitive firm situation, where entry is unfettered, entry barriers in monopoly are assumed to be so great as to preclude new suppliers. There is thus no possibility of additional productive resources entering the industry and in consequence the monopolist will continue to earn above-normal profits over the long term (until such time as supply and demand conditions radically change). Market theory predicts that given identical cost and demand conditions, monopoly leads to a higher price and a lower output than does perfect competition.

Monopoly and Perfect Competition Compared

Equilibrium under perfect competition occurs where supply equates with demand. This is illustrated in figure A.3 where the competitive supply curve is MC (the sum of all the individual suppliers' marginal cost curves). The competitive output is 0Qc and the competitive price is 0Pc. Since the supply curve is the sum of the marginal cost curves, it follows that in equilibrium, marginal cost equals price. Assume now that this industry is monopolized as a result, say, of one firm taking over all the other suppliers but that there are no economies of scale to be gained from rationalizing production into fewer, larger plants. Thus, the monopolist continues to supply the market, as before, from the many small plants it has acquired. It follows that the marginal costs will be the

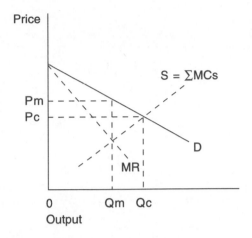

Figure A.3   Monopoly and competition compared

same for the monopolist as for the competitive industry and, hence, their supply curves will be identical. As noted above, the monopolist which seeks to maximize profits will equate marginal cost with marginal revenue, although in the case of monopoly marginal revenue will be below price. In consequence, in equilibrium, market output falls from 0Qc to 0Qm and the market price rises from 0Pc to 0Pm.

The conclusion of competitive optimality, however, rests on a number of assumptions, some of which are highly questionable, in particular the assumption that cost structures are identical for small, perfectively competitive firms and large monopoly (and oligopolistic) suppliers whilst, given its static framework, it ignores important dynamic influences, such as technological progress.

In a static monopoly, a fundamental assumption is that costs are the same for both small competitive suppliers and a single (multi-plant) monopolist. In practice, however, production in a particular market is often characterized by significant economies of scale. In such cases opportunities exist for monopolists to rationalize production and concentrate output in fewer, larger plants (or even a single plant) with consequent reductions in unit costs. Figure A.4 illustrates the reduction in unit costs achieved through exploiting economies of scale.

The downward-sloping long-run average cost curve (LRAC) shows the potential for reducing unit costs by producing on a larger scale. The average and marginal costs of a small-scale plant are shown by ACpc and MCpc, whilst the average and marginal costs of a large-scale plant are shown by ACm and MCm. The unit cost difference between the two plants (Cpc Cm) shows the potential which a large-scale producer has for lowering prices.

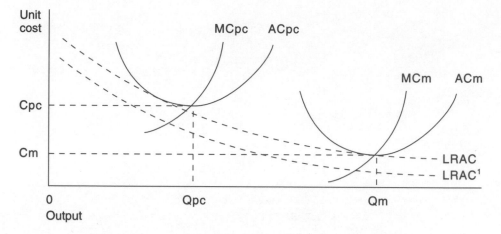

Figure A.4 Economies of scale and unit cost reductions

The fall in unit costs as a result of the rationalization of production by the monopolist lowers the short-run marginal cost curve of the monopolist (MCm) compared to the original short-run marginal cost curves of the smaller competitive suppliers (MCpc). This is shown in figure A.5. Because of the fall in unit costs *more* output is produced by the profit-maximizing monopolist (0Qm) at a *lower* market price (0Pm). There is growing evidence to the effect that the long-run average cost curve (and hence the related MC curve) for many capital-intensive markets is L-shaped as in figure A.4. In these markets total demand and individual market share, not cost considerations, are the factors limiting the size of the firm. The firm may thus grow and find a level of output such that further expansion would be unprofitable. However, in doing so it may become so large relative to the market that it attains a degree of power over price. This is not to deny that the monopolist could further increase output and lower price were it not trying to maximize its profit. Such a position would not, however, be the result of a return to perfect competition. What has happened is that the firm, seeking its best profit position, has abandoned the status of an insignificant small competitor. It has not necessarily done so through a systematic attempt to dominate the market. On the contrary, it is the underlying cost conditions of the market that have impelled this growth. In such a market it is possible that small 'competitive-sized' firms cannot survive. Moreover, to the extent that the unit costs are lower at higher production levels the large firm is a technically more efficient entity.

The analysis developed above also neglects *dynamic* aspects of the market system. In practice, major improvements in consumer welfare occur largely as a result of technological innovations, i.e. the growth of

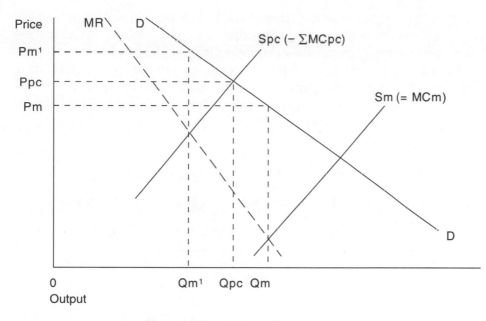

Figure A.5   Progressive monopoly

resources and development of new techniques and products over time rather than adjustments to provide maximum output from a given (static) input; and often monopolistic elements function as a precondition and protection of innovating effort. A monopolist, earning above-normal profits, will have the financial resources to promote technical advance but its incentive to innovate may be weak given the lack of effective competition. However, technological advance is a means of lowering unit costs and thereby expanding profits; and these profits will not be of a transitory nature, given barriers to entry; hence, the monopolist must persist and succeed in the area of technological advance to maintain its dominant position.

Diagrammatically, the proposition that monopoly may lead to a more effective performance can be demonstrated by using figures A.4 and A.5. In figure A.5 the competitive market produces 0Qpc where short-run marginal cost equals price. If this industry were monopolized, the conventional expectation would be a price rise to 0Pm^1 and output decrease to 0Qm^1. However, if the monopolist in such a market introduces cost-saving innovations, the long-run average cost curve in figure A.4 will shift downward from LRAC to LRAC^1 and the marginal cost curve will fall. This fall in the marginal cost curve means that the monopolist may actually produce more (0Qm) at a lower price (0Pm) than the original competitive industry, as shown in figure A.5.

It is, of course, possible that society will remain worse off under monopoly, even if the monopolist innovates; the benefits of innovation may not outweigh the costs of monopolistic exploitation.

Between the extremes of perfect competition and monopoly lie a number of intermediate forms of market which display some characteristics of the two extreme types, in particular 'monopolistically competitive' and 'oligopoly' markets.

Monopolistic Competition

Monopolistic competition is characterized by:

1   many firms and buyers, i.e. the market is comprised of a large number of independently acting firms and buyers;
2   differentiated products, i.e. the products offered by competing firms are differentiated from each other in one or more respects. These differences may be of a physical nature, involving functional features, or may be purely 'imaginary' in the sense that artificial differences are created through advertising and sales promotion;
3   free market entry and exit, i.e. there are no barriers to entry preventing new firms entering the market or obstacles in the way of existing firms leaving the market. (No allowance is made in the theory of monopolistic competition for the fact that product differentiation, by establishing strong brand loyalties to established firms' products, may act as a barrier to entry.)

Apart from the product differentiation aspects, monopolistic competition is very similar structurally to perfect competition.

The analysis of individual firm equilibrium in monopolistic competition can be presented in terms of a 'representative' firm, i.e. all firms are assumed to face identical cost and demand conditions and each is a profit maximizer, from which it is then possible to derive a market-equilibrium position.

The significance of product differentiation is (1) each firm has a market which is partially distinct from its competitors; i.e. each firm faces a downward-sloping demand curve (d in figure A.6(a)), although the presence of closely competing substitute products will cause this curve to be relatively price-sensitive; (2) the firms' cost structures (marginal cost and average costs) are raised as a result of incurring differentiation expenditures (selling costs).

The firm being a profit maximizer will aim to produce at that price (0P)–output (0Q) combination, shown in figure A.6(a), which equates cost (MC) and marginal revenue (MR). In the short run this may result in firms securing above-normal profits (Pxyz).

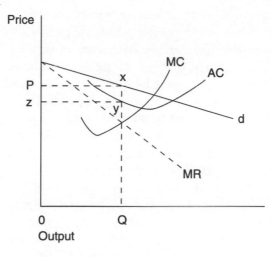

(a)   Short-run equilibrium

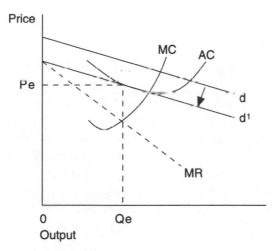

(b)   Long-run equilibrium

Figure A.6   Monopolistic competition

In the long run, above-normal profits will induce new firms to enter the market and this will affect the demand curve faced by established firms (i.e. push the demand curve leftwards from d to d¹, thereby reducing the volume of sales associated with each price level). The process of new entry will continue until the excess profits have been competed away. Figure A.6(b) shows the long-run equilibrium position of the 'representative' firm. The firm continues to maximize its profits at a price (0Pe)–output (0Qe) combination where marginal cost equals marginal revenue, but now secures only a normal profit return. This normal profit position for the firm in the long run is similar to the long-run equilibrium position for the firm in perfect competition. However, monopolistic competition results in a less efficient market performance when compared to perfect competition. Specifically, monopolistically competitive firms produce lower rates of output and sell these outputs at higher prices than perfectly competitive firms. Since the demand curve is downwards sloping, it is necessarily tangent to the long-run average cost curve (which is higher than the perfectly competitive firm's cost curve because of the addition of selling costs) to the left of the latter's minimum point. Firms thus operate a less than optimum scale of plant and as a result there is excess capacity in the market.

Oligopoly

Oligopoly is characterized by:

1   few firms and many buyers, i.e. the bulk of market supply is in the hands of a relatively few large firms who sell to many small buyers;
2   homogeneous or differentiated products, i.e. the products offered by suppliers may be identical or, more commonly, differentiated from each other in one or more respects. These differences may be of a physical nature, involving functional features, or may be purely 'imaginary' in the sense that artificial differences are created through advertising and sales promotion;
3   difficult market entry, i.e. the existence of high barriers to entry which represent obstacles in the way of new firms entering the market.

The primary characteristic associated with the condition of 'fewness' is known as mutual interdependence. Basically, each firm when deciding upon its price and other market strategies must explicitly take into account the likely reactions and counter-moves of its competitors in response to its own moves. A price cut, for example, may appear to be advantageous to one firm considered in isolation, but if this results in other firms cutting their prices also to protect their sales then all firms may suffer reduced profits. Accordingly, oligopolists tend to avoid price competition, employing various mechanisms such as price leadership, and cartels to coordinate their prices. In some cases, those mechanisms are used in order to maximize the joint profits of the firms concerned, leading to industry output and price levels similar to those of a single-firm monopoly.

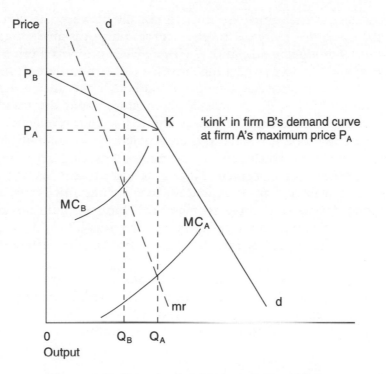

Figure A.7 Price leadership by a low-cost firm

Price leadership

Price leadership results when one firm establishes itself as the market leader and takes the initiative in setting prices and other firms in the market accept its pricing policy. Such leadership can only work, however, where the firm taking the initiating role can be confident that the other oligopolists will follow its lead. This requires a degree of tacit collusion with an implicit recognition by all firms in the market that one of them is taking the initiative with group interests in mind.

Price leadership may be exercised by a 'dominant' firm. The dominant firm price leader may well be the largest firm in the group, particularly if it is also the lowest cost supplier. Such low costs enable the firm to take the initiative in setting price and other sellers have little alternative but to follow because of the power of the dominant firm to punish non-compliance by, for example, subjecting non-following firms to selective price-cutting.

Figure A.7 illustrates price leadership by a low-cost firm. Firm A is the low-cost supplier with the marginal cost curve MC_A; firm B has higher costs with a marginal cost curve MC_B. The individual demand curve of each firm is dd when they set identical prices (i.e. it is assumed that total industry sales at each price are divided equally between the two firms); mr is the associated marginal revenue curve. Firm A is able to maximize its profits by producing output $0Q_A$ (where $MC_A = mr$) at a price of $0P_A$. Firm B would like to charge a higher price $(0P_B)$, but the best it can do is to 'accept' the price set by firm A, although this means less than maximum profit. For given firm B's conjecture about the reactions of firm A to any price change by B, any alternative course of action would mean even less profit. If B were to charge a higher price than $0P_A$ it would lose sales to firm A (whose price is unchanged), moving left along a new 'kinked' demand curve segment KP_B; if he were to cut his price below P_A, this would force firm A to undertake matching price cuts, moving right along the demand curve segment Kd. Firm B could not hope to win such a 'price war' because of its higher costs. Thus, firm B's best course of action is to charge the same price as that established by firm A.

Alternatively, the low-cost firm might be prepared to accept price leadership by a higher cost rival since a price which enables the least efficient supplier to cover its costs and make comfortable profits will allow the low-cost firm to make even larger profits.

Cartels

The centralized cartel case with all its restraints on individual member firms illustrates collusion in its most complete form. Under the cartel arrangement, a central administration agency determines the price and output of the market, and the output quotas of each of the separate member firms in such a way as to maximize the joint profits of the group. Price and output will thus tend to approximate those of a profit-maximizing monopolist.

Figure A.8 shows how two firms can get together and set prices so as to maximize total industry profits. The marginal cost curves of each firm (MC1 and MC2) are summed horizontally to arrive at an industry marginal cost curve ΣMC. Equating the cartel's total marginal cost (ΣMC) with the industry marginal revenue curve (MR) determines the profit-maximizing output (0Q) and the profit maximizing price (0P). Both firms will charge this profit-maximizing price and each firm will determine its output by equating its own marginal cost to the industry profit-maximizing marginal cost level. In this way profits (the shaded areas) are generated between firms on the basis of their individual outputs 0Q1 and 0Q2. It will be noted that firm 1, as the lowest cost producer, receives the largest quota and contributes the most profit to the cartel. However, the profit share-out amongst cartel members is not necessarily in exact proportion to the profit that each generates and the lowest cost producer may contribute some of its profit generated to other cartel

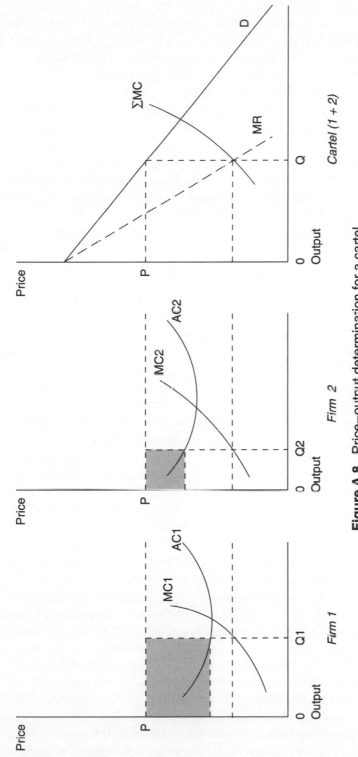

Figure A.8 Price–output determination for a cartel

members to secure group cohesion, on the grounds that the profits obtained by collaborating with competitors is still greater than from going it alone.

Agreement towards a policy of joint profit maximization is easier the smaller the number of firms, the more homogeneous the product, and the more alike the firms are in terms of cost structure. The break-up of a cartel agreement is most likely to arise from the lowest cost firms attempting to increase their profits by 'secretly' exceeding their output quotas.

Disagreement over the allocation of quotas and profits is more likely the greater the number of member firms. In practice, full cartels are rarely encountered. Where collusion is practised, this tends to take the form of price-fixing with firms competing for market share through product differentiation.

Non-price competition in oligopoly

Oligopolists, as has been noted, tend to avoid price competition. Instead they prefer to channel most of their competitive efforts into various forms of product-diffentiation activity, most notably product variations and sales promotion. Price cuts can be quickly and easily met by a firm's rivals – the likelihood of securing a significant increase in market share through price competition is small, whilst there is the obvious danger of reduced profits. In consequence, oligopolists are inclined to feel that more permanent advantages can be gained over rivals through non-price competition because product differentiation strategies are often difficult to duplicate so readily and so completely as price reductions.

Advertising is one main form of differentiation activity and may be usefully examined to illustrate the impact of policies in this area. Advertising is aimed at informing prospective buyers of the product's attributes and persuading them that a particular brand is superior to those offered by competitors. The purpose of advertising is to increase the firm's sales and market share by cultivating and maintaining strong brand loyalties.

The extent to which the firm's sales respond to increased advertising depends on the promotional elasticity of demand. A high promotional elasticity of demand will result in a more than proportionate increase in sales. Whether or not it is profitable for the firm to advertise will depend also on production costs. If the firm is operating under conditions of decreasing production costs, its profits will be increased as sales expand. Assuming the firm to be a profit maximizer, selling costs will be increased to the point where the marginal cost of inducing a further shift in the demand curve is just equal to anticipated marginal receipts.

The conventional approach to the analysis of the relationship between advertising and the position of the firm's demand curve is shown in

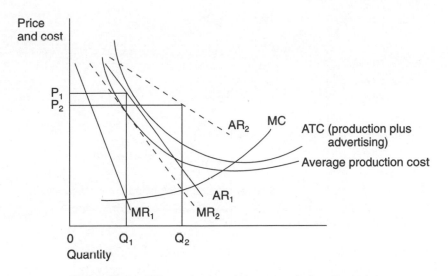

Figure A.9   Effect of advertising on price and output

figure A.9. It is assumed that the promotional elasticity demand is greater than unity and production costs fall (up to a point) as output expands. It can be seen that advertising produces a beneficial allocative effect by expanding demand from AR_1 to AR_2 in so far the level of output is higher with advertising ($0Q_2$) than without advertising ($0Q_1$) and supply prices have been lowered from $0P_1$ to $0P_2$.

If these two conditions are not met, i.e. promotional elasticity of demand is low *and* unit costs do not fall as output expands, the effects of advertising may then be detrimental to the consumer. Specifically the extra costs incurred in advertising may be passed on to consumers in the form of higher prices; and where advertising acts as an important barrier to entry, this can serve to protect excess profits.

Traditional (static) market theory shows oligopoly to result in a 'monopoly-like' sub-optimal market performance: output is restricted to levels below cost-minimization; inefficient firms are cushioned by a 'reluctance' to engage in price competition; differentiation competition increases supply costs; prices are set above minimum supply costs yielding oligopolists above-normal profits which are protected by barriers to entry. As with monopoly, however, this analysis makes no allowance for the contribution that economies of scale may make to the reduction of market costs and prices and the important contribution of oligopolistic competition to innovation and new product development.

Barriers to Entry and Potential Competition

It has been indicated that the 'condition of entry' has an important bearing on the long-run rate of profit earned by the suppliers in a market.

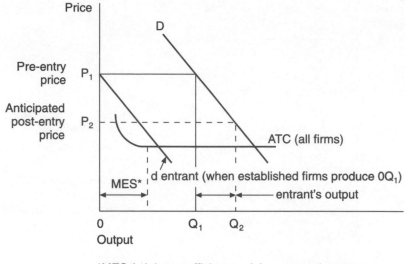

*MES (minimum efficient scale) = entrant's output

Figure A.10   Scale economies and new entry

If new entry to a market can be achieved without impediment (as in perfect competition), the new entrant being at no disadvantage *vis-à-vis* established producers, there will be a long-run tendency for sellers to earn only normal profits. Where entry barriers are substantial, however, persistent excess profits may be earned by established sellers.

Barriers to entry come in a number of forms. Entrants, for example, may be put at a *relative* cost disadvantage because of their inability (lack of finance, low market share) to operate an optimal-sized plant; entrants may be put at an *absolute* cost disadvantage through the ownership of superior technology, and control of input sources and distribution channels, by established firms; entrants may be unable to establish their products in the market because of customer loyalty to existing brands built up by cumulative investments in product differentiation.

Whether or not entry into a market will occur depends upon the profits the potential entrant expects it will earn. These will depend upon its own cost position and upon the post-entry price and demand conditions anticipated by it. These factors, in turn, will depend on the anticipated reaction of established producers to entry.

The existing theory of entry is largely based on the assumption that potential entrants anticipate that established firms will *maintain* their outputs at the pre-entry level following actual entry. This proposition is shown in the context of figures A.10 and A.11, where the 'barrier to entry' is assumed to be one of scale economies. In figure A.10, given the above assumption, the potential entrant's demand curve – d entrant – is

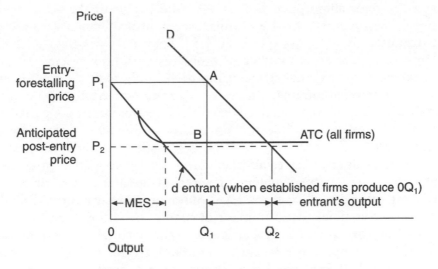

Figure A.11 The entry-forestalling price

the segment of the industry demand curve, D, to the right of the pre-entry output $0Q_1$ produced by established firms. The potential entrant will decide whether or not to enter the market by comparing this demand curve with its own cost position. The potential entrant is assumed to have access to the same average cost curve as that of established firms (i.e. there are no absolute cost advantages accruing to establish firms). Economies of scale, however, are important, such that in order to operate a minimum optimal scale of plant, the entrant would need to supply an output of Q_1Q_2. It will be noted that as a result of the addition of this 'extra' output to the existing market supply, the market price is lowered to $0P_2$. Hence, the price that is relevant to entry decisions is the anticipated post-entry price not the existing pre-entry price.

The existence of substantial scale economies is not in itself sufficient to prevent entry. Entry will occur despite this factor provided that the entrant's anticipated cost and demand conditions permit him to make a profit at the new market price. If the potential entrant's average cost curve is below the post-entry price, as in figure A.10, entry will occur since the entrant can make a profit; entry will not occur if the anticipated post-entry price is below the entrant's average cost curve as in figure A.11, because losses would then be incurred.

The greater the importance of scale economies, the greater is the amount by which established firms can raise prices above the average cost curve (i.e. make 'above-normal' profits) without inducing entry.

If the established firms actively seek to prevent the emergence of new competition then they will aim to produce output $0Q_1$ in figure A.11.

The entry-forestalling price is thus $0P_1$, the height of the scale economies barrier to entry, the size of unit 'excess' profits being measured by the distance AB.

However, there are a number of problems with limit-pricing theory. The theory requires established firms to be fully alert to the 'threat' posed by potential entrants. There is no strong empirical evidence that firms do in fact monitor their environments to the extent suggested by the theory, and lack of information makes it difficult in any case to *identify* potential newcomers and the seriousness of their intentions. Moreover, assuming that established firms do actively attempt to prevent entry, there is the problem of agreeing upon the limit price – a particular difficulty when firms have different cost structures. Finally, static theory assumes that a number of market conditions conducive to limit-pricing are present, in particular static technology and market demand. In reality, however, such conditions are rarely present. Thus, unless established firms are active innovators and sensitive to changes in consumer demand, opportunities for entry may arise. For example, entrants may instal *new* technology in a *new* vintage plant giving them cost advantages over established firms operating older plants, and product innovation may enable entrants to win a viable market share by offering customers products which are superior to those supplied by established firms.

Index